LYNDA
BARRY

Great Comics Artists Series
M. Thomas Inge, General Editor

LYNDA BARRY

Girlhood through the Looking Glass

Susan E. Kirtley

University Press of Mississippi • Jackson

www.upress.state.ms.us

The University Press of Mississippi is a member of the Association of American University Presses.

Illustration on page iii by Lynda Barry. Used with permission.

First printing 2012

∞

Library of Congress Cataloging-in-Publication Data

Kirtley, Susan E., 1972–
  Lynda Barry : girlhood through the looking glass / Susan E. Kirtley.
     p. cm. — (Great comics artists series)
Includes bibliographical references and index.
ISBN 978-1-61703-234-9 (cloth : alk. paper) —
ISBN 978-1-61703-235-6 (pbk. : alk. paper) — ISBN 978-1-61703-236-3 (ebook)
1. Barry, Lynda, 1956—Criticism and interpretation. 2. Barry, Lynda, 1956—
Themes, motives. 3. Girls in art. 4. Girls in literature. I. Barry, Lynda, 1956–
II. Title.
NX512.B37K57 2012
741.5'973—dc23
[B]   2011024295

British Library Cataloging-in-Publication Data available

To George and Dorothy Brelin

CONTENTS

ACKNOWLEDGMENTS

First of all, I must thank Lynda Barry, who sat with me for an extended interview in Rhinebeck, New York, and was incredibly kind and gracious with her art and her words. When I met Lynda in the summer of 2006, we discussed academics, and she explained to me, "I personally love throbbing forehead people. I do. Throbbing assholes, I'm not so into, but throbbing forehead people, I love." I am extremely grateful to Lynda Barry for her assistance, and I strive to be one of the better sorts of "throbbing forehead people."

I am also very grateful to the wonderful people at the University Press of Mississippi, including Seetha Srinivasan, Walter Biggins, and M. Thomas Inge. Tom Inge was a very early inspiration, and I am extraordinarily grateful for the patience, guidance, and insightful comments from Walter Biggins. My colleagues at the University of Massachusetts at Lowell have also been extremely encouraging, particularly Bridget Marshall, Paula Haines, Jonathan Silverman, and Marlowe Miller. I also drew support and assistance from Mary Reda and Mike Mattison, and I thank them profusely. There are many wonderful comic art scholars who inspired me, including Charles Hatfield, Jared Gardner, Isaac Cates, and Craig Fischer. Bill and Pat Kirtley, Kathy and Peter Brost, and all of the Filipos have also been a great support network. Thanks to Ashley Zaniboni for allowing me time to work. I am especially grateful to Tamasone Filipo for his unflagging support, good humor, and belief in me, and to Evelyn and Leone for reminding me to stop and play sometimes.

PREFACE

Lynda Barry is many things—a playwright, novelist, activist, teacher, and lecturer—and, as the creator of numerous comics, including the long-running cult favorite *Ernie Pook's Comeek*, a well-known comic artist. Yet in a personal interview, Barry chose to define her calling more generally as an "image wrangler."[1] Barry's definition of the "image" (and thus her calling) is decidedly comprehensive, following the tradition outlined by W.J.T. Mitchell in his book *Iconology: Image, Text, Ideology*, in which he describes an image "not as any material picture, but as an abstract, general, spiritual 'likeness'" (31).[2] Barry thus expresses images through texts, illustrations, performances, and various combinations of elements, and the image that recurs most frequently throughout the many genres she employs is that of girls on the verge of adulthood. Barry's polyscopic approach challenges romantic ideas of girlhood through various lenses, offering her own comprehensive conception of the subject. Norwegian researcher Else Øyen asserts that a polyscopic approach collects "as much relevant information" as one can and attempts to see the issue "from as many angles as possible" (5). Barry embraces this process, utilizing many different ways of seeing to dismantle idealized "sugar and spice" notions of what it is to be a girl, subverting conventions of beauty, innocence, and maturation, creating instead a vision of girls marked by unattractive, street-smart young women who endure and sometimes thrive when they are able to tap into their creative impulses. In her portrayal of the traps and trials of girlhood, Barry employs numerous genres and perspectives to give a multifaceted representation—looking telescopically and bringing broader issues into focus in her play, studying the distortion as if through a fun-house mirror in an illustrated novel, scrutinizing small details intently as if through a microscope in her weekly strip, and framing and capturing moments as if through a scrapbook in her semi-autobiographical comics. Barry's means of expression creatively underscore her themes, and the relationship between genre and message will be explored in detail in this project. Despite Barry's influence within the comic art world and her recent resurgence in the popular press, only a few scholarly articles have focused on her work.[3] This book fills a gap in current scholarship, giving Barry's work an extended scholarly examination, focusing on defining and exploring the ramifications of Barry's comprehensive expression of girlhood.

This study of Lynda Barry's contributions comes at a pivotal time in her career. Publisher Drawn and Quarterly plans to reissue the entire run of *Ernie Pook's Comeek* in the original four-panel-square format, and as an artist and author her work is gaining additional critical attention. Barry is well known within the comic art world for a childlike, unaffected cartooning style that accentuates a frequent emphasis on childhood, as well as loquacious, often elegant narration within panels and the use of careful, telling details that underscore bittersweet reminiscences of youth. Barry shares her interests with other comic artists focusing on adolescence and girlhood, such as Marjane Satrapi, Miss Lasko-Gross, Julie Doucet, Ariel Schrag, and Debbie Drechsler. However, no other comic artist has examined the essence of girlhood through so many lenses and so many ways of seeing.

In exploring Barry's work, this book draws mainly from the primary sources of Barry's many creations, including her comics, novels, play, and essays, as well as an interview conducted with Barry on July 19, 2006, in Rhinebeck, New York. Secondary sources and scholarship, though uncommon, will be introduced as applicable, along with criticism and commentary from the popular press. Given the wealth of materials created by Barry, the focus here is necessarily limited; and her work bears additional, in-depth scholarly attention, addressing each of her genres and the many themes contained within them in more detail. This book serves to further the conversation, inviting dialogue and discussion of Barry's oeuvre.

To initiate the examination, chapter 1 explores Barry's place within the pantheon of comic artists. Drawing on the history of the discipline, this chapter helps place her within the context of her contemporaries. Chapter 2 provides a profile of Barry, including information from her life story, and considers the shifting focus of her earliest creations. The biographical information provides vital context when considering her later works, given the many details pulled from her life and incorporated throughout her oeuvre. This section further chronicles the scattered, kaleidoscopic approach of her earliest projects, such as her essays, her strip *Spinal Comics*, her work for *Esquire* magazine, and the art exhibition and coloring book *Naked Ladies!*

Naked Ladies! Naked Ladies! During these initial projects, Barry's work in numerous mediums is marked by constantly shifting points of view. Her art style changes from project to project as does voice and content. Yet in these somewhat inchoate nascent endeavors Barry's incipient interest in the lives of young women emerges, foreshadowing her focus on challenging romanticized images of girlhood.

Chapter 3 explores the evolution of the image in *The Good Times Are Killing Me*, chronicling the creation process for its multiple forms and analyzing the means by which significance alters through time and according to the method of representation. The chapter studies how Barry's work in different genres produces images of fluctuating degrees of explicitness. An art show focusing on music and race results in a loose, scattered message, while the text-based novella chronicling two young girls' encounters with racism in the 1960s creates a more direct and intimate experience. The embodied performance of the play provides a more removed, yet more dimensional view that becomes a communal experience, offering a dramatic, focused look at racism in a community. A close investigation of *The Good Times Are Killing Me* thus provides an ideal opportunity for scrutinizing Barry's multiple ways of seeing her subject.

Chapter 4 considers the distorted, hyperbolic perception of girlhood as expressed in Barry's illustrated novel *Cruddy*. Barry's text-based interpretation of one girl's life suggests an image of a girl as mediated through various fun-house mirrors and allows the readers to envision their own picture, drawn from language, thus echoing the idea that the (anti)heroine Roberta's identity is shaped through the reflections of others. This personal collusion with the readers fashions a grotesque reflection of girlhood as a gothic nightmare, further dismantling associations of happy girlhood and arguing that, for girls, survival requires a creative outlet.

Chapter 5 illuminates Barry's vision of girlhood as expressed in her long-running weekly comic strip, *Ernie Pook's Comeek*. In the strip Barry magnifies the lives of a few featured young girls, particularly Marlys and Maybonne Mullens, using the combined text and illustration of comic art. This form asks the audience to fill in the gaps and investigate the contradictions between language and likeness, studying each week's strip deeply and minutely, as one might scrutinize a slide beneath the microscope. This invites the reader to look closely at the small strip printed in the paper, just as the strip itself looks closely at the quotidian happenings of the lives of several girls. The blending of text and art once again disrupts any romantic notions of girlhood, and this chapter studies the ways in which Barry's shifting point of view in the strip creates an unsettled perspective on girlhood.

Chapter 6 studies Barry's creation of a scrapbook of selfhood in *One Hundred Demons*, which brings together comic strips, collages, and a tutorial in order to represent multiple figures of "Lynda" traversing numerous boundaries to converse with one another. In these strips Barry experimented with new technologies, initially publishing the pieces online before collecting them into an anthology. The strips also try out a longer, full-color format, while the anthology brings in elements of collage, composing the narrative with drawn and found objects that suggest a blending of truth and interpretation. These shaped and constructed images of Barry's own life focus on girlhood as mediated through her own memory and her skills as a writer and artist, suggesting a vision that stresses personal history as presented through the mediating lens of time and technology. Barry frames and constructs her own girlhood, showing her idea of a dark, disturbing childhood from which the narrator ultimately survives, utilizing her own creative impulses to emerge victorious over the demons.

The final chapter examines Barry's attempt to shift her gaze to the audience in the workbooks *What It Is* and *Picture This*, considering the dreamlike form that brings artifacts from the past together with Barry's words and self-portrait, offering additional glimpses of Barry as a girl, and suggesting the accessibility of creativity to the masses. This chapter also considers Barry's multiple ways of seeing girlhood, exploring what these many ways of looking offer. What does Barry say about girlhood, and how do these multiple lenses reinforce her vision? As we consider her many texts and genres, all focusing on girlhood, what is the ultimate message? Across her numerous works Barry presents society as a dark, dangerous place for girls, who must make their way alone, without help from adults, who generally appear as villains. Despite the hazards faced by the girls, they are presented as complex, gritty, and capable in appearance and action. These are not pretty girls, but realistic ones who are depicted with freckles and flaws. These girls make both cruel and kind decisions and must face the consequences of their actions. The girls achieve some measure of happiness, if not overwhelming success, when they engage in creative self-expression, as they take control of the stories of their lives, as Lynda Barry does in *One Hundred Demons* and as she encourages the reader to do in *Demons*, along with *What It Is* and *Picture This*.

In closing, this book seeks to examine Lynda Barry's career and contributions to the field of comic art and beyond, exploring her recurrent focus on figures of young girls and examining her skills in a variety of genres. This study makes the case that Barry's oeuvre offers a polyscopic perspective on girlhood, a perspective that examines girls and girlhood through various means of expression. Barry follows the image of the girl through many lenses and many genres—from text-based novels to the hybrid blending of text and image in comic art to an embodied performance to a coloring book and art show—and in doing so Barry expertly represents the correlations and disjunctures amongst these many images of the girl, revealing a comprehensive understanding of the lives of young women.

LYNDA BARRY

1

Outcasts and Odd Ducks

I don't know. I've always been an odd duck. No matter what situation I'm in, I've always been kind of an odd duck. A really friendly odd duck who tries—if I'm just nice enough to people, they'll leave me alone.
—LYNDA BARRY, personal interview

Lynda Barry defines herself as an "odd duck" in an already outcast field—a woman in the male-dominated field of comics, a Filipino-Irish-Norwegian amongst a largely white group of artists, and a cartoonist who makes her audience cry just as often as laugh.[1] Yet Barry also frequently indicates her preference for outcasts, noting that she would rather "hang around odd-balls and losers because they're more interesting and they're always better in bed."[2] How does Barry's position as an outsider influence her style and subject matter as an artist? To better understand this odd duck and her fascination with images of girlhood, it is important to look to her role within the comic world—as a woman, as a minority, and as a descendant of the Alternative comic generation.

An Outsider in Comic Land

Barry came of age in a critical time for comic artists—a time of great change and growth—and she cites key figures of the Underground and Alternative movements such as Art Spiegelman, R. Crumb, Charles Burns, and Matt Groening as sources of encouragement and friendship.[3] Despite her connections, Barry strongly maintains that she is, once again, an outsider, even within this group that defines itself in opposition to the mainstream. And while her work bears some similarities to these compatriots, Barry also demonstrates significant points of departure.

Scholars such as Robert Harvey, Joseph Witek, and Scott McCloud present excellent chronicles of comics history; and a particularly helpful source in outlining recent comics history, Charles Hatfield's *Alternative Comics: An Emerging Literature*, offers a portrait of the Underground comix movement of the 1960s and '70s, which arose in defiance of the Comics Code Authority and which prefaced Barry's entry onto the comics scene. Hatfield maintains that the "countercultural comix movement—scurrilous, wild and liberating, innovative, radical, and yet in some ways narrowly circumscribed—gave rise to the idea of comics as an acutely personal means of artistic exploration and self-expression" (ix). This approach to expressing the self certainly paved the way for nontraditional cartoonists like Barry, though the Underground movement did, for the most part, often seem to focus on challenging the strictly moralistic dictates of "the Code" through macho flights of fancy. Witek argues that while these Underground comic artists "created works in the sequential art medium of unparalleled vigor, virtuosity, and spontaneity" (51), "the unrestrained satire of the undergrounds did at times descend to sophomoric in group smugness" (53). Crumb, one figure from the Underground movement frequently lauded for his innovation and honesty and lambasted for his misogynistic, narcissistic tendencies, made an enormous impression on many working in comics, including Lynda Barry, as well as numerous comics creators focusing on childhood and girlhood.

Barry references Crumb, in particular, as someone she emulated in her early years, although she found his subject matter distinctly unsettling. While she copied his drawings earnestly and found his style "beautiful," she said, "The sex stuff was scary to me" (qtd. in Schappell 52). Barry remembered, in an interview with Hillary Chute, "What R. Crumb gave me was this feeling that you could draw anything" (50). Barry further acknowledges happily imitating cult artist and hot-rod aficionado Big Daddy Roth's rodent caricature "Rat Fink" and remembers of Roth, "Something about his embrace of ugliness . . . made me feel freedom" (qtd. in Schappell 52). Barry drew from numerous sources, not just artists associated with the Underground movement, as she developed her style, including, as she explained in an interview with Joe Garden, "Dr. Seuss, Don Martin, Dave Berg, R. Crumb, Tom Robbins, Grimm's fairy tales, Mrs. Piggle-Wiggle, Anderson's fairy tales, hippie music, Peter Maxx, the Broadway musical *Hair,* Ripley's *Believe It Or Not!, The Family Circus,* Archie, Nancy." Out of this eclectic group, Barry particularly appreciated Bill Keane's *The Family Circus.*

The comic, created by Bill Keane and continued with the help of his son Jeff, debuted in 1960 and appears in daily newspapers as a single, circular panel generally depicting a humorous scene from family life. The Sunday format deviates somewhat from the small, circular panel, but usually retains a singular, rectangular panel, and all *Family Circus* cartoons share a wholesome, moral outlook that emphasizes the importance of family and Christian values. In the introduction to *The Best American Comics 2008,* guest editor Barry reflected, "I didn't love *The Family Circus* because it was funny. I don't think I noticed or cared about that part at all. I loved the very world of it, a world that I could watch through a portal edged in ink every day when I opened the newspaper. It was a circle I wanted to climb through" (xiii). *The Family Circus,* then, provided Barry with solace, a way of escape, much as drawing did as a child. Therefore, while undoubtedly inspired by the freedom and audacity of the Underground comics, it was one of the most wholesome, straight-laced cartoons that truly influenced Barry to create her own comics and to create a window into another world.

Barry continued drawing throughout her youth, concurrent with the growth of Underground comics, but it wasn't until the 1980s and the creation of what some call the Alternative movement that Barry began to showcase her work and to cultivate a wider audience. It was in the 1980s that the Underground movement began to stagnate, giving way to the Alternative movement in comics, and while Barry herself once again resists labeling, she does acknowledge being a part of "the generation right after R. Crumb. Not generation maybe age-wise, but of comics."[4] Roger Sabin notes, "The 1980s and 1990s were indeed a kind of golden age for nonconformist titles; among them were comics that tackled topics never covered before, and which pushed back artistic expectations" (175). At this time Barry clearly challenged topics once considered taboo in her comic art, yet Barry stalwartly resists any sort of connection with the Alternative movement. During a personal interview Barry argued: "I don't feel like I am in any group with comics, certainly in the mainstream."[5] How does one characterize her work? Barry argues that "being called anything (except 'Princess Kitty') bugs me,"[6] and her style and her genre frequently shift, making it difficult to state generalizations about her work. Despite her rejection of labels, Barry does share an interest in expanding the boundaries of comic art to explore challenging topics and terrain with fellow comic artists associated with the Underground and Alternative movements. Still, while Barry's childlike comic art style from *Ernie Pook* has become something of a trademark, and the figure of Marlys with her exuberant pigtails and cat-eye glasses now stands as a cult hero of sorts, Barry doesn't particularly fit neatly with her contemporary comic artists. Barry doesn't create "graphic novels" like Charles Burns, nor does her style align itself with *New Yorker* cartoonists like Roz Chast. Rather, Barry constantly changes styles, techniques, tools, and genres, never quite settling in any one place; and her ever-evolving means of expression frustrates any attempts at classification. While Barry herself resists categorization, she does share at least a common interest with other female comic artists who concentrate on girls and girlhood in their work.

The Tomboy and Wimmen's Comix

A glance at the comics page in a newspaper or at the shelf in the local comic book store quickly illustrates that women are in the minority in the comics world. Furthermore, the 2005–2006 art show "Masters of American Comics" didn't feature a single woman, begging the question, When women do contribute, are they recognized? Do female cartoonists have a different sensibility? And how does Barry, a self-described tomboy, fit in? Barry firmly believes that boys aren't "keeping girls out. I can tell you for a fact no one's ever kept me out, and I can tell you that most of my friends in art and drawing have been guys."[7] Barry does not recognize a sexist boys' club atmosphere in her professional world. Rather, Barry theorizes that boys mature at a slower rate and therefore have more time to cultivate their draftsmanship, whereas girls are quickly drawn into the pressures of adulthood at a younger age. In an interview Barry explained, "So I feel like boys, just biologically, have a longer period of time, and that, if you notice, it's not just a boy's club, but it's a boy's club of socially not-forward people. . . . It's nerds."[8] How did Barry end up amongst these nerds? She speculates it might have been the result of transgressing gender roles as a girl. Barry didn't get caught in the societal trap of abandoning her art for the adult world because, she says, "I was always a tomboy and I was never successful at the girl's stuff, the girly-girl stuff."[9] It is an interesting fact that Barry, a woman who failed at "girl's stuff," would later focus so intently on the lives and experiences of girls. Barry's representations of self clearly struggle with what she calls "girlness" in her comic strip, yet she resists the idea that any misogynist influence keeps women from participating in the comic art world.

Barry is not the only "tomboy" female creating comic art, and although it might not be apparent from the "Masters of American Comics" exhibit, female cartoonists have demonstrated their own take on the world throughout the history of comics. Scholar and comic artist Trina Robbins's work has been instrumental in bringing to light the history of women in comics in her many books, including *A Century of Women Cartoonists* (1993), *From Girls to Grrrlz: A History of Women's Comics from Teens to Zines* (1999), *The Great Women Cartoonists* (2001), and *Nell Brinkley and the New Woman in the Early 20th Century* (2001). As a result of scholars like Robbins, the role women played in the history of comic art is slowly coming to light.

At the time Barry entered Evergreen State College in 1974, women were not well represented in mainstream or Alternative comics, and she had few female comic artists as role models. However, a group of determined female comic artists set out to make a name and a place for their work. As male comic artists rebelled against the narrow dictates of the Comics Code in the Underground movement, and as the Alternative artists took up the challenge to further stretch the form and content of comic art, female comic artists struggled to find a space of their own. Robbins, an active participant in establishing "womyn's comics" recalled:

> Sadly, most of the male underground cartoonists understood as little about the new women's movement as the newspapers did, and reacted to what they perceived as a threat by drawing comix filled with graphic violence directed mostly at women. People—especially women people—who criticized this misogyny were not especially welcome in this alternative version of the old boys' club, and were not invited into the comix being produced. (*From Girls* 85)

When a young Lynda Barry was cultivating her own drawing style and imitating what she saw as pioneer R. Crumb's beautiful aesthetic, she most likely did not condemn outright the Alternative comix pioneer's depictions of women. Yet Barry obviously responded to and was frightened by his graphic and often brutal subject matter; as she recalls, "It was really hard-core because the sex stuff was very frightening" (qtd. in Chute, "Interview" 50). Despite any misgivings or apprehension gleaned from reading these Underground and Alternative comix, Barry maintains that when her career did begin to blossom in the 1980s, she wasn't hindered by a "no girls allowed" atmosphere.

However, some scholars suggest that women entering the field in the 1960s and 1970s might have had a more difficult time breaking into the comics field than Barry did. In his *History of Comic Art* Roger Sabin echoes Robbins's reflections, noting that women at the time were forced to find their own way, apart from much of the Underground comix movement:

> These early women cartoonists were using their strips to protest about a number of related issues: obliquely, about being excluded from the male-dominated underground (especially the big anthologies, which they claimed had a 'Boys Only' atmosphere) and about the sexism that was rife in the movement (particularly comix by Wilson, Crumb and Spain); and more directly about women's politics generally—subject matter included rape, sex, abortion, babies, working conditions and housework. (105)

In 1972 two separate groups took action to provide more outlets and more exposure for female comic artists, resulting in the anthologies *Tits 'n' Clits* and *Wimmen's Comics*. Scott McCloud suggests that these all-female anthologies "were raw, emotionally honest, politically charged and sexually frank" (*Reinventing* 102). Furthermore, "These same qualities, nearly 30 years later, are still present in the works of many leading female cartoonists" (*Reinventing* 102). However, McCloud notes that contemporary female cartoonists

> though a minority still—are far too numerous and their work far to varied, to classify as any one kind of "movement." With years to accumulate large and consistent bodies of work in everything from autobiography to science fiction to urban parables to high fantasy, the worlds of individual creators now far outweigh the novelty of their gender for all but the most close-minded readers. (*Reinventing* 102)

In the years since women like Robbins articulated a space for their work in comics, many more women have taken up the call, creating works fantastic and familiar. It is perhaps not surprising, then, that women comic artists, whether inspired or incensed by the male artists of the Underground and Alternative movements, frequently focused on close examinations of what it is to be a woman and a girl. Hillary Chute suggests that the work of women comic artists "exemplifies how graphic narratives can envision an everyday reality of women's lives, which, while rooted in the personal, is invested and threaded with collectivity, beyond prescriptive models of alterity or sexual difference" ("Comics as Literature" 459). Aline Kominsky-Crumb, Mary Fleener, Phoebe Gloeckner, Debbie Drechsler, and Julie Doucet share with Lynda Barry a place in time as female comic artists working and gaining recognition in the 1980s and 1990s. And though their styles are diverse, they also share key influences as well as interest in depicting female experiences.

Kominsky-Crumb (b. 1948) trained as a painter and worked closely with Underground Comics Artists and was encouraged by prominent figures such as Kim Deitch and her eventual husband, Robert Crumb. She was also an important figure in encouraging female comics through anthologies such as *Wimmen's Comics* and *Twisted Sisters* and edited the series *Weirdo*, in addition to creating the comic *Dirty Laundry* with her husband. Though many know her as Crumb's wife, she was creating her own autobiographical comics well before they met and stated in an interview with the *Guardian* newspaper that she "had a big influence on his style of recording his life." Her 2009 graphic memoir *Need More Love* tells Kominsky-Crumb's life story amidst the backdrop of the Underground comix movement. Kominsky-Crumb focuses primarily on the lives of women, in particular, her own life, creating witty, exaggerated narratives in which droll text pairs with exaggerated images of large, curvy women to tell humorous and sometimes grotesque stories of the self. Barry shares with Kominsky-Crumb an interest in the autobiographical, as well as a willingness to poke fun at herself in her work. While Kominsky-Crumb suggests she had a strong influence on her husband, many prominent female comic artists of the 1980s and 1990s, including Barry, cite Robert Crumb as a strong inspiration.

Mary Fleener (b. 1951), like Kominsky-Crumb, creates autobiographical comics focused on her life as a woman. Fleener utilizes her cubist-inspired style, "cubismo," in many comics, including the collection *Life of the Party* (1996) and the *Slutburger* series. Fleener's bold, geometrically influenced aesthetic creates a particular eye-catching, kinetic style that alternates striking, frenetic, black-and-white cubist panels with more traditional representational panels, resulting in a fascinating mix of fantastic and realistic. As with Kominsky-Crumb and Doucet, these stories are not shy about addressing sex and, in particular, with Fleener, drugs and rock and roll, and they do so with a rollicking sense of humor.

Phoebe Gloeckner (b. 1960) shares an unvarnished approach to girlhood in her work, as well as inspiration from Kominsky-Crumb and R. Crumb, both of whom were family friends. According to an interview with the *Comics Journal*'s Gary Groth, as a teenager Gloeckner spent time with the Crumbs and Terry Zwigoff and approached Ron Turner at Last Gasp to publish her comics. Gloeckner later trained as a medical illustrator and created comics somewhat sporadically through the 1980s and 1990s, but she gained acclaim for her anthology *A Child's Life and Other Stories* (1998) and *The Diary of a Teenage Girl* (2002). *A Child's Life* features seven comic art stories about a young girl, while *The Diary of a Teenage Girl* utilizes a combination of prose, illustration, and comics to tell the coming-of-age narrative of Minnie. Both works depict the harsh, usually brutal sexuality of young girls. The precise details of Gloeckner's black-and-white ink drawings demonstrate her training as a medical illustrator and emphasize the physicality of the characters as well as the rawness of the sexual situations. Gloeckner's work, like Barry's, focuses primarily on young girls, and *The Diary* bears closer consideration in relation to Barry's illustrated novel *Cruddy*, for they both employ a diary format to tell the stories of two adolescent girls on the cusp of adulthood thrust into the adult world. Yet Gloeckner's work, while sharing an approach that does not gloss over the ugliness of girlhood, does not share Barry's moments of fun and whimsy.

Debbie Drechsler (b. 1953) also dwells on the dark side of girlhood in her semiautobiographical comics, particularly *Daddy's Girl* (1996) and *Summer of Love* (2002), which address rape and incest with blunt pictures and prose. Although Drechsler trained as an illustrator, she was inspired by Michael Dougan and Richard Scala to pursue cartooning after moving to San Francisco in the late 1980s. However, in an interview with Gary Groth of the *Comics Journal*, Drechsler cites Barry as her "primary role model for comics," and Barry's influence can be seen in both style and substance. In *Daddy's Girl*, Drechsler focuses on a father molesting his daughter and *Summer of Love* examines an abused teenager dealing with sex and growing up. Drechsler's comic style has a similar feel to Barry's, though Barry's work has a lighter touch and a less representational aesthetic. In *Summer of Love*, Drechsler's images became even more precise and realistic, although in the hardcover edition she experimented with an unusual two-color palette of green and orange that gives the comic art a surreal, dreamlike feeling. Drechsler explained in the interview with Groth that the process of reimagining childhood trauma through her comics was "cathartic," but according to her own website (debdrex.com), she now focuses on illustration work and no longer creates comics.

Canadian Julie Doucet is also known for chronicling the experiences of young women. Doucet, born in Montreal in 1965, created semiautobiographical comics such as the comic book series *Dirty Plotte* (which began as a self-published mini-comic in 1988 and was later published as a full comic series by Drawn and Quarterly, ending in 1998), *My Most Secret Desire* (1995), *My New York Diary* (1999), and *365 Days: A Diary by Julie Doucet* (2002). Barry shares many similarities with Doucet, artistically as well as thematically. While Barry is a few years older and began publishing her comics a bit earlier than Doucet, both cite Crumb as an inspiration. However, Doucet embraces his brutal depictions of fantasy in a way that Barry does not. For example, in one dream sequence from *My Most Secret Desire*, "Julie," a representation of the author, gives birth to a cat, receives a severed penis as a gift, proceeds to eat the penis, and is then jabbed in the eye with a syringe. While Barry tends to tiptoe around detailed depictions of sex and sexuality, leaving genitals and actual images of intercourse out of the panel, Doucet, like Kominsky-Crumb, Gloeckner, and Drechsler, chooses to depict them with meticulous specificity. Aesthetically, Doucet draws in a manner reminiscent of Crumb, with a dense, highly detailed style suggestive of black-and-white lithographs. In contrast, Barry's work, particularly in her comic *Ernie Pook*, demonstrates finer lines and more textual narration. Doucet also works in numerous mediums, at one point even announcing a short-lived retirement from comics; and while her work, like Barry's, addresses the darker side of womanhood, her focus is on young women, primarily a fictionalized version of herself, rather than girls. But perhaps their greatest point of difference remains their treatment of issues relating to young women, for Doucet presents extremely graphic depictions of sex, menstruation, and relationships that distance her from the more oblique references to sexuality in Barry's comics.

Alison Bechdel (b. 1960), creator of the long-running comic series *Dykes to Watch Out For*, also explores girlhood in her graphic memoir *Fun Home* (2006). Like Barry, Bechdel enjoyed success creating a continuing comic strip for alternative newspapers, with her strip focusing on a cast of lesbians and their friends, but it was in *Fun Home* that Bechdel rendered her teen years, examining her relationship with her father, his death and sexuality, and her own coming-out process. The book, a critical and commercial success, combines highly literate and literary text (both in narration and in character dialogue) with Bechdel's crisp, clean, and realistic drawing style characterized by black ink lines along with a grey wash of color. The memoir presents an extremely realistic rendering of a girl and young woman discovering herself and her father through comic art storytelling. Bechdel shares with Barry a love of language and literacy and peppers her memoir with literary allusions, and she does not shy away from extended narration. However, Bechdel's artistic style is much cleaner and more representational, and she has no trouble asserting her memoir is autobiographical.

A new, up-and-coming generation of comic artists has also been exploring girlhood, including standouts Marjane Satrapi, Ariel Schrag, and Miss Lasko-Gross. Satrapi (b. 1969) created the extremely successful graphic memoirs *Persepolis* (2003), *Persepolis 2* (2004), *Embroideries* (2005), and *Chicken with Plums* (2006). In the series Satrapi recounts her childhood in Iran, her flight to France, and her itinerant years as a teenager and young woman before turning her attention to family stories and histories. Her stark, monochromatic style allows for no shading or gradations in color and underscores her straightforward, unadorned narrative voice. The blend of personal and social history resonated with readers and was ultimately adapted into an animated feature film. While Barry and Satrapi have dissimilar artistic styles, in her article "Comic Visions and Revisions in the Work of Lynda Barry and Marjane Satrapi," Theresa Tensuan notes that both artists' "comics highlight the ways in which figures resist, subvert, and capitulate to forces of social coercion and normative visions" (954). Satrapi has a more cosmopolitan narrative that takes place in Iran as well as Austria, while Barry focuses almost all of her genres in the Pacific Northwest, generally within the radius of a street or two. Furthermore, Barry has a more whimsical, sentimental approach to childhood. Even as she depicts children in harrowing situations, there is a sense that the author wants to protect the child, with violence happening offscreen. In contrast, Satrapi pictures the violence in striking black and white.

Ariel Schrag (b. 1979) has the distinction of documenting life as a teenage girl through comics while still a teenager. Her memoirs *Awkward* (ninth grade), *Definition* (tenth grade), *Potential* (eleventh grade) and *Likewise* (twelfth grade) chronicle her development throughout high school, recording her coming-out process, various romantic entanglements, drinking experiments, and graduation. The series is a fascinating record of the artist's development from teenager to adult, as well as from neophyte to practiced comic artist. Perhaps given their topicality, they echo Barry's attention to telling period detail, but artistically Schrag's work more closely resembles Bechdel's black-and-white ink work , though her figures are decidedly less realistic. However, Schrag varies her style throughout the series, sometimes drawing realistically in dream sequences and more fantastically in real-life situations. In an interview with Noah Berlatsky, she notes that she was inspired by *Maus* and used many of Spiegelman's techniques of illustrating the method of recording, such as representing the computer screen or tape recorder, to emphasize the "truth" of the narrative.

Miss Lasko-Gross (b. 1977), like Schrag, is close to her subject matter as a teenage girl creating comics. Lasko-Gross created *Escape from Special* (2002) and *A Mess of Everything* (2009), semiautobiographical short-story collections about her childhood and adolescence. Lasko-Gross is unflinching in her short pieces, detailing her troubles as a loner and outcast, and her style is unusual in that it is designed as two- to three-page vignettes and is created full scale (rather than being shrunk down from the original drawings), often, according to an interview with Daniel Epstein, with markers and ink while racing between dog-walking jobs in New York City. Her style looks very much like watercolors, and the moody, dark palette underscores the somberness of her early life. Lasko-Gross felt her books would be "perfect for someone who's entering junior high" (Epstein), although many libraries and teachers rejected the explicit dialogue, sexual content, and adult situations. Like Barry, Lasko-Gross concentrates on a darker side of a girl growing up, but Lasko-Gross chooses to focus on her personal history alone and does so with these short, sometimes random anecdotes.

Lynda Barry is not alone, then, in creating comic art about girlhood, yet her multiple ways of seeing her subject set her apart from many others working in the genre. Not only does Barry work in primarily text-based formats such as essays and illustrated novels, she also experiments widely with her comics. From her weekly four-panel strip *Ernie Pook's Comeek* to the longer eighteen-panel short stories of *One Hundred Demons* to the loose, dreamy style of *What It Is* and *Picture This*, Barry continually experiments with new ways of depicting girlhood—through comic art as well as other mediums. While Barry shares with many of her contemporaries and up-and-coming comic artists an interest in destroying stereotypes of girlhood, there are borders she does not cross in depicting the horrors of girlhood and images she chooses not present in word or picture.

Race and Ethnicity in Comics Culture

While women clearly have contributed a great deal to the field of comic art, Barry still stands with her female colleagues as something of a rarity in a male-dominated field. She is also part of another underrepresented group in the field of American comic art—an artist of color. As recently as 10 February 2008, several comic artists of color protested tokenism in the newspaper-publishing world by drawing the same strip. Eric Deggans reports, after speaking with cartoonist Darrin Bell, that "most newspapers, it seems, will make room for only two strips drawn by people of color, no matter the subject." Scholars have also noted the lack of minority figures as characters and creators. McCloud observed that while white artists frequently addressed racism in the 1970s, the results were "predictably mixed" (*Reinventing* 107). Scholar Marc Singer studied racism in comic books in depth in his article "Black Skins and White Masks: Comic Books and the Secret of Race," in which he posits, "Comic books, and particularly the dominant genre of superhero comic books, have proven fertile ground for stereotyped depictions of race" (107). While this trend seems to be changing, particularly as "the ranks of comics freelancers began taking on more color" (McCloud, *Reinventing* 107) and creating more realistic portrayals of people of color, the recent protest staged by comic strip artists indicates there is still much work to be done.

Even as American comic art has lacked minority voices, comic books have enjoyed a lively history in the birthplace of Barry's beloved grandmother, the Philippines. The popular contemporary comic artist Gerry Alanguilan states that komiks, as comics are known in the Philippines, "had a very rich history, tracing its roots way back to the late 1800's when national hero Jose Rizal created what would be the very first Filipino made comic strip, 'The Monkey and the Tortoise'" (qtd. in Kean). This rich tradition influenced many Filipino and Filipino American artists drawing comics today, including Alanguilan, Carlo Pagulayan, and Rafael Kayanan. However, most of these artists draw superhero comics for the US market, although some of the artists based in the Philippines, like Alanguilan, continue to "ink American comics" in addition to publishing their own titles with Filipino characters. Men dominate the komiks tradition in the Philippines, and the Filipino American comic artists are generally male. However, Philippines-based comic company Mango produces *Mango Jam* "entirely by Filipinas for young Filipinas," according to their promotional materials. Since the majority of these artists are drawing superheroes, Barry seems to share little commonalities in content or aesthetics with these Filipino and Filipino American artists; and given her conflicted relationship to constructions of femininity, one might conjecture that her thoughts on the extraordinarily stereotypical pretty girls filling the pages of *Mango Jam* would be similarly ambivalent. Barry's identity as a female of Filipino descent sets her apart from many comic artists, yet she seems to enjoy her "outsider" status in may arenas, preferring to remain just outside of the mainstream. However, Barry's ethnicity was not directly addressed in her work until *One Hundred Demons*, in which she explores how her mixed Norwegian/Irish/Filipino heritage set her at a distance from the Filipino community as well as the white lower-class community where she sometimes chose to pass as white. Her later comics, in particular, suggest that Barry did struggle with sexism and racism; and to better understand these issues as presented throughout her career, it is helpful to consider her own life story.

2

"True Stories"

LYNDA BARRY'S EARLY YEARS AND WORKS

But in an overcrowded and unhappy home, it's incredibly easy for any child to slip away.
—LYNDA BARRY, "Sanctuary of School"

When asked about her childhood in an interview with Joe Garden, Lynda Barry responded, "It went on and on. Beyond that, um, I actually don't like to talk about it much. I'm very glad it's over." Despite her reticence to discuss her early years, Barry's childhood experiences clearly resonate throughout her oeuvre. From the keen observations of adolescence in *Ernie Pook's Comeek* to the detailed remembrances of *One Hundred Demons*, Barry demonstrates an acute understanding of what it is to be young. Barry's youthful days were not easy ones, and she struggled, as nearly all of her heroines do, to find a sense of security in a chaotic world. While Barry prefers not to speak of her girlhood, images of girls came to dominate her works in all genres, and eventually her own personal story as a girl began to emerge in later works. Over the course of her career Barry frequently changes lenses, looking at girls through various mediums, yet girls remain central in her oeuvre, regardless of the form. However, Barry's very early works were scattered and unfocused, shifting subjects, mediums, and styles; and although Barry came over time to focus on images of girls, she continues to experiment with genre and style. This chapter examines Barry's early years and works, providing a brief overview of the artist's life and career, and pays special attention to the kaleidoscopic perspective evident in the products of her fledgling career.

Barry was born Linda Jean Barry (she would eventually change "Linda" to "Lynda") on 2 January 1956 in Richland Center, Wisconsin, to Bob Barry, of Irish Norwegian descent, and Pearl Landon, from an Irish and Filipino background. According to the short essay "Picturing Happiness" from 1991, the two met in San Diego, California, while Bob Barry was in the US Navy and Pearl Landon was working in the base PX. Lynda, the oldest of three children, was born in Wisconsin; and several years after her birth the family moved to the Rainier Vista projects, one of the rougher neighborhoods in Seattle, Washington. Barry spent her formative years in the Pacific Northwest with her two brothers, Michael and Mark, who were, as she explained in an interview with Marcia Coburn, "younger and way taller." Barry's father worked as a butcher and "was the exception to the extreme Filipino-ness of [her] family" (Barry, "Pork Memories" 117). According to Barry's 1997 essay "What Pop Fly Gave His Daughter," Bob Barry

> wasn't a mean drunk and he wasn't a nice drunk. He wasn't actually an anything kind of drunk except if you tried to talk to him. Then he was a wave-you-away-like-a-fly drunk, and if you kept trying to talk to him, he was a quick-ditch-you-when-you-weren't looking kind of drunk. I never wanted him to ditch me. Ever. It was awful how much a nine-year-old kid can love her father. (74)

Despite his inattention, according to Barry, "None of what he did prevented me from living most of my life with the unshakable belief that he was the incredible guy he said he was" ("What Pop Fly" 78). It was from her father that Barry gained an appreciation for recording the past. According to Barry, her father treasured the tape recorder that he kept in the basement (another tape recorder makes an ominous appearance in *The Good Times Are Killing Me* as evidence of a father's infidelity). In the essay "Take My Advice" from 2001, Barry writes that Bob Barry "was the one who introduced me to the idea of documenting ordinary things. . . . I've been obsessed with the idea of recovering the past ever since" (109). Barry's fascination with the consequences of small, commonplace happenings, taking tiny moments and details and revisiting them in search of larger meaning, is a key theme that resonates in her work, as is her preoccupation with the past, particularly the period and place of her childhood, the mid-1960s to '70s in the Pacific Northwest.

Barry's relationship with her mother was similarly strained. Pearl Landon grew up in the Philippines, and she is depicted in *One Hundred Demons* as a woman obsessed with her own appearance and femininity while squelching any self-esteem in her daughter. Barry told Coburn, "My mother used to tell me things like, 'You're too ugly to be seen with, so you wait in the car while I go into the grocery.'" After hearing such remarks the young Lynda struggles greatly with feelings of insecurity over her appearance in

One Hundred Demons, and most of Barry's heroines demonstrate a similar anxiety and feeling of unsightliness. In *What It Is*, Barry likens her mother to the mythological Gorgon, a beast so terrifying she could turn anyone to stone if they gazed upon her. As an adult, Barry cut her ties to her mother and father; and in her work, parents are generally depicted as indifferent and absent at best, cruel and violent at worst.

Barry, however, found a friendly presence in her childhood home when her grandmother Rosario Landon moved in with the family when Barry was in third grade. In the 1990 essay "When Grandma Discovered Hotdogs," Barry recalls a great joy at her grandmother's presence, for Rosario Landon "spoke an unusual brand of English, preferred walking around barefoot and possessed the nearly supernatural ability to smoke a cigarette with the lighted end in her mouth" (H13). Barry's grandmother held the family together and developed ties with the local Filipino community. In *One Hundred Demons* Rosario Landon represents a comical and calming presence, one in touch with and unashamed of her Filipino ties. Furthermore, she is one of the few adults who shows affection to the young Lynda, criticizing Lynda's mother and siding with her granddaughter in family squabbles.

Unfortunately, according to Barry's 1995 essay "Pork Memories," the stabilizing influence of Barry's grandmother didn't last; Rosario Landon moved out around the same time that Barry's father "ran off with that checkout girl at the supermarket" ("Pork Memories" H1). During this period Barry also remembers her mother disappearing: "My mother bought a shopping cart load of Swanson's TV dinners and pork pot pies, showed me and my brothers how to heat them and then went to lie down in her bedroom for a couple of years" ("Pork Memories" H1). Barry thus found herself without much of a family and was forced to fend for herself and take care of her brothers with little parental involvement. During this tumultuous time Barry found special solace in the safety and security of school, and in particular in the classroom of her teacher Claire LeSane. It was in Mrs. LeSane's classroom that Barry began to express herself through art. According to Barry's essay "Sanctuary of School" from 1998, Mrs. LeSane "believed in the natural power of painting and drawing for troubled children" (650). Mrs. LeSane gave each of the children the opportunity to "sit apart from the class for a while to paint, draw and silently work out problems on 11 x 17 sheets of newsprint. Drawing came to mean everything to me. At the back table in Room 2, I learned to build myself a life preserver that I could carry into my home" ("Sanctuary" 650). At this time Barry found a lifeline through art that allowed her to endure her troubled home life, and it is to this creative process that Barry would turn to again and again to provide respite in difficult times.

Barry also discovered a friend and mentor in her neighbor Yvonne Taylor, a white woman married to an African American man, an unusual occurrence in Barry's neighborhood. According to Barry's essay "Guardian Neighbor" from 1995, Taylor introduced Barry to many things: the joy of gospel music, the idea of a truly happy family and marriage, and the vocation of artist. Barry's mother was derisive of Yvonne Taylor's calling, but Barry was fascinated. She remembers in particular observing Mrs. Taylor at work on a sign for her church: "As I watched her letter that sign so perfectly, I remember thinking that word. Artist. And when she let me make one of the shining lines of the cross I made a vow in my head that that was what I was going to be. I vowed that I was going to grow up and be great at it" ("Guardian Neighbor" 278). Barry dedicated *The Good Times Are Killing Me* to Yvonne Taylor and Claire LeSane, and their impact lingers throughout her work. In *The Good Times Are Killing Me,* Edna goes to church with Mrs. Willis, where she too discovers the power of gospel music. Though most of the teachers in Barry's work are ignorant and malevolent, at times a kindly teacher will take a student aside and tell him or her exactly what he or she needs to hear.

Junior high was a particularly challenging time for Barry, and it is perhaps no surprise that the girls later featured in her work also straddle the precarious breach between childhood and adulthood, often with disastrous consequences. With her father and grandmother gone, Barry joined her mother as a janitor on the night shift. At this early age Barry took on adult responsibilities and troubles. In *One Hundred Demons* Barry reflects, "When did I become a teenager? Was it when I started shop-lifting? Dropped acid laid on me by hippies in the park? Hitch-hiked in halter tops? Got drunk on wine stolen from a synagogue? I was 13 when I did these things" (71). When she compares her life to the characters in *Good Times,* Barry told Pamela Grossman that she feels that her "struggles as a kid were a little like Edna and Bonna's, but I was much more troubled than they are. I had a very hard time socializing, and although there were racial conflicts on my street, certainly, they were nothing compared to the emotional ones" (P. Grossman). In a recent interview with Carol Kino, Barry revealed that by sixteen she was virtually independent, living at home but supporting herself by her work as a janitor. These emotional conflicts are detailed in depth in *One Hundred Demons* and *What It Is* and include her struggles with beauty, femininity, maturation, and finding her voice, and it is these themes that reoccur to plague the girls she later created.

During the tumultuous time of adolescence, Barry was particularly struck by the power of class in her neighborhood. She recalled in an interview with Pamela Grossman, "The thing that really struck me when I went to junior high was class. . . . I had no idea what was going on off my street until I was 12 or 13, and it really disturbed me to see how much certain people had, how great their lives seemed to be and how I knew that would never happen to me, ever." This disillusionment continued when Barry entered Franklin High School in Seattle. Though she went to school with talents such as cartoonist Charles Burns, musician Kenny G, and choreographer Mark Morris, Barry found the rough atmosphere debilitating. In an interview with Marcia Coburn, Barry remembered that Franklin High School was a particularly brutal environment. Barry was on the verge of dropping out in her junior year. With the help of the counselor, Barry was able to transfer to Roosevelt High School as an Asian transfer student. Barry flourished at Roosevelt, eventually earning a space at Evergreen State College in Olympia, Washington.

Barry entered Evergreen in 1974 and found the nontraditional school a perfect fit for her fractured psyche. In a personal interview Barry suggested that she could not have survived a more traditional academic experience and fondly credits the atmosphere at her alma mater:

> If I tried to go to a traditional college, I wouldn't have made it because I was really in pieces once I left my house, in pieces, so it was good fortune that that school was there and they were dying for students. They really would let anybody in. I'm not kidding. You could just send a one-inch square of elastic from your underwear and they'd be, "This is brilliant!" as your entry thesis. Just glue it to an index card and you're in. I love them for that.[1]

While at Evergreen, Barry was able to pursue her art and her academic interests, and it was there that she met Marilyn Frasca and Matt Groening, two formative influences on her development as a comic artist.

Frasca came to Evergreen as a new faculty member in 1974 and taught a rigorous painting course that Barry likens to "being an apprentice in the Renaissance or Middle Ages."[2] Barry discovered Frasca while she was working as a life-drawing model to earn extra income. Barry enjoyed sitting in the drawing classes while modeling and watching the artists at work, although, she explained to Hillary Chute, "the only bad part was I had to be naked in order to experience this" ("Interview" 49). While modeling one day, Barry said, "[I] started crying because I realized I didn't want to be on the table. I wanted to be in the class" ("Interview" 49). She signed up for Frasca's "Images" class the following year.

For her part, Frasca recalls that the loose, interdisciplinary curriculum of Evergreen particularly suited Barry: "As far as I was concerned the college was designed for her. She joined a number of interdisciplinary programs and learned to find her own way while studying writing, drawing, philosophy, and a variety of other disciplines."[3] As part of Frasca's course, students were required to create "ten finished pieces a week," a practice which inspired Barry to work continuously. In a personal interview, Barry noted that she's working constantly, "but it doesn't feel like work."[4] Barry later dedicated *What It Is* to Frasca and often mentions her as the inspiration for the creative writing process Barry espouses in *What It Is* and *Picture This* and in the "Writing the Unthinkable" writing workshops Barry teaches across the country.

Barry reflects on her mentorship under Frasca in *What It Is* and how it shaped not only her pedagogy but also her art. It is through her work with Frasca that Barry developed a desire to pursue "images," or representations of ideas, through picture and text. Barry found Frasca a particularly "mysterious" teacher, but was drawn to Frasca's silent, thoughtful pedagogy: "I was sure when she looked at my paintings, she was figuring out what she thought of them, but she wouldn't tell me" (*What It Is* 120). While Barry pondered Frasca's silence, her teacher found herself studying her pupil. For her part, Frasca remembered that Barry "was very serious and she paid attention. If you teach, you know what it is like to have a student who is totally present to all that is happening." Frasca explained that she developed a program with Ira Progroff that explored a workshop "process he developed called The Intensive Journal."[5] This process encouraged the students to utilize private journal writing to explore images. Frasca explained that through the writing, "They learned also that their own painting or drawing had a life history as well, a past a present and a future which they were a partner to and so they learned to dialogue with their images."[6] From the beginning, Frasca felt that her student connected through this journaling technique, which helped Barry develop her art:

> Lynda dove into this personal writing and though not required students often read aloud and she would listen as if she were hearing true voices for the first time. In her writing she learned to follow leads given by one drawing to the next and proceeded with courage and good humor to develop a stunning body of work.[7]

This process, emphasizing writing, reading, and creating art as complementary practices, clearly resonated with Barry, who continued to create in a variety of disciplines and asks her own students to read and share their writing in a similar fashion in the "Writing the Unthinkable" writing workshops. Barry also espouses Frasca's philosophy that everyone can and should follow their creative inclinations. Frasca wondered, "Why shouldn't everyone draw, write, make music?"[8] This sentiment certainly informs Barry's philosophy and, in particular, *What It Is*, the 2008 book loosely based on Frasca's process, and *Picture This*, the companion book focused on drawing, published in 2010. Today Barry marks her time learning from Frasca as one of the most "significant" events in her life.

At this time Barry still considered herself a painter, and absolutely *not* a cartoonist. Matt Groening, also a student at Evergreen, urged Barry to pursue cartooning. Through their frequent appearances together and the numerous dedications to one another in various books (even the recent books *What It Is* and *Picture This* carry salutes to "Funklord of USA Matt Groening"), their continuing friendship has become fodder for much speculation. In a 2000 *Life in Hell* strip Groening describes how they met:

> In 1974 I was in college, still raving about "Catch-22." One night somebody said if you like Joseph Heller so much, you should meet this girl in Dorm D. She wrote to Heller and he wrote her back. Where was this girl? I searched Dorm D until I found her. And that's how I met Lynda Barry.

Barry recalls that during their early days at Evergreen she and Groening were "just embryonic."[9] Groening, as editor of the school paper, published Barry's early stories, and from their earliest interactions the two artists inspired and pushed one another. Now Barry can't look back at these early days without reflecting on the friendship that spurred her on: "It's impossible to think about my early work without thinking about some of the very good things like my friendship with Matt Groening."[10]

Groening wasn't the only one impressed by Barry's cartoons. John Keister, a friend who worked for the University of Washington newspaper, the *Daily*, began, unbeknownst to Barry, printing the cartoons that Barry had sent him in a letter. The comics proved popular and Keister asked for more. In an interview with Thom Powers, Barry argued that these earliest comics were "printed by accident" (63). She also explained that her inspiration for the work was being dumped by her "hippie boyfriend" (Powers 60). Regardless of any accidents in the publication process, Barry had begun her career as a creator of comic art.

Barry's first published comics suggest a shifting, kaleidoscopic approach, and they stand apart from her later works in style and substance. Her drawing at the time is more representational and realistic than later projects, and the young girls who figure so prominently in her career are noticeably absent, though there are numerous immature women struggling to resist the charms of spiny, sweet-talking, succulent plants. Later chapters will outline Barry's major works and favored genres in more detail, providing expanded context and analysis and exploring her multiple ways of visualizing girlhood in various forms. However, as these early efforts are so much a part of her personal history and trajectory as an artist, they bear additional attention in relation to her biography. Thus the remainder of this chapter examines Barry's projects in correlation with her life story.

In her early cartoons Barry emphasized adult concerns, particularly in regard to relationship woes. The cartoon in figure 2.1 features one of these nascent efforts, depicting a troubled relationship between a woman and a cactus. Stylistically, these comics differ from later endeavors. These single panels feature finely drawn images directly facing the audience. The realistic characters are drawn with precision and deftness; the pen's lines are fine and detailed. There is a sense of depth and dimension, as in the cartoon starring a plaintive woman covered in spines and a prickly cactus sharing coffee. The two sit together, the woman gazing out as the cactus reaches for her, the perspective suggesting that the reader sits directly opposite, peeking in on the drama. Unlike her more stylized and abstracted images from later years, this image is much more realistic, in direct contrast to the absurdity and unreality of the situation depicted. The woman's delicate, overdrawn hands, for example, indicate she is fiddling with the table and her face. These comics also lack Barry's trademark loquaciousness. Although some have marginal commentary, most of the text is in the form of dialogue, lettered in capitals in clearly illustrated speech balloons. These comics, sometimes known as the *Spinal Comics*, focus on amplifying the import of the ordinary, as much of her later work does—here mocking mundane and silly courtship rituals, particularly the poor choices of women.

Just as her style was, at the time, peripatetic, Barry, too, was wandering after graduating from Evergreen in 1978. Upon leaving school Barry returned to Seattle and continued cartooning while juggling a number of jobs. She told interviewer Tod Olson that she did, however, have a strong inclination *not* to work for other people. In Seattle, Barry approached the new alternative paper *Seattle Sun* with her comic, and although her work was initially rejected for being racist by an editor who interpreted the cactuses as racist caricatures (Chute, "Interview" 51), another staff member at the *Sun* decided to run the comic. While Barry juggled a variety of jobs in addition to creating her strip for the *Sun*, her friend Groening was employing his

Figure 2.1. "Ernie Pook's Comics."
The University of Washington,
Daily, 5 May 1978.

journalism skills at the (now defunct) *LA Reader*. In 1979 he wrote an article entitled "Hipness and Stupidity" that touted Barry's talents. In an interview with Joe Garden, Barry recounted that after seeing the article, "Robert Roth at *The Chicago Reader* called me in Seattle and picked up my comic strip. The *Reader* paid $80 per week. My rent was $99 a month. Lordy! I was rich." Barry could now pay her way as a cartoonist.

Barry's first book, *Two Sisters Comeek*, a self-published, xeroxed book, came out in 1979. The book featured twins named Rita and Evette, and, as Barry recounted to Hillary Chute, "people loved the hell out of that strip" ("Interview" 52). Barry copied the strips, packaged them in an envelope, provided her own decorations, and sold the small books for ten dollars (Chute, "Interview" 52). These misunderstood girls foreshadow the more developed characters in *Ernie Pook's Comeek*, but the strip "kind of just ended because sometimes they do" (Chute, "Interview" 52). Given her success with *Two Sisters Comeek*, Barry continued to self-publish the strips with the help of Printed Matter, a store in New York. These books, sometimes known as the "Little Pink Books" because of their pink covers, came out from 1979 to 1980. Barry reflects that an unknown worker at Printed Matter had a profound influence on her when he or she wrote her an enthusiastic note saying that the store wanted more copies of her books (Chute, "Interview" 54). This personal connection with her audience and the affirmation that someone understood and appreciated her work inspired Barry to continue creating comics.

Exposure in the *Chicago Reader* acted as a "bellwether," according to editor Robert Roth, and *Girls and Boys*, as the strip was then known, was soon syndicated in numerous alternative weeklies. Building on this popularity, Real Comet Press published two collections of her strips, *Girls and Boys* in 1981 and *Big Ideas* in 1983. What did Roth see in Barry's work that inspired him to publish her in the *Reader*? What made her strip stand out? Frankly, Roth isn't quite sure. "How much do you remember about 1979?"[11] he asked when prompted for specifics on Barry's early career. While Roth cannot recall exactly what encouraged him to take a closer look at Barry's work, these initial comics demonstrate Barry's wit and humor, her appreciation for the absurd and strange, and her frank depiction of the lives of women, certainly all qualities that would stand out in 1979. A close examination of these early efforts also reveals fleeting images of the adolescent girls who would later come to dominate Barry's work amongst what she told interviewer Thom Powers were her "more editorial strips" (66). These comics would form the basis for the collection *Girls and Boys*, and as her focus shifted once again to these more adult strips her style also changed from the soft, flowing drawings of the sisters to a more boisterous, raucous style.

At the time of *Girls and Boys* Barry demonstrated her changeable perspective, moving on to new topics and experimenting with different drawing techniques. Barry told Powers that the comics from *Girls and Boys* were "editorial; they were opinions, real explaining kinds of strips: break things down and explain how things work" (66). But even in these more mature strips Barry was continually drawn back to childhood. Barry recounted to Powers, "When I did *Girls and Boys* there was a lot of childhood stuff that moved into relationships, and then moved out of relationships back into childhood stuff. I think that the two things are really tied to each other. I think the reasons we choose the people we choose have a lot to do with our childhood" (66). At this time Barry wrestled with the notions of relationships and childhood in her comics; although these more "editorial cartoons" differ in style and humor from her later work, they certainly catapulted her into the public eye.

The early comics (from 1979 to 1981) that were eventually printed in *Girls and Boys* in 1981 by Real Comet Press feature simply rendered profiles of figures, generally engaged in spirited conversation about relationships. The highly stylized approach is much different from the softer, more realistic

Figure 2.2. "But Milk and Cookies." Excerpt from Lynda Barry, *Girls and Boys* (Seattle: Real Comet Press, 1981), 74–75.

lines of the *Spinal Comics*. Barry's primary focus in her work of the time was relationships, and for a while she even took on the role of a relationship expert in the popular media. Barry recollected, "For some reason I thought I knew a whole lot about love and dating at the time and wrote quite a bit about it. The joke was on me, of course."[12]

Rueful meditations on unfair relationships frequently appear, as they did in this strip from 1981, which is typical of many of those of the time. The strip depicts a pleasant doormat of a woman being abused by her undeserving boyfriend (fig. 2.2). The woman, Lisa, depicted in profile, wears a matronly dress, pearls, and large, busy earrings as she offers a plate of cookies to her boyfriend. Her dialogue is lettered in straightforward capitals as she placates him, "But milk and cookies are good for you honeybunny," yet the lettering tilts to the right when she becomes angry: "Oh! You nasty little boy! Shame on you! I'll bring you some nice broccoli!" This visual shift suggests an exaggerated, maternal scolding from the girlfriend. The boyfriend, a rougher looking figure, sits at a table, tiny lightning bolts of anger over his head, his words shooting out of his mouth. His dialogue is encased by an angry, jagged speech balloon, and the lettering begins to tilt to the right and is eventually underlined as he exclaims that he's "Leavin" and he's "Had It."

Only the "SLAM" of the door remains, and Lisa wonders, "He left without his jacket! Gosh.-maybe I should bring it to him. I guess I should pack a lunch for him so he wont be hungry when he looks for his new girlfriend." A warning at the bottom of the final panels queries, "How many times has this happened to you?" The admonition invites the audience to place themselves in the scene, presumably identifying with the female, pondering their own relationships and perhaps laughing at the ways they, too, have been mistreated. The woman, however, is no one to admire. She actively supports this treatment, alternately debasing her boyfriend and coddling him. No one is a winner here, a theme echoed in many of the strips addressing romance.

The flattened, somewhat frenzied drawings reinforce Barry's caustic commentary on relationships. Miriam Harris notes that Barry's drawings "possess a deliberate eccentricity and looseness that recalls the art of children, and of other 'outsider' artists, such as the art of the insane" (130). Critic Rob Rodi commented, in his 1989 review of the early life of the strip,

> Her art style too, was anarchic and primitive. The panels looked as though they'd been scratched out by a particularly vicious six-year-old, which, again, suited the strip perfectly. Like medieval religious paintings, the strongest passions warranted the largest depictions, without regard to perspective or proportion. (59)

Not only do the drawings suggest Barry's intentions, the lettering of the dialogue also plays a significant role in telling the story. In this strip, as in most of the early cartoons, the dialogue is lettered entirely in capitals. Joseph Witek argues that "freehand lettering, no matter how precisely done, always betrays the calligrapher's hand, and thus more closely approximates the nuances of the human voice." (23), and it is through Barry's lettering that we glimpse the voices of her characters. The lettering here is not perfect and mechanical, nor is it childish. It is, if anything, sparse and somewhat raw, though the capitalization indicates an emphatic quality, an urgency to the conversations. While the straightforward, capitalized lettering of the dialogue remains much the same for many years, Barry soon introduced an element that has become characteristic of much of her work, a narrative voice accompanying the action.

Barry typically split panels horizontally to allow for a line of commentary at the top or bottom of the panel. These commentaries were most often written in cursive, though they were occasionally printed. In a strip from 1980, the story is told by a first-person narrator whose script is carefully

Figure 2.3. "I Remember."
Lynda Barry, *Girls and Boys*
(Seattle: Real Comet Press,
1981), 31–32.

lettered in cursive throughout the first three panels (fig, 2.3). The placement of the narration on the side of the panel (rather than the top or bottom) is unusual, but this subject reappears frequently in Barry's work, as does the narrative voice accompanying the action.

Text assumes primacy in this strip, with the female figure remaining static and pensive. The cursive here contrasts with the louder, more insistent lettering in the previous strip. The soft lines of the informal cursive lettering imply a letter from a friend or perhaps a midday reverie. This panel demonstrates two key hallmarks of Barry—her obsession with retelling the past (that returns full force some twenty odd years later in *One Hundred Demons*) and her desire to invite readers to participate in the strip. In an interview with Mary Hambly in 1982 Barry reflected on the strip, commenting that the character is in "the process of remembering and then it stops and in the final square you fill in with your own memories and in that way it becomes personal, it's your own cartoon."

Most of Barry's cartoons of this period circle around the theme of relationships, twisting around the subject of romantic entanglements and exploring different angles of male-female relations; yet children and, in particular, girls still make appearances, as they do in this strip from 1980 featuring two young girls, Vivian and Francine (fig. 2.4).

Figure 2.4. "Yuk." Lynda Barry, *Girls and Boys* (Seattle: Real Comet Press, 1981), 16–17.

The cruelty of children is a common theme for Barry, and in this 1983 panel the snobby Francine rebuffs Vivian, who smells like "P" and is actually drawn with tiny letter *P*s radiating from her body. Miriam Harris comments on Barry's mischievous use of the letter *P*, suggesting that "Barry playfully puns on another liquid substance, P, so that it may be read as a sound, signifier, and pictorialization of a pungent emanation" (136). This silly, slightly naughty witticism plays on numerous levels, engaging the reader in a childish joke. Vivian, the malodorous girl, reacts violently to the teasing, choking and spitting on Francine. These figures are depicted with little regard to perspective, giving a flattened appearance, something like paper dolls. The characters at this time almost always appear in profile, facing one another, and very rarely face forward, fostering the illusion that the viewer is peeking through a keyhole into another world but is being held at a distance. Backgrounds are sparse, though the characters are drawn with many telling details, such as elaborate hairstyles and complicated clothing. The figures, with their oversized heads and strangely geometric bodies, are abstracted in such a way as to emphasize the flaws and incongruities. Most characters show rows and rows of teeth and look as if their features have been stuck onto overlarge heads like a Mr. Potato Head toy. While some might accuse Barry of poor draftsmanship, these figures serve to underscore her themes.

These are not heroic figures saving the world, nor are they sweet children frolicking in picturesque landscapes. These are adults and children fighting and crying and eating too many doughnuts. They are the audience abstracted and pressed under glass for all to see, even as the readers are invited to see themselves in the reflection.

The exaltation of the ordinary is maintained in the dialogue; the figures speak in the vernacular. Francine asks, "Yuk. Why do I gotta be partners with Vivian stink-face. She smells like 'P.'" Francine responds, "Pssst. Francine. We don't really have to do it. We can fake like we are holding hands but we won't be 'K?'" The characters converse in everyday dialect, what one might hear if eavesdropping on the playground. The hand-lettered font and the shape of the speech balloons further underscore Barry's ideas. David Carrier comments that a balloon "is not just a neutral container but another element in the visual field" (45), and the bumpy speech balloons suggest the agitated nature of Francine. The smoothest balloon encases Vivian's "OK OK OK OK", and indicates the quick, rushed nature of the outburst.

Strips like "Phobia-Phobia" from 1982 presage Barry's personal reminiscences in *One Hundred Demons*, with a fuzzy-haired narrator who looks much like Lynda from *Demons* reflecting on the fears of her childhood. This strip differs from most others of the time period in the drawing style. The figures are finely rendered in thin, scratchy lines—as if to emphasize the veracity of the strip through a more realistic style. Unlike the thicker outlines and exaggerated profiles of other strips, the textured characters stare out from the strip, challenging the reader to interact with them. The narrator is also present, voicing the story from the bottom of the panel. The strip plays out like a series of snapshots from the memory of the narrator—a filmstrip of phobias (fig. 2.5).

Fear is just one of the issues facing the children in these early strips; they also confront the cruelty of other children, the stupidity and apathy of adults, and the great anxiety of straddling the divide between adult and child. Foreshadowing a major theme in her later works, these children are not depicted as innocent or naïve. In one strip originally published in 1979 an anxious Karen is propositioned by a "BLONDE + CUTE" Bill. Karen looks anxiously to the lower left side of the panel, her teeth stretched tight in a grimace. In the next panel Bill gropes Karen's tiny breasts, his hands drawn over and over to indicate a twisting motion. Bill's tongue sticks out and he salivates in earnest. Shown in profile, his single eye with double pupils connotes a sort of mania. Karen, in contrast, once again looks to the lower left shamefully. Small, shaded bubble clouds and the phrase "She thinks" tell us that she has "The Creeps." And yet after Bill departs Karen dissolves into

Figure 2.5. "Phobia-Phobia."
Lynda Barry, *Big Ideas*
(Seattle: Real Comet Press,
1983), 38–39.

tears wondering, "Why do I keep <u>doing</u> this? It makes me feel so gross. Im <u>not</u> gonna come here tomorrow. Im gonna go straight home. But what if he quits liking me." Karen wants to be liked, to fit in, yet she finds the adult sexual activities and the casual pawing of Bill disgusting (fig. 2.6). At this juncture she is both child and adult, a young girl used as a woman. Barry explained to Mary Hambly that the figure of this girl was meant to address women young and old: "I was criticized once by a 'very intelligent' woman who said that one of the reasons she didn't like my cartoons was 'cause they portray things as they are instead of as they should be. I thought, 'Oh, holy cow, how is anybody going to get out of anything without seeing where they are first?'" Even early in her career, Barry demonstrated a willingness to recognize criticism and take risks to create work not widely accepted or lauded.

In these early strips Barry's perspective is kaleidoscopic in nature, constantly revolving and shifting as she looks at romance and sex, adult concerns, and the world of children. Her artistic style also shifts from finely detailed and realistic to abstract and unrefined. In her early career Barry's attention frequently changed and she often experimented with different styles. Barry noted in an e-mail that looking back on these early forays into the cartooning world is impossible without also reflecting on her "early self, and the early 80's! And the arrogance I had then that is particular to

Figure 2.6. "C'mon Karen." Lynda Barry, *Girls and Boys* (Seattle: Real Comet Press, 1981), 32–33.

some artists in their twenties, the 'gonna change the world, man!' feeling, and there is chagrin about that."[13] Drawing on her confidence and bravado, Barry took on another challenge, depicting life from the male perspective in a moneymaking assignment with *Esquire* magazine that ultimately left her cold.

Barry's success in the alternative weeklies brought her to the attention of a much wider audience, ultimately landing her a job for a full-color, full-page spread in *Esquire* magazine in 1983. The strip, entitled *Modern Romance* until March 1987 and later renamed *The Home Front*, featured a male take on work and relationships (fig. 2.7). A magazine for "Man at His Best" might seem an awkward fit for Barry, and indeed her style and subject matter is tightly constrained—with her favored young female protagonists noticeably absent.

While the brightly colored images draw immediate attention, the strip is extremely controlled and composed, almost stilted in contrast with Barry's weekly strip. The figures, although reminiscent of the abstracted men and women depicted in *Ernie Pook*, appear more conservative and less exaggerated. The lettering, all in capitals, is uniform and clear; and though this might seem like praise, amongst Barry's work this gives the impression of a lack of character. The narrative voice, evident in the harried, sometimes messy let-

Figure 2.7. "Out Clean" from "The Home Front." *Esquire Magazine* 110.2 (August 1988): 144.

tering of *Ernie Pook*, is tamed in the tidy font. Even the speech bubbles seem to be carefully, symmetrically drawn. The characters in the *Esquire* strips are rendered more precisely than the figures in the alternative weeklies, and the result is more forced. The *Esquire* strip featured adult men dealing with life. When asked about her work for *Esquire*, Barry responded, "I hate that stuff with all my heart. I really was broke and I was working with an editor."[14] The editor, Jay Kennedy, directed Barry and guided her to material appropriate for the *Esquire* audience. According to an interview with Thom Powers, Barry recounted she "was really unhappy because I couldn't think of a group of people I had less in common with than rich, white males between the ages of 35 and 45—and I had to write it from a male's perspective. After a while, my brain just felt frozen or shriveled up" (73). The process of drawing the pages, something Barry likened to "having my period" in an interview with Rosemary Graham, was a creative struggle. She revealed her goal to Graham—to show men, "This is how stupid you are." Though often funny, the results feel strained, and Barry eventually quit *Esquire* in 1989. Resisting the constraints of a forced perspective from *Modern Romance,* Barry found another vehicle for her talent and a familiar voice—the adolescent girl.

Perhaps in reaction to the male-centered project for *Esquire*, in the summer of 1984 Barry turned her attention to a decidedly female-centric project, the art exhibition *Naked Ladies! Naked Ladies! Naked Ladies!*, which was translated into a coloring book published by Real Comet Press later that year. In this enterprise Barry painted fifty-four naked women and, inspired by these images, created the voice of what she told interviewer Thom Powers was her "first character," Ann, an adolescent girl reflecting on her experiences with images of naked ladies.

Barry described the genesis of *Naked Ladies!* to Powers, reminiscing that she purchased a deck of "nudie playing cards" for her little brother, which promised pictures of "52 different girls"; but her brother protested, asking, "Is it 52 different girls, or is it five girls with 52 wigs?" Barry noticed that the nude women were essentially interchangeable and felt "it would be fun to do a deck of cards—because I love naked women—with every type of body. It would be fun to just draw it. . . . It turned into this *thing*—it turned into a show; it turned into some paintings; I turned into this coloring book. And then I wrote this narrative to go with it" (Powers 65). The show opened at Seattle's Linda Farris Gallery and featured fifty-four paintings of nude women of all shapes, sizes, ages, and backgrounds, including Barry's self-portrait as the Ace of Spades. The controversy was, according to Barry "more anticipated than it was actual" (qtd. in Rochlin 120), and the exhibit even got positive reviews from such contradictory sources as the feminist publication *Ms.* as well as the decidedly tawdry magazine *Screw*.

The coloring book based on the exhibition presents an alternative to the women of *Playboy* and features all fifty-four nudes in black and white in an oversized volume complete with a full-color, fold-out centerfold reprinting all the nudes in miniature. The opposing side of the centerfold is printed with a repeating card-like pattern featuring shells and fish, so the owner of the book could, ostensibly, cut out each of the nudes and have his or her own complete deck of *Naked Ladies!* cards. The women, varying from extremely realistic to a cubist abstract, are drawn with solid, dark lines and are depicted in a variety of poses from sexually charged to maternal to comical. Some are, indeed, hyper-sexualized in the style of pornography, exposing their vaginas and gazing suggestively at the viewer. Other women look playful, angry, and/or amused. There are women breastfeeding, pregnant women, vampire women, Asian women, and African women with spears. Paired with the oversized images, a typed narrative creeps along the bottom of the pages, with no more than four lines of text underneath each portrait. Barry juxtaposes the idea of "naughty" pictures for adults with a coloring book for children, shattering the illusion that children are removed from such images. Barry further challenges the idea of children's innocence in the narrative accompanying the pictures, for these short vignettes portray a girl's impulse to see "forbidden" women's bodies, and consequently reject her own body as a result.

The narrative accompanying *Naked Ladies!* begins when the protagonist, Ann, is "five years old" and sees her "first boner" and describes her changing feelings for women's bodies throughout childhood and adolescence, ending in high school.[15] While Ann maintains a consistent voice throughout, her perspective shifts drastically over the course of the piece, moving from being thrilled by the figures of naked ladies to being horrified by them, including the sight of her own naked body. Ann's language is the uncensored vernacular of most children, and she speaks frequently of "dingers" and "tits." Her language seems particularly apt, given that the accompanying images are also of ordinary women, both crude and exquisite.

Though Barry confided to Powers that the scene that opens the narrative was true, "A lot of it's just made up. Good old fiction" (65).[16] In fact, the process of composing the narrative was for Barry her "first encounter with the fact that you can take a character, and then they'll do all the work, and you just sit behind them and jot down everything they're saying" (qtd. in *Current Biography* 43), and thus it was a turning point in her work. In the opening story that was based on Barry's own childhood experiences, Ann does not actually see a naked lady, but a naked boy. A group of children gather around a boy named Vernie "laying on the ground . . . Vernie pulls his dinger out and Marty says 'On your Mark, Get Set, GO!' and everyone starts going 'Naked Ladies Naked Ladies Naked Ladies' and then I saw it. It did not disturb me." Thus the title of the book is derived from the children's chant, meant to invoke the image of nude women to titillate and entice a young man. In this scene Ann appears calm about the matter of Vernie's erection, and even a bit disinterested. In contrast, in the next sequence she relates how much she

Figure 2.8. "Jack of Diamonds."
Lynda Barry, *Naked Ladies! Naked
Ladies! Naked Ladies!* (Seattle:
Real Comet Press, 1984).

loves looking at *Playboy*s with her friends, until a religious neighbor discovers them and forces them to pray for salvation.

The young heroine particularly delights in the image of a woman on the Tijuana Brass album: "She made my pants itch. So what if I was a girl? Girls can like naked ladies." This portion of the narrative is accompanied by a particularly sultry portrait of a woman lying on her belly, her skirt pulled up to expose her buttocks and vagina. The woman's expression is reminiscent of the actual woman from the album cover, evoking the sexy naughtiness of the original (fig. 2.8).

After confessing her appreciation of naked ladies, Ann comes to another realization, but one fraught with disappointment: "I found out I could be a naked lady." She makes "a deal to show each other" with the boy next door, only to be disappointed when he reneges and teaches her the shame of her body, demanding she make "him a sandwich and let him come into [her] house and watch TV" or he would tell her mother what she'd done. While she admires the woman on the album cover, Ann learns that not only does her body not measure up, but also that it is dangerous and immoral. Through the encounter she learns that males will use her for her body and then make her feel guilty about it. This portion of the narrative is framed beneath two portraits, the Queen and King of Diamonds. The King of Diamonds appears to be a tiny, young, white girl wearing high heels with a bow in her blond hair, her swimsuit pulled down to reveal fake, conical breasts stuck to her chest. The other portrait, the Queen of Diamonds, features an alluring, dark-skinned woman of around twenty, who might be a stripper or exotic dancer, with small tassels affixed to her full breasts, her tan lines indicating sunning in a bikini. The juxtaposition of the undeveloped girl faking her sexuality contrasts sharply with the lush confidence of the older woman (fig.

Figure 2.9. "Queen and King of Diamonds." Lynda Barry, *Naked Ladies! Naked Ladies! Naked Ladies!* (Seattle: Real Comet Press, 1984).

2.9). Ann is like the young girl, attempting to assume the sexuality of the mature women but failing, feeling used and embarrassed.

Ann progresses to sixth grade and views a film on "Your Special Day" and learns, "One day I would wake up and find a red flower in my underpants and that's when I would be a woman. I figured that's when I would get the tits as well." In seventh grade, according to Ann, "Everyone thought they were ugly. Everyone thought they were too fat." At this time "the world was divided by who had gotten their periods and who hadn't," but by high school "we all knew we were naked ladies. We knew it and some of the girls started being called sluts and some of the girls started being called prudes." The girls gaze furtively at one another in PE, comparing their bodies, but they are now afraid to look at *Playboys* "because you might be a lesbo by accident." In fact, the narrator concludes:

> By then the girls in Playboy were clearly the enemy. They were going to get all the guys and we'd never get any guys, not even the creeps, and even if we ever did get a guy, they could take him away from us just like *that*. Because every man in the world would always want them way more than they would ever want us because they were beautiful and we were ugly. It put us in a bad mood for the next ten years.

Ann's statement echoes the images of the Queen of Diamonds and King of Diamonds, for although the young white girl pictured on the King of Diamonds might occupy the higher position in the hierarchy of race and class as well as the deck of cards, it is the lushly sensual woman depicted on the Queen of Diamonds who will "get all the guys." Ann, like the little girl on the King of Diamonds, is an imposter, attempting to assume sexuality too

Figure 2.10. "The Jokers." Lynda Barry, *Naked Ladies! Naked Ladies! Naked Ladies!* (Seattle: Real Comet Press, 1984).

soon and believing herself to be in competition with the eroticized images from *Playboy* magazine.

The conclusion is accompanied by two final portraits: the jokers. The first features the profile of a woman spraying herself with a garden hose, an image strongly reminiscent of girlie magazines. The woman holds the nozzle to her lips and, with eyes closed, showers herself (fig. 2.10). Once again the sexual subtext is quite blatant. The final image, however, presents the most cartoon-like woman in the series: an Egyptian woman in the ancient hieroglyphic style: her arms raised at right angles and her breasts facing opposite directions (fig. 2.10). The two women suggest the divide between the women of *Playboy* and the awkwardness of girls like Ann, who feel "deformed," flattened and pressed into clumsy, uncomfortable positions. Where is the image of Ann? Is she the hieroglyph or the unattainable beauty?

In the beginning, "from looking at all the naked lady pictures," Ann was convinced "that [she] was going to have huge tits. Everyone was going to have them." As she enters adolescence this certainty fails and the narrator despairs, "It seemed like nearly everyone was deformed without ever even having a chance to be normal. Nobody could stand how they looked even if there was nothing wrong with them." While Ann is initially thrilled by the figures of nude women, her commentary indicates that as she grows society teaches her that such likenesses are shameful and immoral. *Naked Ladies!*, like a kaleidoscope, takes women's bodies and splinters them into numerous reflections; and in focusing on the images of nude women, including her own body, Barry found yet another voice of girlhood—that of a young girl growing up and comparing her body to those of the women of *Playboy*. As Barry shows the heterogeneous group of women, the text contracts into the voice of one young girl.

Figure 2.11. "Insomni-Yak." Lynda Barry, *Everything in the World* (New York: Harper and Row, 1986), 86–87.

This narration marks a turning point for Barry; it was the introduction of her first "true character," one of the first of many young women who would come to dominate her work. As with many others that appear in Barry's later works, Ann struggles, and her particular challenge is accepting herself as a naked lady amongst all the others. And as with the others, there is no grand and happy ending. Ann states, "It put us in a bad mood for the next ten years," indicating her individual disappointment as well as solidarity with other women. But then what happens? Does she accept herself? How? Given the unhappy, conflicted women depicted in the early years of *Ernie Pook*, it seems unlikely that Ann found acceptance in adulthood. Rather, the text of *Naked Ladies!* suggests that the exaggerated women of *Playboy* create a permanent and impossible standard of beauty that damages the psyches of girls and the women they eventually become. Ultimately, Barry leaves the audience to decide Ann's fate, but she certainly was not done telling the story of young women.

After the *Naked Ladies!* exhibition and book in 1984, Barry's career was on the rise. Barry continued to create her comic for *Esquire* until 1989, and more and more weekly newspapers picked up her syndicated weekly comic strip. The strip, first known as *Girls and Boys*, was eventually dubbed *True Comeek* and finally named *Ernie Pook's Comeek*, a joke involving Barry's brother. Apparently, as Barry explained to Lynn Neary in a 2002 interview for *Talk of the Nation*, Barry's brother called almost any object "Ernie Pook." Barry, hoping to please her brother with their inside joke, decided to name her strip after his favorite childhood phrase. Unfortunately, as Barry related to Neary, when she revealed the name to her brother, he replied, "'Yeah. Who's Ernie Pook?' And he was too little. He doesn't remember. So nobody knows." As the named changed from *Girls and Boys* to *Ernie Pook's Comeek*, the tenor of the strip evolved as well, and Barry began to settle into the style and subject matter for which she is most known. Barry attributes the change in tone to a change from pen to brush around 1984 or 1985. She explained to Powers that "something happened. One of the things that happened was that my hand started to really hurt when I drew, so I had to use a brush instead of a pen, and there was something about using a brush that made it so I couldn't draw that same kind of strip; they just didn't look right in brush to me" (66). Thus the tools of her craft, moving from ink to brush, profoundly changed Barry's style and subject matter. This transition is well documented in two collections of her work, as she explained to Powers in 1989: "*Everything in the World* is transitional; you can see brush and pen. That's the transitional. *The Fun House* is all brush" (66). *Everything in the World* represents a particularly wide-ranging assemblage, demonstrating Barry's shifting style and subject matter.

The collection presents some of Barry's pen work focusing on relationships and adult problems, such as the strip entitled "Insomni-yak" from 1982 (fig. 2.11). But the collection also showcases Barry's incipient fascination with childhood. At times *Ernie Pook* seemed more autobiographical than fictional, with the character "Linda Barry" starring in "Hula Memories" in 1985 (fig. 2.12).

However, as time went on, distinct characters began to emerge. Barry pointed to one strip as a turning point in which Arna's voice begins to emerge. When Powers asked Barry to look back on these early strips, she noted "a lot of echoes or portent to what I'm doing now: the lack of punch-

Figure 2.12. "Hula Memories." Lynda Barry, *Everything in the World* (New York: Harper and Row, 1986), 43.

line; no real story." The text in this key strip, written in a straightforward, capitalized font often associated with Barry, advocates the tenets of friendship, but these concepts are challenged by the images juxtaposed just beneath the somewhat preachy lessons of the narrator. The two boys have clearly violated the rule not to call friends "Butthead." Furthermore, who exactly will befriend the frightening girl who actually emanates smelly "p's" in her "I need a hug" T-shirt, bowl haircut, and tremulous smile? The narrator sounds like a little girl playing teacher to an audience of her dolls, lecturing them on true friendship, while the images show a more accurate expression of the reality most children experience (fig. 2.13). At this point in her career Barry felt compelled to follow her instincts, leaving the adult world behind, but she did so knowing her new focus would alienate some readers. Barry indicated concern about repelling her audience: "If you made your reputation doing these sorts of snappy jokes about relationships and then you move into some other field, you're going to definitely lose a lot of people who feel there's something wrong with you" (qtd. in Geyh, Leebron, and Levy 211). Yet she felt she had to follow her instincts. For Barry, this darker turn to the inherent drama (and melodrama) of childhood was not as much a matter of choice as necessity, as she explained in an interview with Pamela Grossman: "My strips are not always funny, and they can be pretty grim at times, and I know I lose readers because of it but I can't do anything about it—my work is very much connected to something I need to do in order to feel stable."

This move to chronicling the trials of adolescence through her new brush style caught the attention of critics such as Rob Rodi, who commented that

Figure 2.13. "What Is Friendship." Lynda Barry, *Everything in the World* (New York: Harper and Row, 1986), 28–29.

as her tone has shifted, "her art style, too, has softened, has become distinctive. It's rounder and more careful, still earmarked by the appealing crudity, but with a real cartoonist's eye for faces and body language" ("Repeat" 60). The *Washington Post* argued that "Barry's busy boxes and askew lines reflect the scuffed look of childhood" (X16), while Inga Muscio observed that the "pictures are drawn as if, perhaps, one of the characters drew them" (20). Paula Geyh, Fred G. Leebron, and Andrew Levy, the editors of *Postmodern American* Fiction, commented, "The cluttered and sinuous appearance of her ink lines within the square panels suggests the tension between the limitations of the format and Barry's efforts to expand what can be expressed within them" (194); and Shaenon Garrity suggests that "Barry's comics are often crude on the level of draftsmanship but beautiful in all the ways that count." Jeanne Cooper notes:

Barry's unique visual style also finds its source in childhood: scrawls, stick figures, doodlings. Dialogue in the cartoons is barely punctuated and brazenly misspelled. Barry says she actually can draw in a representational style, but decided in college to draw "like when I was a kid, when I was real happy." Not that her childhood was happy, she amends, but "the actual act of drawing made me very happy." (G1)

Thus, while some have criticized Barry's draftsmanship, numerous critics lauded her style as reflective of her unique focus on childhood. Taking into account Barry's artistic style across many different genres, including painting, collage, and drawing, as well as her early comic art as seen in the *Spinal Comics*, it is clear that the rough, unfinished comic art style she is most associated with is a deliberate choice, not an artistic failing or shortcut. Barry chooses to render the world in this way, and the raw, edgy aesthetic underscores the bumpy, jarring experience of childhood.

Barry's writing in the child-focused strip also drew praise, with Muscio exclaiming, "Her command of language is breathtaking" (20). A 1998 *Washington Post* review argued, "Her prose—and yes, such a thing does exist in the comic-book genre—captures the idiom of the playground" (X16). Speaking more generally of her work, friend and fellow cartoonist Matt Groening confided in a 1991 interview, "Lynda's stuff is just incredible. It's about as close to literature as comic strips have ever gotten, and I think she's really on to something new" (94). The *Washington Post* declared in a 1987 review, "To call Barry a cartoonist is to diminish her work; the best of the four- and six-panel stories here are almost literature, literature that culminates in an unbearably poignant insight" (X12). While these comments certainly applaud Barry, they also sound a bit abashed about admiring a comic strip.

Whatever they might think of the literary merit of comics, most critics agree that Lynda Barry's work represents a particularly authentic conception of childhood. Jeanne Cooper notes Barry's genius for rendering the painful, awkward, and absurd truths of childhood: "By retrieving the everyday discards of conversation and experience, and mixing in remnants of her personal life, Barry has created a found art of children's souls, one that can veer from harrowingly poignant to wildly funny and never go off course"(G1). Novelist Dave Eggers concurred with the prevailing sentiment that Barry presents a realistic depiction of childhood, insisting, "Her ear for how kids talk (and how they try to destroy one another while trying to survive) is flawless; and her artwork, crude as she chooses it to be, serves her agenda well—of course stories about 8-year-olds would be homely and pretty in only the most awkward way" (10). Thus Barry's comic serves not just to tell stories of childhood, but also to invoke the feeling of being a child through the intersection of content, artistic style, narration, and dialogue.

When she first began narrowing her focus on children, *Ernie Pook's Comeek* had a wide cast of non-recurring characters; but over time the recurring characters of brother and sister Arnold and Arna Arneson and their cousins Marlys, Maybonne, and Freddie Mullens took center stage, and for over twenty years they were at the forefront of *Ernie Pook*, becoming cult figures and favorites, much as their creator has taken on a cult-like following, as evidenced by the many enthusiastic fans in attendance at her lectures and workshops. *Ernie Pook's Comeek* remains Barry's most famous creation and will be examined in greater detail in chapter 5.

As the Mullens and Arneson families took center stage in the flourishing strip *Ernie Pook*, Barry felt particularly exhilarated in her personal life. In a 1985 interview Barry explained to Margy Rochlin that she was "in love right now . . . and this time I can say it's the real thing" (120). In September of 1986 Barry married carpenter Gregory Lee Lester, but the relationship was troubled and ultimately short-lived. Even as her relationship foundered, Barry's creativity flourished, and she immersed herself in creating a collection of portraits of jazz musicians that would eventually become the inspiration for her novel and play *The Good Times Are Killing Me*, which will be analyzed in detail in the following chapter. Real Comet Press ultimately published *Good Times* as a novel in 1988, the same year that Barry and Lester divorced. It was a difficult time for Barry, who, as Marcia Coburn revealed, was forced to give up "her savings, her car, and the furniture in order to keep all the rights to *Good Times*." After the separation, Barry moved from Seattle to New York. As *Good Times* gained accolades, it caught the attention of the theater world and was adapted for the stage in Chicago in 1989 and later revised and performed off-Broadway in New York in 1991.

At this time, Barry moved frequently, following the development of the play and living briefly in New York, Chicago, Washington, D.C., and Minneapolis. During this frenetic time she also appeared on *The David Letterman Show* numerous times from 1987 to 1990 and began to cultivate a more public persona. According to Barry, Letterman even offered her a job, and initially she thrived on the attention.[17] During this tumultuous time, Barry maintained a high degree of productivity and publicity. With the success of *The Good Times Are Killing Me* and *Ernie Pook's Comeek*, Barry flirted with Hollywood glory. *Good Times* attracted considerable notice, and film producers expressed interest in a movie version of the play, an experience

Barry likens to being a "woman with a pork chop on her head in a room full of dachshunds."[18] Noted director Norman Jewison was set to direct, but the project never made it to the screen.

In the midst of the attention and adulation, Barry began to balk at maintaining this larger-than-life public persona, and in 1992 she retreated from the public life and withdrew to the Ragdale Foundation Artists' Colony in Lake Forest, Illinois. In a 1999 interview with Pamela Grossman, Barry clarified, "My going into the background was something that has happened quite naturally over the last five or so years. I noticed that it took longer and longer to recover from the public persona I put on to get through the interview or a lecture or some of the other things I was doing." Maintaining such a high-profile persona pushed Barry to exhaustion. Although her star had been rising higher and higher during the 1980s and '90s, she eventually chose to turn to a slower, more introspective existence. At Ragdale, Barry found a perfect retreat away from an increasingly flamboyant lifestyle. The artists' colony offers a residency program where artists in a variety of disciplines are provided "time and space," as well as food and shelter and the opportunity to create, uninterrupted by the outside world. At Ragdale, Lynda Barry met her future husband, carpenter and naturalist Kevin Kawula. With Kawula, Barry found a slower, quieter lifestyle. After pulling away from the hectic allure of Hollywood, Barry settled into a time of peaceful introspection and creative expression.

After her sojourn at the Ragdale Artists' Colony, Barry left behind a "manic" lifestyle to concentrate on more important matters. Barry reflected, "To take that all away and get to the thing that really mattered to me all along was a good, really good thing. And I think my work—yeah—my work changed dramatically because of it."[19] One of the things that really mattered was Barry's relationship with Kevin Kawula. The couple married in 1997, and in contrast to the unhappiness of her first marriage, Barry's bond with Kawula remained stable and contented. After they married the couple moved to Evanston, Illinois. Kawula is depicted as a kind and stable influence in *One Hundred Demons,* and he served as a "guest watercolorist" for *Picture This* in 2010.

During this fulfilling time, Barry was exploring new creative outlets but was disappointed to discover that the publishing world was changing in disturbing ways. In 1997 the famous alternative weekly the *Village Voice* dropped Barry's strip along with Matt Groening's and Jules Feiffer's to feature more sports coverage.[20] Other papers followed suit, and *Ernie Pook's Comeek*'s readership dwindled. Her book publisher, Harper Collins, also dropped her just before she was supposed to deliver her collection of strips entitled *The Freddie Stories*. This new publishing environment caused Barry to doubt her work and even her calling: "That was a dark time. I was getting dropped from papers all over the country and was getting broker and broker and sadder and sadder. I even made homemade books to sell by mail, with hand-colored covers. I spent a lot of time trying to figure out what I was going to do for a living" (*Independent Publisher Online*). Help arrived from an unexpected source—Barry's high school classmate Gary Luke, an editor for Seattle-based Sasquatch Books. The two had not been close friends in school, nor had they maintained contact. However, Luke was a fan and leapt into the breach, and Sasquatch Books reissued *The Good Times Are Killing Me* in 1998 and published the revised collection of *Ernie Pook* strips featuring Freddie Mullens as *The Freddie Stories* in 1999. Around this time Simon & Schuster expressed interest in the illustrated novel *Cruddy*, and Barry's works were once again in the public eye.

Cruddy, which will be further explored in chapter 4, marked a serious departure for Barry, who had made her reputation as a comic artist known for loquacious comics that nevertheless still maintained (for the most part) the traditional four-panel layout. Instead, this altogether alternative fairy tale was very much a novel, with the accompanying illustrations serving only to support the text. *Cruddy* also demonstrated a change from Barry's past work in that it explored extremely dark, gruesome images and themes. The focus on a girl, however, was not new, and the public seemed ready to embrace Barry's prose venture after *Cruddy*'s publication by Simon & Schuster in 1999. The book introduced Barry to new audiences and paved the way for Barry's next breakthrough, *One Hundred Demons*, which will be examined in detail in chapter 6. Barry began *Demons* while working on *Cruddy* and polished it over the next few years. In 2002 Kawula and Barry moved to a small farm in Footville, Wisconsin, the state of Barry's birth.

Moved by her surroundings and her newfound contentment, Barry began experimenting with new painting techniques, including sumi brush painting, and the results were transformative. The strips that would eventually make up the *Demons* collection were inspired when Barry discovered, according to one of the demons from the introduction to the book, "a hand-scroll painted by a Zen monk named Hakuin Ekaku, in 16th century Japan" while reading *The Art of Zen* by Stephen Addiss. She shared,

> I got interested in kind of tracing the history of the brush and learning more about it, and also just getting every book I can about how to just use that stuff technically, and it opened up my world. I have to say that the most significant thing in my life since Marilyn Frasca has been the

brush, and it's—I don't know. It turned me back into a person of faith, the faith in the brush.[21]

During this time of experimentation and exploration with the brush, editor Jennifer Sweeney approached Barry about doing a strip for Salon .com. The result was a semi-monthly strip that ran online from 7 April 2000 to 15 January 2001. The professional relationship was a fruitful one, as Barry told *Independent Publisher Online* in 2003. Barry then worked with Sasquatch Books to collect and publish the strips in book form in 2002. The book was well received and was notable for its excellent reviews as well as the collages interspersed between each comic strip. The interstitial collages foreshadowed Barry's next direction, the dreamy do-it-yourself writing workbook *What It Is* and the companion drawing book *Picture This.*

Before the publication of *What It Is,* Barry was in the process of redefining herself as an artist. She has always proven herself willing to experiment with her artistic means of creative self-expression, but Barry's struggles with the changing publishing climate forced her to find new avenues for her creative energy as well as alternative sources of income. Despite the success of *Demons,* fewer and fewer papers were willing to pay for *Ernie Pook's Comeek* and many of her books had gone out of print. Barry suffered another blow when Sasquatch Books, the Seattle-based publisher of *One Hundred Demons,* refused a proposal for the book that would eventually become *What It Is,* a setback, Barry confided to *New York Times* columnist Carol Kino, that was like "an ax to the forehead." In this process of reinventing herself as an artist, Barry embraced new technology, as evidenced by her strips for Salon .com, and endeavored to connect with her fan base by publishing *Ernie Pook's Comeek* on the fan site marlysmagazine.com. Barry also sells her art on eBay, which she has found to be a valuable means of supplementing her earnings and a source of pride. This approach aligns with Barry's frequent suggestion that art belongs to all, not just the elite. In selling her work on eBay, Barry maintains a direct link with her fans, supplements her income, and snubs the snobbery of the art world.

Barry ended the fan-favorite, long-running weekly strip *Ernie Pook's Comeek* in 2008 after the strip was dropped from all but a handful of papers, although the characters live on in other projects. And, despite what Barry has called her "hermit" tendencies, she also ventures out several times a year to teach her writing workshop, "Writing the Unthinkable," a program drawn from her work with Marilyn Frasca. But teaching to small groups of students around the country was not enough for Barry, who collected her teachings into the writing guidebook *What It Is,* published in June 2008 by

Montreal-based Drawn and Quarterly Press. Barry followed *What It Is* with the companion book *Picture This: The Near Sighted Monkey Book* in November 2010, and the book also encourages readers to express themselves through various artistic exercises. These most recent books by Barry will be followed by reissues of the entire run of *Ernie Pook's Comeek* in their original four-panel-square format, also to be published by Drawn and Quarterly. The reissue promises to open Barry's world to new readers. Barry plans to continue teaching, traveling to support her books, and selling her art on Ebay. She also told *Vice* magazine that she hopes to develop a musical with a close friend, singer Kelly Hogan.

Looking from her most recent endeavors back to her earliest works, it becomes evident that Barry has progressed and matured. While her early days suggest a kaleidoscopic vision marked by a scattered style and unfocused subject matter, Barry eventually settled into a constant subject matter for her weekly comic *Ernie Pook's Comeek*. And while the weekly strip stabilized, Barry extended her artistic energies and continued to experiment with various creative outlets. Furthermore, even as she worked in numerous genres, Barry ultimately chose to narrow her focus and settle in on the subject of girlhood, seeing young girls through multiple lenses and ways of seeing.

3

Evolution of an Image

THE GOOD TIMES ARE KILLING ME

In her book *What It Is*, Barry strongly emphasizes the importance of following and realizing an image through the creative process, which in her approach is a representation that may be realized through various mediums. Barry's multiform project *The Good Times Are Killing Me* provides an ideal opportunity to trace her process of interpreting an image through various genres, in this case, following Barry's representation of girls experiencing racism through an art show, novel, and play. A close analysis of *The Good Times Are Killing Me* reveals an evolution of message and medium, with the early versions circling around ideas of race and ethnicity and the final form concluding as an argument that racism is inevitable and that even young people bear responsibility for perpetuating prejudice. In the initial series of portraits of blues musicians, the theme was a scattered, loose idea revolving around music, race, and loss; but when Barry translated the work into an intimate, text-based novel about a young girl growing up and experiencing racism, the focus on children's understanding of prejudice became clearer. In the final incarnation as a play, the project transformed into an even more concentrated narrative focusing on two young girls who find and lose one another and discover the impact of prejudice and realize the consequences of their own choices to perpetuate racism, presented in an embodied performance that creates a shared experience with the audience. This chapter follows the evolution of *The Good Times Are Killing Me*, examining the history and process of creation of the various incarnations and studying the ways in which the meaning shifts over time and as a consequence of the means of expression. Ultimately, Barry employs various ways of seeing that result in varying degrees of clarity, from the casual browsing of the art show and its correspondingly inchoate message to the close scrutiny of reading a novel that reflects the narrative's theme, chronicling racism within the realm of one summer in a young girl's life, and, finally, to the binocular view that brings the larger issue of racism into sharp focus through the three-dimensional performance of two girls and their families. After examining the evolution of the image for *Good Times*, the analysis narrows further, contemplating the theme of duality as portrayed in the most polished version of the image, the play, as well as addressing the idea presented in the drama that racism is inevitable and all parties bear responsibility in continuing discrimination.

The Origins of *Good Times:* The Exhibition

Barry did not initially set out to examine racism through *The Good Times Are Killing Me*. Her early plan was to immerse herself in music, particularly blues and jazz, paying tribute to some famous and some little-known musicians through a series of paintings. In 1986, while struggling in her marriage to Gregory Lee Lester, Barry found solace in her work; and in addition to her cartooning jobs, she occupied herself creating a collection of portraits of musicians like Cleoma Falcon, Amedée Ardoin, and Jimmie Rodgers. When Thom Powers asked about her inspiration for the pictures, Barry explained that one of her favorite artistic exercises in the eighth grade, aside from copying R. Crumb, was imitating album covers. Much later in her career, Barry still enjoyed reproducing album covers (Powers 71–72) and felt moved to create portraits after seeing various album covers and hearing the music. The resulting series of portraits was eventually displayed at the Linda Farris Gallery in Seattle, Washington, in 1986 and at the Nine Gallery in Portland, Oregon, in 1988. Full-color reproductions of the portraits were included in the initial printing of the novel *The Good Times Are Killing Me* as a "Music Notebook" when the book was published in 1988.[1] Barry was drawn to the heartbreaking stories behind the music during her creative process. In a conversation with Powers, she further clarified that for musicians to be considered as subjects, "they also had to die; most of them had to die in some quick, funky way, which I think is mainly *how* people die. And then if I could find their music, then I would do the painting" (72). Inspiration, then, for Barry was a process of choosing images based on music and tragedy, the elements that would later weave throughout *The Good Times Are Killing Me* in all its other incarnations.

The mixed-media portraits featured bright colors and collage elements juxtaposed with hand-printed, paragraph-long narratives about the featured artist (including Gertrude Rainey, Otis Redding, and James Brown) or style (such as "Blues Style," "Girl Groups," and "Gospel Style"). Most figures smile

Figure 3.1. "Iry LeJeune" from "Music Notebook." Lynda Barry, *The Good Times Are Killing Me* (Real Comet Press Edition, 1988), 91.

cheerfully at the viewer, the winsome expressions and lively colors belying the tragic histories of those depicted (fig. 3.1).

The striking pictures are notable for their bold colors and richly layered design and for the arresting aluminum frames. The pounded metal frames evoke Mexican punched-tin folk art and do much more than simply encase the portraits, instead interacting with the subjects, adding additional dimensions and continuing the narrative. For example, the tribute to Iry LeJeune features two small angels holding LeJeune's beloved accordion, while Cleoma Falcon's portrait highlights Falcon's "loud, steel bodied guitar" (*Good Times* 96) as a contrasting element to the portrait itself.

It is impossible to recreate the circumstances of the exhibitions, but one can speculate that when shown as a collection, the experience was both communal, as viewers moved together through the galleries, and individual, as viewers studied the pictures from a distance. The viewer was guided by the space and the arrangement of the portraits as well as the lengthy explanatory captions, but in such a moment the audience maintains control when interpreting the collection. The series of paintings lacks a point of view or an overarching narrative other than that which the viewer creates for them, although the individual captions provide text-based descriptions of the biographies of the musicians and movements. The musicians and musical trends portrayed skip around in time and place and, consequently, in focus. While most of Barry's works in other genres have a clearly defined narrator, the paintings, most likely as a result of their genre, lack a strong narrative thread, and the only girls depicted are those in the portrait of "Girl Groups," who appear to be adult women rather than adolescents.

Thus, while the series of pictures is extremely aesthetically appealing, with smiling, colorful characters, layers of mixed media, and playful tin frames adding depth even while belying the tragic conclusions, an overarching message or focus is difficult to discern. The series addresses music and misfortune, but a more focused insight remains elusive. The pictures, while pleasant to observe, remain vague in terms of theme, offering only an inconclusive message. The next incarnation of the project as a novel, however, introduces a strong female heroine, a young girl who becomes the focusing lens and narrates a story of friendship found and lost as two girls encounter racism and eventually come to accept prejudice as predestined and inevitable. The novel sharpens the ideas hinted at in the paintings into a text-based narrative that is intimate and domestic in tone, an intimacy and domesticity that is reinforced by the solitary, private process of reading.

The Novel Approach

The novel began as a companion piece to the paintings, for after the exhibition, Real Comet Press, which had previously published *Girls and Boys*, *Big Ideas*, and *Naked Ladies!*, expressed interest in putting out a catalogue of the paintings. However, they wanted Barry to compose an introduction to the series. While Barry told Powers that she initially planned to "write about the history of American music" (67), after two months she came to the realization that the portraits were "also about loss" (68) and decided to focus on that element of the narrative. This "accident" (Powers 68), as Barry called it, took only ten days to write. In an interview with Marcia Coburn, Barry remembered, "I sat down and that just flew out. Boom! Done! And I

Figure 3.2. Book cover. Lynda Barry, *The Good Times Are Killing Me* (Seattle: Real Comet Press, 1988).

thought, 'Great. I'll take ten days every year and write a novel.'" Barry had found a way to tell a larger story about racism through a much smaller, more intimate narrative—that of the young girl Edna Arkins and her best friend, Bonna Willis.

In its first printing by the Real Comet Press in 1988, the cover of the novel features a painting entitled *The Good Times Are Killing Me*. While the painting shares the colorful, mixed-media feeling and busy, eclectic, punched-tin frame of the other paintings from the exhibition, this rendition differs in that it features neither a musical style nor a musician, but rather two young girls, one black and one white (fig. 3.2). The painting, unlike the others contained within the novel, resonates particularly with the written text, suggesting the themes to be explored in Edna's narrative. The blue background of the work implies a nighttime scene in a neighborhood comprised of five rectangular houses, suggesting the importance of the dark and divided neighborhood. The central house has a larger red house encompassing the smaller structure. The girls, gliding with angelic wings, fly above the house, each with a foot and hand tied to a record situated in the center of the house. One girl clasps records while the other holds a red record player. The image suggests the duality of the girls and their joining through music. Interestingly, the floating girls are upside down, as if falling back to the earth rather than ascending heavenwards, and their grim expressions imply a shared seriousness rather than a joyful unification.

The front pages of the novel (also called a novella or, as Barry herself described it to interviewer Steve Johnson, a "novellini") indicate dedications to Mrs. Yvonne Taylor, the kind neighbor featured in the 1995 essay "Guardian Neighbor," who took Barry to a gospel church and first exposed her to a career in art, and Mrs. Clare LaSane, the teacher depicted in the 1998 essay "The Sanctuary of School," who nurtured Barry and encouraged her creativity in elementary school. Given its slightness, the book is truly more of a novella than a novel and is comprised of a series of loosely structured vignettes narrated by twelve-year-old Edna Arkins. This version of *Good Times* doesn't follow traditional story arcs or structure, instead skipping around in a stream-of-consciousness style. In the 1988 Real Comet Press edition, the paintings that inspired the story are reprinted in full color and presented in a "Music Notebook" at the end of the book along with Barry's brief commentaries. The original portraits are not included in the later 1998 reprint from Sasquatch Books, although that edition featured additional illustrations to accompany the text. After publication, critics were generally complimentary, and the book went on to win a Washington State Governor's Award. Deborah Stead of the *New York Times* called it a "deft and deceptively simple first novel" and commented, "Ms. Barry has an impeccable ear, and this funny, intricate and finally heartbreaking story exquisitely captures an American childhood."

Lynda Barry insisted to Peter Goddard that *Good Times* isn't a "girls'" story, but rather a story about race that simply happens to feature girl protagonists (H3). However, while the themes of racism, friendship, music, and the loss of innocence clearly resonate for boys, men, and women, and not girls alone, the narrative undoubtedly reflects a girl's experience of racism in a certain place and time. Featuring girls changes the story to reflect their unique experiences, and the girls' friendship and families in *Good Times* offer a more domestic, more intimate view of racism within the female sphere.

As Gwendolyn Brooks's *Maud Martha* presented the story of an "ordinary" protagonist, according to Jacqueline Bobo's *Black Women as Cultural Readers* (194), so too did Barry create two very commonplace young girls as leads. Both the novel and the play versions of *The Good Times Are Killing Me*, like *Maud Martha*, internalize racism through the experience of a few characters and present racism from the gendered (and aged) perspective marked by the experiences of young females. It would be difficult to conceive of many key scenes in the narrative, such as singing and dancing and bonding over records in Edna's basement, fighting over Girl Scouts, or arguing about a sleepover, with two male protagonists. While the story does not deliberate on gender so much as race, the work itself is undoubtedly influenced by the choice of two female leads, girls treading the treacherous boundary between childhood and adulthood and experiencing racism for the first time.

In the novel version of the story, the text assumes primacy, and the act of reading echoes this private, largely domestic story about racism as experienced by two girls. While the novel speaks of and to the power of music, by virtue of the medium, the music remains imagined but unheard. The novel creates a magnified, virtual image of racism through the narrative of Edna Arkins. In contrast with the less-focused portraits that inspired the work, the novel puts a magnifying glass up to the issue of racism, relying primarily on text and asking the audience to create pictures based on their own imaginations and experiences.

As with the later play, the novel centers on a young girl named Edna Arkins and her friendship with Bonna Willis. Both the novel and the play take place in a "lower class neighborhood making a transition from mostly white to mostly black," "sometime in the mid-sixties."[2] The novel opens with Edna introducing herself in the chapter entitled "My Street":

> My name is Edna Arkins. As usual I'm stuck sitting around watching my sister and my cousin Ellen's baby until my mother gets home from work. Come over here and look out this window. You see that street? That's my same old street. I know everything that has ever happened on it and everything that is ever going to happen on it. (9)

The opening establishes Edna as the autodiegetic narrator and creates a confessional dialogue between Edna and the reader, who is invited into the action with the second-person "you." The initial paragraph also identifies the small radius of action; all of the events are limited to the neighborhood where Edna lives and, furthermore, her own narrow point of view as the internal focalizer who perceives and presents her environment. Edna also determines the domestic nature of what is to come; Edna is babysitting, again, while waiting for her mother to return home. The direct address of the narrator suggests confinement within the domestic world, looking through the window and out at the neighborhood, as well as a sense of predestination. Edna knows all that has happened and all that will happen, in this case the racial strife that Edna finds inescapable.

After introducing herself, Edna goes on to chronicle the changing character of her street from "mainly white" to "Chinese, Negro, Negro, White, Japanese, Filipino, and about the same but in different orders for down the whole street and across the alley" (9), thus quickly establishing the focus on race relations that will dominate the latter half of the novel. The next few chapters of the novel center on Edna alone, discussing in particular her favorite songs and passion for music, as well as introducing her family's troubles, with small flashes of Bonna interjected. This is clearly Edna's story; she discusses her overbearing Aunt and Uncle, her failure to learn the flute, Music Appreciation class, her cousin Ellen's illegitimate and interracial baby, her mother's miscarriage, and her father's departure. The novel continues to jump around, introducing Mrs. Loximana, the Filipina neighbor who takes care of Edna and Lucy when their father leaves; Mr. Madsen, the racist music teacher; Ranette, a "white trash" girl who is ostracized after calling Bonna "The Word" (56); and Uncle Raymond, a playboy who briefly lives with the Arkins family. Amidst the disorderly narrative, Edna and her sister Lucy bond with Bonna and her younger brother Elvin over music in the basement, dubbed by Edna as "The Record Player Night Club."

The narrative of *Good Times* lacks the rising tension that builds to a dramatic conclusion characteristic of most novels; the vignettes seem to hold together loosely until the final four chapters, "The Camping Trip," "The Projects," "Girl Scouts," and "Seventh Grade." While these chapters are among the longest in the book, they assume a rushed, hurried quality as they barrel forward to the conclusion. In these final chapters the focus shifts from a somewhat muted, oblique story of a young girl's reveries and interests to a more focused story of racism and friendship. In "The Camping Trip," Edna's Aunt Margaret watches a "TV special on racial prejudice" and decides her "new hobby [is] improving the conditions of the life of the underprivileged Negro," that is, "until she started taking the hula" (62). Aunt Margaret thus decides to bring Bonna on the family camping trip and is heartily disappointed to discover that Bonna has, in fact, gone camping many times before. "The Camping Trip" and "The Projects," in which Edna follows Bonna into a rough neighborhood where a local boy calls Bonna an "UNKA TOM," follow a very similar pattern in the play, with only minor variations and edits. The chapter "Girl Scouts," which chronicles Edna's choice to go to a segregated party, is also faithfully reconstructed in the play, as it builds the tension and creates the rift that leads into the final chapter and scene, "The Seventh Grade," where an estranged Bonna slaps Edna in the hallway at school. The novel ends with the girls sitting outside the principal's office, two best friends now divided.

The novel assumes a very narrow point of view through the first-person narration of one individual, Edna Arkins, and the action remains rooted in her experience. It is her voice and unique vernacular that shape the audience's understanding of the neighborhood. The musical origins of the narrative filter through the text as Edna frequently philosophizes on her love of music and the way it makes her feel, although these musings often distract from the forward momentum of the developing plot. As opposed to the exhibition of paintings that lacked a unified narrative voice, the novel finds focus in a singular narrator, as the audience is invited (quite literally with her command to "Come look") into Edna's head and her world. Yet the structure of the novel includes roundabout reminiscences and daydreams and is thus unedited and unfocused. Further disrupting the forward motion of the book, the narration frequently jumps back and forth awkwardly through time, and Edna's anecdotes lack cohesion or a sense of purpose until the last third of the book in which Edna's relationship with Bonna becomes the central focus.

While the novel poses structural challenges, it does allow readers to create their own pictures based on Edna's words, creating in collaboration with the author's words a window into one girl's life. Music, family, and race reverberate throughout this intimate conversation, but the tenor of the dialogue with Edna changes considerably when adapted for the stage, with the play version improving on the lax structure of the novel and bringing the message into sharper, more critical focus.

Playing with *Good Times*

The final version of *The Good Times Are Killing Me*, the play, portrays racism through the performance of two young girls, invoking a binocular or "double vision" that retains the intimacy of the novel, reclaims the musical/aural origins of the art, and strengthens the structure and focus of the message through an embodied enactment. Barry fashioned the adaptation after the novel created considerable attention in the theater world, particularly in Chicago; and according to the play's publication notes, it "was first adapted for the stage in Chicago with City Lit Theater Company at the Live Bait Theater in 1989" and was first directed by Arnold Aprill.[3] According to Mervyn Rothstein's *New York Times* review, in 1991 Barry came to New York at the request of the co-directors of the Second Stage Theatre, Robyn Goodman and Carole Rothman, and further developed the play, eventually working with Erin Sanders, Second Stage's literary manager, and Mark Brokaw, the director of the play (C11).

In the move from Chicago to New York, Goddard noted that "the play went from being an adult's-eye-view to one centered on the two 12-year-old protagonists, Edna (Barry more or less) and Bonna" (H3), thus closely following the structure and feel of the original novel. Unlike many authors who prefer to work in one medium or genre (particularly comic artists), Barry found little difficulty moving between the novel and play. When asked about the challenges of working in different genres and adapting the novel into a play, Barry explained in a personal interview, "The work just presents itself. But it all seems exactly the same to me."[4]

The production of *Good Times* garnered a great deal of attention, and its first-time playwright also received her fair share of the spotlight. In an homage to Barry's effusive style, critic Louise Kennedy could not contain her enthusiasm, proclaiming, "Lynda Barry! You are so completely great! As a playwright you are just IT! Excuse me, I seem to have mislaid my critical detachment. But that's what a play like "The Good Times Are Killing Me" can do to a person. . . . She's a kid! Totally! Except she can tell us what it's like!" Terry Morris pronounced it "one of the best-written contemporary scripts around" (2C). Iris Fanger even likened the play to a theater classic: "It's the play Thornton Wilder might have written if he had updated 'Our Town' by a quarter of a century and moved it to the city streets" (S20).

Of course, the reviews were not all quite so fulsome, and Barry herself admitted to being a theater neophyte as evidenced, she said, "by writing 27 scenes in the first act" (qtd. in Gates and Kuflik 54). She further confessed that the "main character steps forward to tell parts of the story not as a tip of the hat to 'Our Town' but because 'I didn't know how to do it without a narrator yet'" (qtd. in Gates and Kuflik 54). Other critics also mentioned Barry's faults as a novice playwright; Misha Berson asserted, "The play feels sketchy in spots, and ends abruptly. One might chalk that up to experience; this is, after all, Barry's first play. But it is a tribute to her off-kilter talent that Barry never panders to nostalgia here, nor does she make children sound like mouthpieces for a clever adult" (E1).

Several critics, such as Steven Winn, Frank Rich, David Gates, and Abigail Kuflik, commented, as Berson did, on the loose structure of the play, which is actually quite a bit more orderly than the novel. Yet in comparison to most plays, and to the tight organization imposed by a comic strip, it is clear that Barry's prose tends to digress when freed from limitations, as both the novel and the script for the play for *Good Times* exhibit a propensity to wander. Geoff Chapman offered much harsher criticism, stating, "Barry has barely fleshed out the comic characters who might populate her cartoon strips. . . . A look at the racism issue could not be more timely, you'd imagine, but this play merely scrubs the surface with a J-cloth" (B1). Chapman condemns what he believes is Barry's superficial treatment of racism, and does so with an obvious swipe at her dubious pedigree as a comic artist. While the play does have flaws, particularly in structure, perhaps Gates, Kuflick, and Chapman are noting the smallness of the setting and scene as opposed to a deficiency in capacity. *Good Times* is not a grand, global examination of racism in the world. Rather, it is an exploration of two girls finding one another and falling away from one another within the confines of one small neighborhood. *Good Times* tells a limited story, one of small sadnesses and slights in a primarily young, female sphere.

While other reviewers criticized various aspects of the play, in particular the structure of the work, for the most part the consensus was clear that Barry excelled at capturing the careful, specific details of childhood; and critics Louise Kennedy, Michael Kuchwara, and Frank Rich all commented specifically on Barry's skills at portraying childhood. Rich noted, "Barry captures the innocent abandon of childhood with the wit of a mature writer but without letting go of the uninhibited child still lurking deep within herself." This refrain is familiar when examining criticism from Barry's entire oeuvre, as many critics have observed Barry's ability to accurately reflect the world of children.

Given Barry's well-documented propensity for depicting childhood, many felt that the play was largely autobiographical. Barry acknowledged drawing from her background, but with key differences. The play is set in her old neighborhood, the Rainier Vista projects in Seattle, and she acknowledged in an interview with Tim Appelo that the street is modeled on her own. Time and again Barry returns to her old neighborhood, re-examining it as raw material from various angles and through various tools and mediums, fashioning and refashioning this landscape of childhood. Despite utilizing her own background growing up in the Pacific Northwest, there were key differences from her own experiences. For example, as Barry told Pamela Grossman, in her neighborhood race was not such a divider as class.

In a departure from earlier versions of *Good Times*, race is the predominant theme of the play rather than one of many threads woven throughout

Edna's life, and the resolution is not particularly optimistic. As she continued to adapt *The Good Times Are Killing Me* from medium to medium, the idea of exploring the history of race relations in the United States through the story of two girls inspired Barry, who created what she termed a "feel-bad comedy" about a "war" in which the girls are the "first casualties" (qtd. in Rothstein C11). In this "feel-bad comedy" Barry creates a corporeal event, a moving performance of text in the flesh that invokes sight and sound.[5] In the play *The Good Times Are Killing Me* Barry assumes a binocular or "double vision" that plays out in the process of experiencing the play as well as the double images of the two main characters, young girls Edna and Bonna. Binoculars utilize two lenses to improve on the monocular telescope, providing a doubling of images that results in a three-dimensional picture; Barry also draws on a doubling of images in her principal characters as well as her choice to present her images through the medium of performance that invokes sight and sound to offer a three-dimensional, communal experience.

The play retains the intimacy of the novel, as it is still located within a very small sphere, the street where Edna lives, and focuses on the narratives of just two girls. Yet the play is expansive and more public. The audience participates and adds its energy to the production, and although Edna is still the principal narrator, the individual characters speak for themselves, moving the narrative beyond Edna's first-person (and second-person) point of view in the novel. Edna functions as a focus point, acting as a character in the drama and stepping forward as the narrator to offer her meta-cognitive commentary. She is both insider and other, serving as a bridge between the performers onstage and the viewers in the audience. Edna becomes, in essence, the tool or technology through which we perceive the action, the lens or focusing device that brings racism into view.

While Edna's purpose as commentator and participant expands in the play version of the story, the point of view also widens considerably, as more time is spent on and with the other characters. In a key difference from the novel, the audience sees Bonna's home and the other characters speak for themselves—offering their first-person perspectives rather than being mediated by Edna's stream-of-consciousness recollections in the novel. Bonna becomes a much more powerful and key figure in the play, a parallel individual to Edna, who speaks and sings and fights for herself, rather than the important, but more peripheral character of Edna's memory as presented in the novel. The play also develops other characters more fully. The plight of the two girls' mothers is more poignant when voiced by the two women themselves.

Even as the play suggests a wider, more comprehensive worldview, it also comes together as the most complete version of the *Good Times* narrative. The play is a shared story and one that focuses on the duality of the girls as friends and foes. When performed as a play, *Good Times* creates a shared experience. The experience is fleeting and transitory, much like the small choices an individual makes that are remembered and sometimes regretted but cannot be revisited. As a singular performance *Good Times* cannot endure; the memory of the act is all that remains. This form, in particular, echoes the plight of the characters, for Edna and Bonna make quick decisions that have larger implications; and these determinations, once made, cannot be undone, leading to what Barry felt was the inevitability of the racial divide.

The music that first inspired Barry's investigation of race now plays a prominent part in the dramatic interpretation of the story. The performance and the music bring levity and significance to the production, underscoring key moments of the play and offering commentary on the characters. In her cartoon work Barry will often draw pictures that undercut the veracity of the narrator's voice, denying the truthfulness of the text-based telling of the story. In this performance of *Good Times*, the songs also work with Edna's narration, sometimes reinforcing the action as played on the stage, such as the song "I'm Black and Proud" playing when Bonna first visits Edna's home, and sometimes refuting it, such as the moment when the romantic song "Pledging My Love" plays as Edna and her mother sit on their stoop, waiting for the philandering father and husband who will not return.

Barry also uses movement to emphasize her message of racial disquiet in the play; the characters dance and fight and circle one another, echoing the idea that though the girls come together into a perfect unit like "magnets," as Edna explains in her narration, once "pointing the wrong way" (99), they are compelled to push farther and farther away. The girls come together through music and movement, dancing the "Tighten Up" in Edna's basement, and their final parting is emphasized by the physical violence of Bonna's slap and solidified as they sit together outside the principal's office, facing forward but unable to face one another. The movement and proximity of the characters shapes the audience's understanding that the girls, once together, inevitably fall apart. When looking at art, the viewer creates his or her own story or narrative, while a reader deciphering a novel invents his or her own pictures, but in this image, Barry's vision comes to life—singing, dancing, and moving, bringing the issue of racism into focus through physical performance.

Double Vision: Racism and Real Girls

Barry plays on this idea of a binocular or double vision throughout the performance of the play, creating mirror images of the girls who play out this "feel-bad comedy" of race relations and act as the lenses through which to view a narrower, more domestic view of racism. Initially, Edna and Bonna find happiness mirroring one another, before they pull apart and enter a sadder, older, adult world. Each girl finds in the figure of the other a sense of wholeness. They do not see a twin, a duplicate self, but rather another image that completes them. As Terry Morris argues, "Like the 45 records best friends Edna and Bonna spin on the hi-fi in a humble 1960s basement, everything in Lynda Barry's two-act play *The Good Times Are Killing Me* has a flip side: funny and sad, white skin and black skin, cartoon fantasy and real social commentary" (2C). The Manichean story of *The Good Times*, in both of its incarnations, as a theatrical performance and novel, plays with duality in theme and in the figures of its two heroines, Edna and Bonna. As previously noted, in the novelized version of *Good Times* Bonna appears only as a secondary character as described by Edna, yet in the play Bonna becomes a true foil. This duality of figures, this either-or perspective, also points to the ultimate argument of the play, that once the naiveté of childhood is breached by the adult concept of racism, a turning away is inevitable. The following portion of the analysis of the evolving image in *The Good Times Are Killing Me* focuses in more depth on the final and most cohesive rendering of the project, the play, scrutinizing Barry's use of a doubling of vision through dramatic performance as a way of vividly and physically enacting the racism as experienced by two girls.

For Barry, adolescence represents a crucial juncture, a fissure particularly appropriate for exploring questions of race, as she told Mervyn Rothstein: "I wanted to paint a picture of adolescence . . . because one of the things that's incredible about adolescence is that you start to see the problems of the world, and when they first hit, you think you know how to fix things" (C11). In the play adolescence represents yet another dualism, a separation between child and adult. On the childhood side of adolescence Edna and Bonna experience deep loss and find in one another a reflected image that helps them feel stable again. When with their counterpart, they are not bothered by racism, seeing in one another only a completed unit, despite the prejudices in the world at large. However, as they traverse the breech, maturing into adults, both girls become more conscious of the social pressures associated with race and both make choices that shatter their cohesive unit. Their actions push them apart and, like the magnets Edna refers to, they seem doomed to repel one another even after such a strong initial attraction.

Visually, the girls as described in the "Cast Description" certainly do not appear as identical twins, clearly one is black and the other is white. Nor do they appear as exact opposites. Rather, they give the impression of being different but complementary to one another. Bonna, according to the directions for costume design, wears a blue blouse and jumper, yet the first thing Edna notices about Bonna is not her attire but "that for earrings she had little pieces of broom straws with the ends burnt off stuck through her ears" (30). This small but memorable detail points to Bonna's background, for, as Stephanie Rose Bird points out in *Sticks, Stones, Roots & Bones: Hoodoo, Mojo & Conjuring with Herbs*, broom straw bears particular importance in the African American community and is known for its curative and healing powers. Bird explains that "this special practice of piercing, knotting, and inserting broom straw was used to fight infection and scarring" (49) when piercing ears. From her very first impression, Edna marks Bonna as different and exotic, distinguished by her African American heritage. Ear piercing also traditionally indicates female beauty, further emphasizing Bonna's maturity as a female. Edna does not seem dismayed by these markers of gender and race, but rather attracted to Bonna's difference.

Bonna's first impression of Edna as bearing a striking resemblance to the "what-me-worry guy off of Mad Magazine" (30), however, suggests that Edna appears to be more boyish and, furthermore, connects her with mainstream popular culture. The Alfred E. Newman reference also connotes a humorous, fanciful bent appropriate with Edna's personality. Bonna's statement is delivered "almost flirtatiously," according to the stage directions, implying an immediate affinity between Bonna and Edna as they begin a modified courtship ritual. While Bonna wears blue, Edna wears a brown-and-red plaid blouse and orange jumper. Yet Edna's jumper features blue buttons, hinting that at her core she is drawn to the blue worn by her new friend, much as magnets are pulled together when correctly aligned. The girls are further linked by their "pale yellow knee highs." Obviously, choosing to wear the same conspicuously colored knee-high socks despite the differences in their wardrobe provides a colorful visual link between the two characters.

The characters are also coupled by parallel family ties, and their respective relations are first introduced in contrast to one another, emphasizing the happiness and stability of the Willis clan as opposed to the simmering discontent and incipient infidelity in Edna's own home. While Edna pretends "to be a secret agent named Henry Moscow" to spy "on everyone in the neighborhood without them ever once seeing me" (12), she sees Mr. and Mrs. Willis singing "Don't Let Temptation Turn You Around" along with the Hank Ballard recording:

DON'T LET TEMPTATION TURN YOU AROUND
NO, NO
DON'T LET TEMPTATION TURN YOU AROUND
IF YOU START FEELING FANCY FREE
CLOSE YOUR EYES AND THINK OF ME. (12)

Mr. and Mrs. Willis sing together, and though the song speaks of temptation, ultimately the message is to reject other enticements: "close your eyes" and think of the other. Throughout the play, despite the tragedies, Mr. and Mrs. Willis remain committed and faithful to one another, unlike Mr. and Mrs. Arkins.

The introduction of the Willis family is mirrored by the introduction of the Arkins clan, though Edna's family is markedly less connected and convivial than Bonna's. As Edna spies on her own relatives, her mother and sister Lucy emerge from their house singing "It's All in the Game." Dad joins the singing but remains separate, standing behind the screen door. They sing:

MANY A TEAR HAS TO FALL
BUT IT'S ALL IN THE GAME. ALL IN THE WONDERFUL GAME
THAT WE KNOW AS LOVE. (12)

The song resonates throughout the play, for in this not so wonderful "game of love" Edna, Lucy, and their mother will suffer greatly when Mr. Arkins abandons them for another woman. For him, it is indeed simply a game; but for the women, the losses are very real, causing, as the song suggests, "many a tear to fall." The placement of Mr. Arkins behind the screen, disconnected from the women, further points to his distance from his family and foreshadows his eventual departure. The quick, juxtaposed introductions to the Arkins and Willis families swiftly sets up the contrasting home environments, one husband and wife steady and devoted and the other already divided. In Bonna's parents Edna glimpses wholeness, a complete contentment lacking in her mother and father's relationship. Although their parents demonstrate contrasting relationships, the girls share many family similarities. Both are older children responsible for their younger siblings. Both have somewhat meddling, powerful aunts with the similar-sounding names of Martha and Margaret. Both of the girls are bidden by their families to stay close to home, unlike many of the other children in the neighborhood.

Not only do the girls' families and appearances suggest a replication of images, even their speech reinforces a double rhythm. In the following dialogue they both remember "the exact first time" they ever saw one another, and their conversation sets up a pattern of repetition and completion:

> EDNA. I remember the exact first time I ever saw Bonna Willis.
> BONNA. I remember it too.
> EDNA. She was wearing a pink dress.
> BONNA. It was blue.
> EDNA. And I wondered if she was my same age because there weren't any girls my age in our neighborhood.
> BONNA. I wondered about you too.
> EDNA. I stood up and shouted "Excuse me girl!" but she didn't answer me, so I figured either she was hard of hearing or boy was she ever stuck up.
> BONNA. I heard you.
> MRS. WILLIS. Bonna Willis! You better get your brother back over here! If he gets hit by a car whose fault will that be? Don't let me have to tell you twice! (14)

This early dialogue from act 1, scene 4, sets up a call-and-response pattern, with Edna calling out a statement and Bonna echoing the original call in her response, sometimes affirming Edna's thoughts and sometimes challenging them. Even when Bonna challenges Edna, the rhythm and pattern of her speech replicates the call, her dialogue forming a poem of sorts: "I remember it too / It was blue / I wondered about you too / I heard you." In this poetic excerpt the girls create a shared memory of their first meeting, in which Bonna cannot be sure whether Edna is shouting a derogatory comment or simply calling out to another girl. Edna, though assuming the more powerful position in the call-and-response pattern, seems oblivious to any racial overtones in her call, only identifying another girl and possible friend, and imagines that Bonna is simply uppity or unable to hear her. Either way, Bonna assures the audience that Edna was heard. The exchange closes with an interruption from the adult world, a prophetic warning for Bonna to look after her little brother, for if anything should happen to him, she would be held responsible.

Both girls stay home to care for their younger siblings, and both demonstrate, despite any grumblings, affection for their young charges. However, for the most part, the demeanors of the two girls are quite opposite, though once again harmonious. Edna is a dreamer who invents an alternate ego as a spy and indulges frequently in fanciful reveries. She imagines herself as Maria from *The Sound of Music*, exclaiming, "Beautiful me with the British accent who can sing so beautifully that everybody knows I am God's first pick, no contest" (14), and daydreams about "leaning over our president who had just been shot in the head and his last request was to hear me sing which would perform a miracle on him and bring him back to life" (85). While Edna cherishes her extravagant dreams, in the real world she acts much more as an observer and follower. Edna fears many things, including her neighbor Bonna.

Bonna is more pragmatic than Edna. If she has dreams or fantasies, they remain hidden. Bonna, however, despite her feminine earrings and skirt, has a well-deserved reputation as an "ass beater" and tough girl. In act 1, scene 15, Bonna rises to defend her brother Elvin from the neighborhood bully and big shot, Earl. She chases Earl down and threatens him. Edna recalls, "Back then, all I knew about Bonna Willis was that I had to watch out for her" (34). In fact, Edna relates:

> She would get after you, swearing to beat the asses off everyone in our neighborhood on a rotating basis. That was the main topic of conversation. Ass beating. And it wasn't just all talk and no action either. I guess she's just about the best ass beater I have ever met in my life. Boys included. (34)

When Earl tries to tell Bonita, another neighborhood girl, that he got the best of Bonna in their confrontation, Edna waits until she's in a "safe" zone close to her house and shouts, "Psyched you out Earl! I was lyin'! Bonna can beat your ass any day!" (35). Edna, unlike the more assertive and physical Bonna, only challenges Earl from a safe distance. While Edna wants no part of a physical altercation, she feels compelled to vindicate Bonna even before they are friends. Bonna witnesses Edna's championing of her, and thus the two girls continue circling one another, advancing in their dance toward a symbiotic friendship. While Edna occupies center stage as the main character, she is also the more fanciful, cerebral character, while Bonna inhabits the role of the more physical, aggressive being, falling into conventional stereotypes of white and black behavior.

It is Bonna who takes the lead, initiating the friendship by making the move to visit "The Record Player Night Club" that Edna and Lucy have created in their basement with the help of the red record player given to them by their father (which was actually taken from his new girlfriend). Bonna knocks on their basement door with records (and Elvin) in hand and introduces Edna to the great bond between the two girls: music. Safely ensconced in the privacy of Edna's basement, the girls become close friends, but it isn't until they experience great loss that they become a complete unit.

It is parallel tragic events, the loss of loved ones, that ultimately orient the girls to one another, connecting them as intimates and completing their bond as double images. In contrasting scenes culminating in the climax of act 1, it is revealed that Bonna's little brother, Elvin, has drowned, and at this same moment in time Edna's father has left the family. Edna waits on the porch for Bonna after hearing the news of Elvin's death, even as Edna's mother waits outside for her husband. Neither one will return. When Bonna finally comes back, Edna reaches out to her, offering comfort.

> BONNA. (*To everybody.*) What are you looking at?
> EDNA. (*Spoken as a greeting.*) Hey Bonna. Hey.
> BONNA. I said what are you lookin at?
> EARL. Nothing man. Hey. For real.
> EDNA. Hey Bonna. Want to come over? Why don't you come over? (60)

At this point in the play Edna touches Bonna for the first time, drawing her to the porch, where Bonna exclaims, "It wasn't my fault" (60), and Edna responds, "Shoot. I know that. Who doesn't know that. Heck, everybody knows that" (60). This physical action connects the girls as a unit, a pair bonded by loss and personal choice. When Bonna leaves to go home, Edna calls to her, offering, "I'll walk you" (61). Thus, in this moment of greatest despair, Edna calls out to another wounded soul, seeing in her the reflection of her own sadness. The girls are very different in temperament, background, and ethnicity, yet somehow through these variations it is as if, like magnets, their poles are attracted to that point of divergence: a north pole to a south. It is this absence, this lacuna, that orients the girls to one another, and like magnets they finally touch and click together to form an integrated unit.

At the beginning of act 2 their shared loss provides a center of gravity for the relationship, and Bonna and Edna are perfectly balanced in their relationship, paralleling one another in actions and dialogue. In this moment they remain in the innocence of childhood and race matters little to them, rather, they transcend their grief together, focusing on one another. They establish a new rhythm, filling in gaps and losses with their friendship. Edna states of their daily routine:

Everyday it was like that. I would get up every morning and go to her house or if she got up first she would come to mine and we would just spend the day together doing it didn't matter what. She was all I thought about. Every day and every night I would say it in my head. "My Best Friend Bonna." (66)

The two best friends mimic each other's activities, walking back and forth across the street and the stage, back and forth between their houses. They also have corresponding speech patterns, completing one another's sentences and replicating the rhythm of the other speaker:

EDNA. Every night she would walk me to my house . . .
BONNA. Then we would turn around . . .
EDNA. And I would walk her to hers . . .
BONNA. Then we would turn around and . . .
MOM. Would you knock it off and come inside!
BONNA. Good night, Mrs. Arkins.
MOM. Good night, Bonna.
(Bonna walks away backwards so SHE can keep waving at Edna.)
EDNA. I remember standing on my front porch watching her and waving
   goodbye until the last possible second.
BONNA. Bye!
EDNA. Bye!
BONNA. Bye!
EDNA. Bye!
BONNA. Bye!
MOM. *(Off.)* Enough!
EDNA. And I thought it was going to be like that forever. I thought we
   would grow up, get married to twins, and live next door to each other
   for the rest of our lives. (65)

Edna illustrates her naïve hope that they will mature and prosper in adulthood together "forever," without complications, including race. Through the voice of Edna's mother, once again the adult world interrupts their balance, but ultimately at this midpoint in the story the girls act in perfect synchronicity. They walk and talk alike. They begin crossing over into their respective communities, Edna and Lucy accompanying the Willis family to their gospel church and Bonna coming with Edna on a camping trip with Aunt Margaret and her cousins.

However, the reciprocal arrangement between the girls cannot last, and Barry's *Good Times* suggests that as Edna and Bonna enter adulthood neither one is innocent. Yes, society, at large, and racism, in particular, conspire to turn the girls away from one another, but they also make decisions that pull them apart, leaving the former friends spinning away from one another. Several key incidents depicted in both the novel and the play mark turning points in the characters' separation, though the play's performance implicates the girls even more fully in the final estrangement.

Two incidents/chapters, "The Girl Scouts" and "The Projects," are key events in which the girls make choices that deny the friendship and join them with the actions of racist counterparts. These scenes, though similar in the novel and play, bear additional attention as they are structured slightly differently in the two versions, and these small changes result in considerable differences. In the novel, Edna and Bonna visit the projects in a chapter by the same name, then Edna joins the Girl Scouts and attends a party at Joycie Mercer's house all in one chapter, while the play divides "The Girl Scouts" and "The Party" episodes into two scenes, separated by Edna and Bonna's visit to the projects. The structure of the novel sets Bonna up as betraying Edna first, while the play hints at Edna's betrayal in "The Girl Scouts," then shows Bonna's perfidy, followed by the Edna's ultimate treachery in "The Party." The play's structure argues for a mutual and eventual parting, with both girls taking an active role in their unraveling, while the novel implicates Bonna's betrayal as the catalyst for the breakdown to come.

In the play the first incident that pulls them apart takes place at the Girl Scouts. When fellow Girl Scout Theresa Doucette tells Edna that the famous Joycie wishes to speak with her at a Scouting event, Bonna knows she is being slighted. Bonna notes Edna looking "*in the direction of Joycie Mercer*" (89) and senses Edna's longing. Bonna storms off, but the rift isn't yet permanent, for Bonna "just paid me back by acting like she hated me for around two days and then things turned pretty much back to normal" (90). Edna didn't act on her desire to be with Joycie, and thus this event would be only a minor breach between the two girls. However, perhaps discerning the changing attraction of Edna, Bonna soon makes a choice of her own that further damages their bond.

When Bonna must go to "the Dunbar Vista projects. The ones with all the laundry hanging everywhere and the kids standing around in the dinky brown yards giving the finger to every car that goes by" (91) to find her increasingly unstable mother, Bonna begs Edna to come along as well. Edna knows her mother would not approve; while Mrs. Arkins seems to tolerate Bonna within the small sphere of their racially mixed neighborhood,

to enter the projects is to cross a racial divide. Edna nervously agrees to accompany Bonna; Edna is coming to understand that her relationship with
Bonna cannot exist outside the narrow, childhood space they have created
but clearly wants to maintain her friendship despite the intolerance of the
outside world. When Bonna and Edna arrive at Aunt Martha's house and the
girls are told to wait outside, Bonna suddenly can't take the pressure any-
more and begins walking, in no particular direction other than away from her
family. Edna realizes that Bonna doesn't need or want her at this moment,
reflecting, "I don't know if you have ever been with someone who you can
suddenly tell really does not care what you do with yourself" (93). Instead of
turning to Edna for comfort as she did before, Bonna walks away alone.

Not only does Bonna turn from Edna, she finds new companionship in
Marcus, a young black boy from the projects. Initially, Marcus sees Edna following Bonna and shouts, "Hey! Uncle Tom! Oreo! Uncle Tom!" (91). While
Edna urges Bonna to ignore the boy and return to Aunt Martha's, Bonna
states that she needs to "kick this little sucker's ass first" (91). Edna wonders, "What I will do if I have to go in there and help Bonna beat that boy's
ass. I'm no good at ass beating. I'm not even good at tetherball" (93). But
Edna isn't called upon to assist her friend, in fact, she seems conspicuously
out of place in this neighborhood and, suddenly, in Bonna's life. Edna witnesses Bonna's other life, another world she has not experienced and has no
place in. Here she is a liability. Bonna underscores her contempt for Marcus
by snatching a cigarette from his hand before demanding that Edna "get
over here" (93). In this locality Bonna immediately assumes the dominant
role, commanding Edna come to her.

Bonna indicates Edna and asks, "This why you calling me Uncle Tom?
Because I ain't no Uncle Tom" (94). When Edna once again pleads with
Bonna to leave, Marcus taunts her:

MARCUS. (*To Bonna.*) Ummmm hmmmmm and I see she tell you what to
   do now too.
BONNA. Better shut your mouth Marcus Davis before I shut it up for you.
MARCUS. Ummm hmmmm.
EDNA. Bonna, let's go back.
BONNA. (*Looks at Edna to shut her up. To Marcus.*) These cigarettes your
   mama's?
MARCUS. They was.
BONNA. Can I have a pack of them, then?
MARCUS. You must be high.
BONNA. Can I have one, then?

MARCUS. Maybe yes and maybe no.

BONNA. Dag Marcus, don't be so tight.

(*Marcus gives her a cigarette.*)

BONNA. What do I do with this? (*Bonna holds up the one she snatched from him.*)

MARCUS. (*Looks at Edna.*) Make her.

(*Bonna hands Edna the cigarette. Edna smokes it.*)

EDNA. Take a puff. . . . It's springtime! (95)

In this scene from act 2, scene 8, when called an Uncle Tom, Bonna chooses to befriend Marcus and embarrass Edna. When Marcus colludes with Bonna, perhaps attempting to make Bonna prove herself to be his compatriot rather than Edna's, while asserting superiority over the weaker Edna, Bonna complies, handing the cigarette to Edna. Edna attempts to clown around with Marcus and Edna in order to connect with the others and maintain some dignity, but her subjugated position in the scene is clear. The demand to "make her" and Bonna's complicity in handing the cigarette over to Edna mark an interesting departure from the novel, in which Bonna asks Marcus what to do with the cigarette and he suggests she put it in the toilet, while Bonna herself says, rather ambiguously to Edna, "You," after which Edna smokes the cigarette. This exchange exerts more power in the play, as Bonna takes a position with Marcus and chooses to dominate Edna. The cigarette stands to represent the adult world that has intruded on their friendship; it is clearly destructive, a weapon of maturation Bonna pressed upon Edna.[6]

This power imbalance offsets the girls' duality, and once the girls return home Edna makes it clear that Bonna's slight has not gone unnoticed. The disruption in the relation becomes obvious through their movements onstage as well as their dialogue. In retaliation for Bonna's rebuke, Edna bids Bonna good-bye, forsaking their tradition of walking home together and creating a physical symbol of their separation. Furthermore, although their speech patterns still mirror one another, they are no longer affirmative and supportive, instead repeating variations of "no" over and over.

EDNA. OK Bonna. See you.

BONNA. What do you mean. You're not walking me?

EDNA. If you want.

BONNA. No that's alright.

EDNA. No Bonna, I'll walk you.

BONNA. No, no that's OK. No.

EDNA. Ok. Fine. (96)

At this point both girls refuse to acknowledge anything has changed, repeating it is "OK" and that all is "fine" and "alright," while their actions indicate their relationship is far from satisfactory. Their symmetry has been disrupted by the emotionally charged trip that brought into sharp focus how the world viewed their interracial friendship, and though both make small gestures toward reconciliation, offering to walk the other only "if you want," something has changed. They are no longer opposite but equal in the relationship; instead they seesaw back and forth, one assuming dominance over the other. The aural and visual elements of the scene illustrate through several senses and three dimensions the small rifts and tears wrought by racism on the connection between the two girls.

Bonna's decision to side with Marcus and denigrate Edna sets the stage for the final betrayal that turns the girls from one another and sets them on a path that ultimately leads to violence. When Edna's dream girl Joycie Mercer of Circle View and the canopied bed invites "only certain girls" to her party and Edna chooses to attend despite the segregated invitations, Bonna cannot forgive her. Onstage, the two girls sit on their front steps, now divided by impenetrable physical barriers, arguing and lamenting their fractured friendship. Edna still maintains that she isn't prejudiced:

> It's a built in fact that there was way you can be prejudiced and a Girl Scout at the same time. . . . I mean, I had never been to a party on Circle View before and I always wondered what it would be like. Her big house and gorgeous sounding doorbells. Glass bowls of free candy sitting every- where. Dogs that got haircuts. And I just couldn't believe the incredible- ness of how out of everybody in our troop, Joycie Mercer suddenly picked me to start liking. (99)

There are many factors at play in Edna's choice to attend Joycie's party. Clearly, Joycie represents a different world and social class. The big house with "gorgeous" doorbells and the luxurious images of sweets in decorative bowls and pets receiving haircuts signify a world away from Edna and her family. Lynda Barry acknowledged in an interview with Pamela Grossman, "The thing that really struck me when I went to junior high was class," and as the girls are just about to enter junior high, the idea of aspiring to another class obviously appeals to Edna. Bonna, as an African American, can never attain this level of class and social status and is thus discarded.

As she gets older and begins entering the adult world, Edna has taken on this new dream of popularity; she no longer searches for an equal, comple- mentary partner, but instead looks to be part of the hierarchy, preferably the top of the pecking order. Unfortunately, this power structure holds no place for Bonna. Though Edna fervently avows her belief that she isn't racist, arguing that it simply is not possible to be a Girl Scout and be prejudiced simultaneously, her statement also indicates her awareness of the racist overtones of the invitations. Edna proclaims her innocence too passionately, acknowledging that she "wanted so bad to believe" that Joycie simply chose "who would get along best" rather than segregating her party. The audience sees that despite her protests, Edna knows the truth of the situation and makes a choice to leave Bonna behind.

After these mutual betrayals, the girls never find their way back together. Edna knew, "She wanted to talk to me as bad as I wanted to talk to her but whenever I saw her I got this feeling in my stomach of two magnets pointing the wrong way and I couldn't get them to point back right" (99). In act 2, scene 9, the song "Weak Spot" plays over the two girls sitting on their respective porches, now turned away from one another. Both girls showed their "weak spots" and made decisions to participate in the prejudice of society, which inevitably and irrevocably pulls them apart. As they mature neither one can claim to be without blame. While a racist society worked against their bond, each of the girls chooses to betray and belittle the other. In this production, no one is innocent.

The final scene completely and violently fractures the coupled nature of the girls, breaking their doubled nature and setting them spinning apart, the audience acting as witnesses. A bell rings, signaling Edna's and Bonna's entry into the adult world and the institution of seventh grade, when childish things, including friendships, are put behind, a theme that plays out throughout Barry's oeuvre. The transition to junior high is a perilous one, from innocence to adversity. Visually, this scene is marked by children pushing and shoving, a sharp contrast to the singing and dancing of earlier scenes. Edna explains to the audience that upon entering junior high, "we all automatically split into groups of who was alike. . . . This was our new main rule of life, even though it wasn't us who created it" (100).

While the students are strictly divided along lines of race and class, the seventh-grade curriculum ironically stresses equality; and in a poignant exchange reminiscent of their earlier call-and-response dialogues, Edna explains:

EDNA. We had to constantly read books and poems about equality in English and I wondered sometimes if Bonna thought of me the way I thought of her when I read them. *To Kill a Mockingbird. A Raisin in the Sun.*
BONNA. "What happens to a dream deferred?" Yeah. I thought of you. (100)

Bonna responds to Edna's query, and yes, she too thinks of her former friend and of their dreams, old and new. But they both know that "no puny little poem or story could change anything" (101), thus begging the question, Will this play, this story, change anything? The ending seems to suggest, as Barry herself did, that it is "too late."

In the halls of school, two of Bonna's friends, Kimmy and Jackie, push Edna, who tries to walk away, responding to conflict through her usual technique of passive avoidance. But Kimmy and Jackie won't let Edna go, and Kimmy shoves her while Bonna watches. Once again the black characters are depicted as the physical aggressors, and this time the aggression is directed at white Edna. Something in Edna snaps, causing her to cross the boundary between them, and she calls out, "Why don't you tell them? Why don't you do something, stupid?" (101). Edna can't believe her best friend, her partner in grief and loss, could hurt her: "I couldn't believe she was really going to hit me because I knew that inside we were still friends. We are! Rules or no rules!" While childhood best friends might call one another stupid, the new system dictates that Bonna cannot let this insult stand, and the rules are in place despite whatever the girls might feel inside. Bonna slaps Edna, and they are both taken to the office, where they wait to be disciplined. Edna tries to look at Bonna, who will not meet her gaze. Edna concludes, "In the vice principal's office, we acted like we had never met. Like all it was any black girl slapping any white girl that mouthed off to her. Something that happened every single day and would just keep on happening world without end" (103). In the final tableau the girls sit silently, side by side but unable to speak. Edna weeps, a visual and aural reminder of her grief. Aunt Martha's voice begins singing "Uncloudy Day," and the others join in, singing:

Oh they tell me of a home far beyond the sky
Oh they tell me of a home far away
Oh they tell me of a place where no storm clouds rise
Oh they tell me of an uncloudy day. (104)

"They" speak of a home without conflict or clouds, but the lyrics contrast with reality of two lonely girls who sit together, but turned away from one another.

Though some, like Mira Friedlander, criticized the "rather down ending" (Friedlander WO13), the conclusion seems appropriate for what is in essence a tragedy, albeit with comic moments. The only conclusion for these two girls at this point in time is to go their separate ways, and one imagines they will forever feel this loss, a lack of the wholeness they found for one summer. Terry Morris argues:

> When Edna and Bonna are driven apart by the inexorable force after their
> sweet summer of friendship, it's nobody's fault. It's something that hap-
> pens to them rather than being something they cause. Only an adult can
> look back and wonder why it happened then, yet know full well it would
> probably happen again now. That's where the sadness in this play comes
> in. It lingers like the blues, but points no fingers. (2C)

While Morris believes that the girls are pushed apart by a larger force, I
would argue that *Good Times* does not absolve Edna and Bonna of culpability. As they mature and understand racial divisions, they are no longer innocent bystanders. Something does happen to them, but they choose how
to react to these happenings. In the first half of the play the girls look to one
another to fill losses in their lives, as a kind of mirror reflection that offers a
sense of plenitude. There is no denying the causality of Edna's and Bonna's
actions, large and small, that devastate their relationship; and as they traverse the chasm from childhood to maturity they make choices—to go to a
segregated party, to share a laugh at the other's expense, and to participate
in the divisions of society at large. Yes, many things happen "to them rather
than being something they cause," but they are not without blame. Barry
explained to David Friedman in an interview for the *Los Angeles Times*, "The
minute you understand racism, you're responsible for being racist. It's like
eating from the tree of knowledge." In all their dualities these two girls,
Edna and Bonna, are human, complicit, and complicated. Rather than taking
the position that "it's nobody's fault," both girls in the play bear responsibility, as do all who participate in perpetuating racism, which, unfortunately,
feels much like a foregone conclusion in *Good Times*.

Tracking the Progress: The Transformation of *Good Times*

Exploring Barry's uncommon (particularly among comic artists) commitment to a multi-genre rendering of the image demonstrates her versatility
as a creator. This evolving project furthermore highlights how the figures
of girls, in particular, come to act as focusing lenses in her work. *The Good
Times Are Killing Me* also points to several continuing concerns of Barry's
that work throughout her oeuvre, such as the importance of examining the
everyday, in this case exploring racism through the tiny window of two girls
in a small neighborhood rather than on a larger, macroscopic scale. This is
the racism enacted at slumber parties and Girl Scout jamborees, something
easily relatable to most. The project also addresses the dark side of child-

hood with wistful humor, suggesting the dashing of childhood hopes and dreams.

As Barry employs various mediums to invoke a multifaceted vision of girls experiencing racism, what is revealed about her perspective on girlhood and race? Racism, Barry suggests, is ineluctable. Barriers will be thrown up and tragedy will result. That is not to say that individuals do not bear responsibility for prejudice. Rather, the victims are depicted within a small sphere of friendship, and these girls, once introduced to the adult concept of judging by color, demonstrate that they are flawed and fallible and not innocent, but rather accountable for their decisions. However, throughout this project's numerous incarnations, it does bear some significant differences from the majority of Barry's projects. While most of the adults in Barry's works range from unfriendly to cruel, the adults in *Good Times* are largely sympathetic. Although Aunt Margaret and Edna's father have negative qualities, both mothers and Bonna's father are generally kind, if somewhat sad and misguided adult figures, suffering alongside their children. Unlike other Barry heroines, Edna and Bonna display relatively little concern over beauty and appearance, a common fixation for most of her female characters. Despite Edna's resemblance to Alfred E. Neuman, she seems unbothered by her attractiveness or the lack thereof. One prominent difference from other Barry projects is the bleakness of the narrative. While other stories, such as *Cruddy*, are much more brutal, there is a measure of success and individual triumph at the end, whereas the inevitability of racism is unusual when compared to Barry's later works. Furthermore, in many of Barry's works girls survive and find happiness when they find a creative outlet of some sort—writing, drawing, or creating in some way. While Edna and Bonna bond over singing and dancing, they abandon music as they settle into the adult world, thus sealing their failure. In her later efforts Barry stresses the power of stories and story making to make a difference in her own life and in the lives of her fictional characters. Barry often implies that the creative process can save the girl, but not in this work.

Barry began her evolving project *The Good Times Are Killing Me* as a series of paintings with a floating, unfettered quality—the vivid, colorful, mixed-media portraits chronicled little-known singers and performers and musical movements united by a poignant, wistful sense of loss. This medium invites a casual, introspective viewing that allows the audience to create (or reject) an overarching narrative and/or message guiding the works. As she adapted the play into a novel, Barry invoked another mode and another way of seeing, this time using a text-based narrative to invoke the image. The intimate and individual experience of decoding prose and creating one's own pictures through the reading process echoes the project's refined focus on exploring racism through the domestic, localized narrative of two young girls and the devolution of their friendship over the course of one summer. In the final incarnation of the project Barry sharpens her gaze, invoking a binocular vision that brings the issue of racism into three dimensions by creating a play that calls upon the viewers' senses and presents a doubling of figures who enact and inhabit this vision of girlhood and prejudice. I would argue that this final version, the play, offers the most comprehensive image, not implying any inherent superiority of drama, but rather proposing that in this particular play, Barry's binocular vision as presented through drama best expresses her image. In the play, the structure and plot are tightened and the medium creates an intimate yet communal and embodied, multisensory experience that underscores Barry's message: when community pressures conflict with an individual, that individual makes choices in the moment, choices that he or she cannot undo, but for which each person is ultimately responsible. Edna and Bonna, as presented on the stage as double figures, demonstrate the joy and hope of young girls who find happiness with one another but eventually succumb to societal pressures and knowingly choose to betray one another. Though each of the mediums employed by Barry has value, the message of culpability is at its most profound and pronounced in the play. Despite her success in the medium, Barry has as yet not returned to writing for the stage, instead pursuing her representations of girls through other mediums, such as her long-running strip *Ernie Pook's Comeek* and her novel *Cruddy*.

4

Through a Glass Darkly

CRUDDY'S GIRL IN THE FUN-HOUSE MIRROR

A novel is a mirror carried along a main road.
—HENRI B. STENDHAL, *The Red and the Black*

What is the use of a book, without pictures or conversations?
—ALICE, in Lewis Carroll's *Alice in Wonderland*

Lynda Barry employs her multifaceted perspective on girlhood throughout her career, tackling the image of the girl through various lenses and ways of seeing, but the most grotesque, macabre vision of girlhood emerges from her darkly comic, illustrated novel *Cruddy*. This chapter considers the distorted, hyperbolic perception of girlhood as expressed in the fun-house hall of mirrors as represented in *Cruddy*. Barry's text-based interpretation of one girl's life creates a warped journey through a maze of twisted mirrored images, a vicious road trip that invites the reader to envision his or her own picture of the girl as drawn from language, thus echoing the idea that heroine Roberta's various identities are created through the reflections of others. This intimate collusion with the reader fashions a monstrous reflection of girlhood as gothic nightmare and aggressively dismantles any associations of happy young ladies enjoying a peaceful transition into womanhood. Barry's approach in *Cruddy* suggests that a fragmented sense of self for girls is undeniable given the pressure to conform to the conflicting demands imposed by the gaze of others.

This chapter begins by touching upon Barry's career as a text-based writer (apart from her work in comic art and theater) before briefly outlining the genesis behind Barry's longest textually based work, the novel *Cruddy*. The next sections explore the twisting, confusing hall-of-mirrors quality that characterizes *Cruddy*, examining the ways in which Barry obfuscates the boundaries of truth and fiction and dismantles the romance of girlhood through an extremely horrific narrative. The analysis then turns to scrutinizing the many identities that Roberta, the young girl at the center of the work, must create in response to the gaze of others, studying how she uses these identities to her ultimate advantage. Finally, the investigation considers Barry's choice of a novel to tell this story, pondering the ways in which Barry fragments and distorts the image and identity of the girl through language. Rather than relying primarily on pictures of her own creation, by choosing to render the narrative in a novel Barry calls on the reader to fashion his or her own mental image of the girl, acting as yet another mirror, another interpretation, another illusion.

Lynda Barry as Author

Many critics, such as Nick Hornby and Alice Sebold, have commented on the high quality of the writing in Lynda Barry's comics, although others, such as Art Spiegelman, Pulitzer prize–winning creator of *Maus*, argue that she can err on the side of loquaciousness, crowding out the pictures with her extended narration and speech balloons.[1] Rarely, however, do scholars study her as a writer of prose separate from her comic art. Despite this, Barry enjoys a rather successful career as a writer in numerous forms. Her coloring book *Naked Ladies! Naked Ladies! Naked Ladies!*, published in 1984, featured a lengthy monologue from Ann, a young girl who was, as Barry told Thom Powers, her "first true character." The 1988 novel *The Good Times Are Killing Me* received favorable reviews and received the Washington State Book Award before Barry adapted it into a play. Although few consider her an essayist or short-story writer, Barry has quietly written in both forms for many years.

Barry has written essays and short, autobiographical pieces for newspapers and magazines throughout her career. The works are, as with her comics, richly detailed and self-reflective in nature. These little-known essays might be considered her "truest" reflections of self, as they are published as nonfiction (not drama or fiction or, as Barry called her work in *One Hundred Demons*, "autobifictionalography") and consequently considered to reflect the real. The essays appeared in newspapers such as the *Los Angeles Times*, magazines like *Newsweek* and *Life*, and anthologies such as *The Armless Maiden and Other Tales of Childhood's Survivors* (1995) and *Home Field: Nine Writers at Bat* (1997). While these written works are obscure even for Barry aficionados, the themes she addresses in them echo those featured in her fiction and comics. The 1997 essay "What Pop Fly Gave His Daughter," for example, tells the heart-wrenching story of Barry as a young girl, betrayed by her father when he abandons his family, much as the fathers do in the comic strip *Ernie Pook's Comeek* and the novel and play *The Good Times Are Killing Me*. Barry also addresses problems with her mother and discusses adoring her grandmother in the short essays "When Grandma Discovered Hotdogs" from 1990 and "Pork Memories" from 1995, both of which appeared in the *LA Times* and feature photographs and recipes along with the text. The accompanying photos and recipes tender veracity, while the style of the essays is unembellished and unadorned, not at all the fanciful, fictional renderings of *Cruddy, One Hundred Demons, What It Is, Picture This,* or even *Ernie Pook's Comeek*. A particularly poignant example of her short, autobiographical writing is the essay "Oh, Christmas Tree," which appeared in the *LA Times* in 1992. In the piece Barry recalls searching for the perfect Christmas tree and finding, for a brief time, a moment of happiness in a very troubled childhood. Barry also wrote an especially personal piece for *Harpers* in 1992 in which she recounts the "night I found out I was pregnant" and her subsequent abortion. If *Cruddy* represents text as the distortion through a fun-house mirror, it is these short pieces that act as the most sincere reflections.

Barry also penned a series of short, fictional stories that served as a bridge from her essays and play to the longer, more developed novel *Cruddy*. From February 1989 to June of 1991 Barry wrote a series of single-page short stories for *Mother Jones* magazine entitled "1619 East Crowley." The short stories consist of eight to twelve paragraphs with a single illustration in the center and Barry's embellishments around the borders of the page. The narratives continue the story of Edna Arkins from *The Good Times Are Killing Me* and maintain a structure similar to a comic strip—a short introduction to a situation that resolves within a few paragraphs. While the episodes carry on Edna's story, outlining the death of Bonna Willis's mother and delving further into Edna's trials in junior high, the focus gradually shifts, and shades of the story that would become *Cruddy* emerge. Vicky Talluso, one of the main characters from the novel, makes her first appearance in the story "Getting Saved" from May 1989 and appears frequently throughout the run of the series. The story "Blue Cross" from February–March 1989 echoes the opening of *Cruddy*, with the narrator lamenting moving to the "cruddy beige house on this cruddy dirt street" (68). These pieces are transitional in nature, moving from the undercurrent of violence hinted at in the novella *The Good Times Are Killing Me* to the outré and reckless *Cruddy*.

Barry explained to Benny Shaboy that in her early sketches for *Cruddy*, "At first I thought it was Edna Arkins, the character who was in my first

little novel, *The Good Times Are Killing Me.* But it wasn't her, it turned out."
The main character in Barry's novel wasn't Edna Arkins, but rather Roberta
Rohbeson. *Cruddy* presents a heroine who adventures in strange lands and
sees gross exaggerations of identity in her search for self. Reading the novel
gives the impression that Roberta has entered a hall of mirrors and must
stumble through the maze of distortions. She is confronted at each turn
with individuals who act as mirrors that warp her image, reflecting their
own imperfections. *Cruddy* echoes another famous story of girlhood, *Alice
in Wonderland*, in which Alice enters an alternative reality and asks, "But if
I'm not the same, the next question is 'Who in the world am I?' Ah, that's the
great puzzle!'"[2] Roberta, too, travels to curious places, puzzles over her identity, and struggles to find herself; and readers of *Cruddy* accompany Roberta
on her journey, creating mental pictures from Barry's words.

The vast majority of Barry's comic art focuses on young girls, and the
novel *Cruddy* is no exception. However, the processes of creation are somewhat different for the various forms, and the differing methods of production also appear to be reflected in the structure of the works. As a novelist
Barry was freed from page constraints and criticisms of wordiness, but given
that liberty, Barry's work takes on a rushed, saccadic nature. Barry explained
to interviewer Tod Olson:

> With a comic strip I can see all of it at once, but after page 25 in a book I
> have to believe the story has its own DNA that will keep it together. The
> comic strip has to make instant sense. With a novel it's more like a road
> trip—you expect to run into things on the way to where you're going but
> they don't have to totally fit in with the goal of the trip.

Cruddy chronicles several road trips, but the rushed, meandering style also
mimics the feeling of a journey. Some might argue that these diversions that
Barry admits don't "totally fit in" with the purpose of the narrative detract
from the focus and structure of the work, preferring the tightly controlled
structure of Barry's comics. Barry, however, clearly indulged in the freedom
of the text-based novel, arguing that the digressions do not diminish from
the "goal" of the final product.

The messy, wandering feeling of the book parallels Barry's eclectic writing process when no longer limited by the rigid panels of a comic created
for newspaper publication. In an interview, Barry recalled that she initially tried to draft the novel on a computer but eventually painted the entire
manuscript with a paintbrush, and then took the story and "typed it up on a
manual typewriter and then typed that manuscript again."[3] At a certain point

in this long, laborious process, Barry knew that with *Cruddy* she had gotten, in her words, "to the end. I didn't know the whole story, but I got to a place where it felt like it was the end, and then when I started typing it . . . My idea of editing is to expand."[4] Barry retyped a third and then a fourth draft, which, with the exception of one chapter that was cut,[5] ultimately became the novel *Cruddy*, published by Simon & Schuster in 1999.[6] The resulting book is, according to author and critic Alice Sebold's review "Writing Outside," "an extremely physical novel," not surprising given that "Barry's process is so clearly a physical one" (26). This hyper-kinetic, dynamic process of painting, writing, and typing, and of calling up what Barry told Benny Shaboy was a "living thing," is reflected in the reckless energy of *Cruddy*. The pace of the book, the characters, the illustrations—*Cruddy* crackles with intense emotions, and the center of these fierce feelings is Roberta Rohbeson, the heroine of *Cruddy*, and yet another of Barry's young female protagonists.

Blurring the Boundaries of Real and Imagined

Cruddy offers a particularly unstable vision of girlhood, and, as previously noted, the reading experience is akin to struggling through a fun-house maze of mirrors; both reader and narrator struggle amidst the illusions. The book puts forth deception after deception, yet also introduces elements that imply the real, blurring boundaries of truth and fiction. Even as she looks to others to show her reflected identity, Roberta plays with that identity through her narration, resulting in numerous distortions of selfhood. The twisted, convoluted novel conspires to create confusion as it tells the story of Roberta Rohbeson, a sixteen-year-old misfit girl who is "writing the cruddy book of her cruddy life and the name of the book was called Cruddy" (4). Parallel narratives tell the story of Roberta's past and present. In the past narrative, eleven-year-old Roberta goes on a hair-raising, uber-violent road trip/rampage with her father, during which they search for money the father believes is due to him. Along the way the pair wreak havoc, leaving a trail of murder and destruction. Ultimately, Roberta murders her father and is left alone, wandering in the desert and covered in blood. She eventually returns home to her mother and sister. Several years later, in the narrative present, sixteen-year-old Roberta decides to take her stoner friends, including rebel Vicky Talluso, to return to the site of the stolen money. The trip fails and the end of the book implies that Roberta has committed suicide.

A fascination with the gruesome and macabre pervades the book, offering a hyperbolized vision that contrasts with any "sugar and spice and all things nice" notions of girlhood. Brian Miller argues that "Lynda Barry seems determined to pluck off the very last ribbons and bows from our conception of girlhood"; and *Cruddy* doesn't simply remove the imagined "ribbons and bows" associated with sweet dreams of girlhood, it slices them to bits and drenches them in blood. Roberta's account bears no trace of young female frivolity; the tale is influenced by her adoration of pulp drama, horror movies, and *Stedman's Medical Dictionary*. This is not a girlhood of Disney princesses, frilly dresses, and canopied beds; this is a girlhood of Grimm's monsters, "Little Debbie" the butcher's knife, and rotting, mutilated corpses. The mythology of girlhood falls prey to *Cruddy*'s wake of destruction, and although Barry's perspective certainly offers an alternative image from the happy, glossy stereotype and a significantly darker look at girlhood, this story cannot qualify as realistic either. *Cruddy* exaggerates the lurid and violent to the extreme, suggesting the most sinister reflection of girlhood imaginable.

From the onset, *Cruddy* challenges the reader with artifice, the opening pages setting the tone for a book of distorted reflections. The illustrated novel features original cover art by Barry as well as illustrations and two maps, one located on the frontispiece and the other found on the end pages. Following the dedication, an epigraph is featured below a small illustration of the silhouette of a figure writing, housed in an ornate, curlicued frame. The tiny frame resembles an object one might encounter even in the original Hall of Mirrors at Versailles—intricate, ornate, complex. It is unclear whether the profile contained within represents Barry as the author of the text or Francesco Redi as the author of the epigraph or even Roberta, the story's narrator. Perhaps, given the manuscript's concentration on a multiplicity of selves, it stands for all of them.

The epigraph offers no resolutions to the question of the identity of the figure, only foreshadowing the dark, gritty story to come. The quote, an excerpt from Redi's dithyrambic poem "Bacchus in Tuscany," published in 1685, refers to the wines of Tuscany, though this may not be apparent at first glance.

> Such bright blood is a ray enkindled
> Of that sun, in heaven that shines
> And has been left behind entangled
> And caught in the net of the many vines.

In the original verse, the "bright blood" likely signifies the wine grapes brought to life by the fiery nourishment of the sun and then "left behind," snarled amongst the web of vines. Yet in relation to *Cruddy* the quote takes on larger significance, playing with ideas of "son" and "sun" as well as "Ray" and "ray," for protagonist Roberta Rohbeson is the progeny, or "son," of her father Ray; and, of course, Roberta's life is marked with a great deal of blood, tangled as she is in the troublesome web of violence initiated by her father.

The biography of Francesco Redi also offers subtle hints as to several of the more gruesome themes to come: maggots, flies, death, decay, and meat. While Redi was known as a poet, and the epigraph that opens the book refers to his verse about the pleasures of wine, Redi was also known as a physician and scientist who studied decay and, in particular, the origins of maggots. Redi disproved a popular theory of the time known as "spontaneous generation," the idea that maggots would arise naturally from the flesh of decaying meat. Through his experiments, Redi proved that the maggots were introduced from the outside environment and did not arise from the meat itself. Maggots and flies appear throughout *Cruddy*, as spectators to the horrors of rotting flesh. Butchers and meat cutting also appear throughout the book: Ray Rohbeson butchers meat and people with alarming frequency, and Roberta unfortunately bears witness to a mysterious, Sweeney Todd–like butcher shop in the grisly town of Knocking Hammer. The idea that maggots are introduced rather than arising spontaneously also points to Roberta's position, not a direct product of the death, but rather a creature living from the spoils of mortality. Roberta's selfhood arises not from the decaying matter itself, but as a symbiotic creature responding to the environment, adapting herself to endure.

This curious image and epigraph are followed by a startling dedication that continues to blur the lines between fiction and reality. On the left side of the book is an imprint of a left hand with part of the index finger missing. This, apparently, is Roberta Rohbeson's mark—an impression of her identity and a symbol that this document is one of her possessions. The facing page brings the reader into the narrative, addressing the audience:

> Dear Anyone Who Finds This,
> Do not blame the drugs. It was not the fault of the drugs. I planned this way before the drugs were ever in my life. And do not blame Vicky Talluso. It was my idea to kill myself. All she did was give me a little push. If you are holding this book right now it means that everything came out just the way I wanted it to. I got my happily ever after. Signed,
> Sincerely Yours,
>
> The Author,
> Roberta Rohbeson
> 1955–1971

Figure 4.1. "The Father." Lynda Barry, *Cruddy* (New York: Simon & Schuster, 2002), 46.

The signature and years are written in a scrawled, childlike cursive. This self-referential note and stamp lead readers to believe that they have happened upon the not-so-secret diary of a young girl who has committed suicide and that her death indicates the happy conclusion of her fairy tale. Benjamin Weissman noted that for Roberta, the "reader is her essential confidant" (55). As she does with her comics, Barry finds another way to draw the readers in, demanding that they play an active role in bringing this narrative to life and, as the case may be, death. Furthermore, Roberta the character pushes the fourth wall to make direct contact with the reader as an author. She leaves a physical impression when no body remains. From the onset Roberta (through Barry) crafts her most important identity—that of author and shaper of her perception. *Cruddy* continues to obscure the boundaries between fact and invention with other created artifacts, such as the treasure maps and an ending annotation, presumably by Roberta's sister Julie. These sleights of hand serve to confound the reader, who must examine the text closely: Are these inscriptions graffiti? A part of the text? Genuine artifacts? In answering these questions the reader must interrogate his or her own understanding of the text as imagined, creating dissonance as the audience is forced to ask whether such a gruesome narrative could be true.

Over forty illustrations appear in the novel, further compounding the sense of dismay and confusion.[7] While the illustrations are not integral for understanding the novel (in contrast with Barry's comics, which require text and image for full comprehension), they do provide an additional layer of feeling to the terror and fear of the narrative as well as a glimpse into the fun-house mirrors that Roberta encounters that marginalize her, resulting in a fragmented, subaltern self. The loose, smudged style of the images, a considerable departure from the clear lines and jubilant, frenetic energy of much of Barry's comic art, suggests a dark, muddled fear, the result of a warping and disfiguring of the image. As Alice Sebold argues, *Cruddy* is an extremely "physical" book, and the images show evidence of fingers, as if a child had been finger painting in the dirt and muck.[8] The masterful craft and the intensity of the pictures, however, clearly indicate that these are not the work of an amateur. One of the most terrifying characters in the novel, "the father," is depicted as a ghastly, menacing specter (fig. 4.1). The man stares out directly, as if framed in an oval mirror. Smudged streaks obscure the image, implying a haze of gore or grime. The father's teeth clench in a menacing grimace, and the heavy, lidded eyes promise darkness, while the swirling tendrils left by Barry's fingers give the portrait a distinctly macabre feeling.

These are fun-house mirrors in picture form: gruesome, distorted, terrifying. Weissman lauded the power of the pictures, stating, "They are equal parts spontaneous, gothic and raw—not a single belabored picture" (55). There are very few pictures of Roberta herself, as her reflection is primarily text-based. However, the rare pictures of Roberta imply a dark, despairing visage. One of the few images of Roberta, rather than from her perspective, is located on the front cover and intimates a somewhat distorted reflection (fig. 4.2). The image depicts a young woman with broad features and heavy, lidded eyes; her face appears almost too flat, too wide, as if it has been stretched horizontally through the reflection. Her teeth are chipped and her expression is vacant, caught in a stare. The cover is the color of muddy brown finger-paint, with black ink lines adding definition to the features. Green vines surround the image, spiraling upward. At one point in the book Roberta's love interest, "the Stick," comments, "You have such a fucked-up nose. And your teeth and your finger. All of you is so fucked up. I have never seen such a fucked-up person and it makes me so sad" (241). The cover image makes it clear that Roberta is no princess, no pretty girl, and that is precisely what Barry intends, for Roberta must struggle with her

Figure 4.2. Book cover. Lynda Barry, *Cruddy*
(New York: Simon & Schuster, 2002).

own desire to be beautiful despite society's condemnation of her exterior, utilizing her unattractive outer shell as yet another tool for survival.

Another illustration of Roberta appears in a portrait before chapter 1 officially begins. In the grim image, also framed as though in a mirror, the rough, vertical strokes of the ink highlight Roberta's broad, flat nose and the wrinkles and creases of her worried face. Her posture is hunched as she looks suspiciously over her shoulder, her arm curled around her body protectively (fig. 4.3). In the upper right corner Roberta's sister Julie looks angelic, set off from her sister by much lighter ink and delicate horizontal strokes shading her face. Julie's eyes are closed and her expression beatific. Is Roberta turning away from her sister or to her? In either case the little sister shines down on the older one; Julie, still young and innocent, is unpolluted and bright, in contrast with the slashed lines and murky shading of Roberta's guilty misery. However, these two illustrations picturing Roberta are the exception; the vast majority of illustrations appear to be from Roberta's vantage point, either looking out on the scene or staring at a reflection in a mirror,[9]

Figure 4.3. "Roberta and Julie." Lynda Barry, *Cruddy* (New York: Simon & Schuster, 2002).

while the gaze of the text-based focalizer and the voice of the narrator shift, creating disorientation as the narrative unfolds.

Shifting Floors: Focalization and Narration

In *Cruddy* the gaze is a variable one, alternating between an internal focalizer, present Roberta's perception of events unfolding at age sixteen, and an external focalizer, sixteen-year-old Robert relating and commenting on her past at age eleven.[10] As an internal focalizer, Roberta describes the setting: "Now you need to know the scenery. First the house. The address. 1619 East Crawford. A rental in a row of rentals all the same, all very hideous on a dead-end road between Black Cat Lumber and the illegal dumping ravine" (5). This passage demonstrates Roberta's internalized perception of her neighborhood, with an emphasis on the bleakness of the environment. At other times, *Cruddy* demonstrates external focalization within the embedded narrative, as Roberta renders her past from a seemingly removed, distanced point of view: "The authorities said, 'Who are you? Where have you come from? What tragedy has occurred?' But the child could not answer. The child's bloody face could only stare without blinking for the child was in the medical condition known as shock." (13). While the focalizer is always Roberta, the shifting focalizers, internal and external, create a feeling akin to the rolling floor in the fun house; the reader, though aware of the center of the room, finds his or her sense of equilibrium shifting back and forth throughout the novel, swaying and buckling, inspiring a vertigo not unlike what Roberta feels as she struggles to find herself amidst her past and present experiences and the many identities foisted upon her.

Roberta is not only the focalizer but also an autodiegetic, overt narrator who addresses the audience directly, blurring lines between public and private. In contrast with many of Barry's heroines and young female narrators, rather than maturing gradually through the course of the story, as with Edna and Bonna in *The Good Times Are Killing Me*, or remaining frozen in time like the children of *Ernie Pook's Comeek*, Roberta's childhood and burgeoning adulthood are shown in parallel narratives at the ages of eleven and sixteen. Roberta recounts an embedded narrative of past adventures to her new friends. She further records the sessions with her friends in her diary, layering a story within a story within a diary, creating a Chinese box of concurrent and retrospective narratives. The accounts flash back and forth rapidly, and the reader shifts with Roberta across the expanse of time and space, traversing the rift between a child forced into an adult world and a young woman still struggling with all that she has experienced. The structure of the narrative thus sets up the divided nature of the narrator from the onset: the girl Roberta and the young woman Roberta represent very different people.

Roberta, as focalizer, narrator, and character, clearly operates as the locus of the narrative, yet as *Cruddy* unfolds Roberta's numerous reflections through others reveal themselves. Roberta is made and remade through the reflecting surfaces of others. In a rare, quiet moment of reflection toward the end of the book, Roberta sits with her unrequited crush, the Stick. He asks her, "Who are you?" (216). It is a question that echoes that of Alice in her adventures in Wonderland, and Roberta reflects on her identity for much of the book. Roberta answers the Stick "with all of [her] names. Roberta, Clyde, Ee-gore, Mystery Child, Michelle, then Roberta again, and recently Hillbilly Woman" (216). She is all of these people and more. In *Cruddy* Barry presents another compelling image that dominates the narrative, that of a girl who creates multiple selves based on the reflections of others but eventually gains control of her own reflection and remembrance with deadly finality. The following section examines the images of Roberta as reflected through the warped mirrors of others and explores how Roberta ultimately twists these images to her own satisfaction.

Warped Images: The Girl through the Gaze of Others

Roberta assumes numerous identities based on the distorted impressions of others; she is Roberta, Clyde, Ee-gore, Mystery Child/Michelle, and Hillbilly Woman, amongst others. However, the most prominent and important identity is reflected by the narrator, and is that of author and creator of the text. The narration holds the status of "the Author" of preeminent importance, and it is the author who begins and ends the book. Roberta creates for herself a "Roberta as author" in control of the telling of her life story and, ultimately, in control of her own life, including deciding when that life will end. Roberta Rohbeson is prominently named as "the Author" of the diary in the suicide letter that opens the book, and it follows that the mutilated handprint is evidence of her possession of the diary and her hand that has recorded this journey. The letter gives her year of birth and death (1955–1971) immediately placing the narrative in time and revealing the fate of the narrator/character. However, she tells her readers, "If you are holding this book right now it means that everything came out just the way I wanted it to. I got my happily ever after." This book, this story, is the conclusion of Roberta's fairy tale and her means of achieving immortality.

Roberta as author finds transcendence through her words despite death:

> In this book the truth will finally be revealed about the horrible murders and then the author must die. And people may be sad about that and wishing there were more books by the author, Roberta Rohbeson, but sadly it will be too late. There will be only one Dewey decimal system number for her. Sadly only one. And if they ever find her body, and if she could have one final request, that number is what she would like engraved on her gravestone. (13–14)

Roberta as author tells the hard, painful truths, but then having purged herself of this evil, she can no longer live. She will be immortalized, though, through the safety, security, and permanence of the Dewey decimal system.

The direct address of the diary once again blurs lines between public and private, the diary implying a hidden, secret tale, while the direct address breaks the frame and argues for an implied, decidedly public audience. This act of what narrative theory scholar Gérard Genette would characterize as *metalepsis* (234–35) positions the reader as witness, confidante, and friend. She addresses the readers with a convivial "you," as in "Now you need to know the scenery" (5) and the following description:

> The author knows there is a lot of details to remember for your reading comprehension but the author badly wants to give you the who, what, when, where, and how of this story right away because the author very badly wants to get to the question of why. The burning question of why she turned out the way she did and why she ended the way she ended. Ask a burning question, get a burning answer. (11)

Roberta, as author, wants the audience to know all of the details immediately so that she can answer the question of why she exists.

Roberta as author is interrupted, however, in recounting the tale by the "experiencing I" Roberta. While Roberta as author attempts to maintain authority and narrative distance, the exigencies of life intrude. Roberta indicates this multiplicity when alternating between first and third person, as she does in the opening pages when her mother, a nurse, tries to convince Roberta that she might step on a needle and die if she goes barefoot: "And the author sat very still but she was thinking AS IF!!! As if I wouldn't feel a needle go into my own foot. As if I don't have enough vein biology information to know a needle would never make it to my heart. AS IF! AS IF! AS IF!" (9). Roberta strives for a detached distance from the narrative with her third-person commentary on "the author." This is the imagined tone of great literature with a capital L, but the reality of interfering little sisters and severe, deceitful mothers intervenes; and Roberta the teenager cannot help but interrupt, loudly and angrily, as indicated by the interjection "AS IF," her emotion emphasized by the capital letters and the numerous exclamation marks. It is the "experiencing I" Roberta who acts to connect with her friends and attempts to recreate her father's road trip. Roberta as author is thus divided as well; she is the authoritative, detached chronicler of events and a teenager immersed in the world. The narration reveals the struggle for dominance, with the young girl overwhelmed by the present usually taking control of the narration, with the voice of the distanced third person appearing only occasionally.[11]

While Roberta as narrator and shaper of the text is the most prominent identity, Roberta learns a great deal about survival as "Clyde."[12] When Roberta accompanies her father on his road trip at the age of eleven, she becomes Clyde, a twisted reflection of the man identified only as "the father." Clyde exists only in the past narrative and is a violent, dangerous boy, a warped, mirror image of the father, who comes to resemble the father more and more as the trip progresses, eventually becoming the dominant figure. After Roberta is bundled into the back of the car by her mother (identified only as "the mother"), she becomes her father's partner-in-crime. The father has taken off on a violent crime rampage in hopes of regaining the money he felt his father owed him after selling their butcher shop and committing suicide, and the father anoints Clyde as his partner and son. Roberta explains, "Clyde is what he called me. He wanted a son to pass his wisdom to. Me being born a girl was just a technicality. The world spun a lot smoother once you understood what you were bound to live by and what you weren't" (16). The father wants a son and therefore Roberta is remade into Clyde. Roberta accepts this transformation, having learned the important life lesson of which rules she must follow and which she can ignore.

Roberta is very rarely a girl when with her father, only assuming her biological sex when it is convenient. It is safer for her to remain a boy in her father's company, so they remain in their roles of father and reflected son. The father reinforces the naming of Clyde through repetition. Over and over, he calls Roberta "Clyde," as he does when he explains that he killed a man for burning Clyde/Roberta with a cigarette many years ago (although this crime was actually committed by the father), trying to cement their bond as partners: "I killed him for you, Clyde. No hesitation. . . . I killed him five times over for you Clyde. . . . That's what it means to be partners. Are we partners, Clyde? . . . Look at me, Clyde. Can I count on you?" (67).

Clyde is the father's stooge and partner, but definitely not a child:

> The father never treated me like a kid unless there was someone around. When the father looked at me, I do not know what he saw. Maybe a midget. Maybe an elf. I don't think it ever entered his mind that I was a kid. He knew it, but he never thought it, and it was what a person thought that mattered. That was the stuff you could twist a dream around. (63)

The narrative makes an important distinction here: while the father clearly knew that Clyde was a child, just as he knew Clyde was really a female, it made no difference because he "never thought it," preferring instead to create his own reality; and thus Roberta/Clyde comes to reflect the intentions and imperfections of the father, and it was that reality that governed their lives. The father's mythical image became true, so true that he could "twist" or distort his hopes and dreams of a fine son, a real partner, and a legacy between generations. For the father the legacy had been disrupted when his father, "Old Dad," committed suicide and sold the butcher shop, robbing him of his inheritance and breaking the bond between father and son. And so Clyde is created as everything the father lacks: a friend, partner, confidante, and son. The truth, if such a thing can be discerned, matters not so much as what one believes.

Roberta/Clyde reflects her father not only in disposition but also in appearance, resulting in a distinctly unattractive girl/boy, a fact that the father uses to gain sympathy in their cons. For Roberta/Clyde, her resemblance to her father further binds them as reflector and reflected. She states:

> I'm what a person might call a dog. Very much a dog. Guys have actually barked at me and offered me Milk-Bones. My face cells divided into the shape of the father, who even for a man was on the homely side. Jug ears and no chin and a wide nose and hooded eyes. Bad skin. Thin Hair. All of it revisited in me by means of somatic mitosis, *Stedman's Medical Dictionary*, page 954. (60)

Roberta/Clyde looks like a boy, so much so that she is a miniature version of her father, giving her a prophetic vision of the future as reflected in his appearance. Clearly, whatever deficiencies he carries, the ugly ears, nose, eyes, skin, and hair, are all the genetic legacy of her father. The father also links them by making Roberta a boy, Clyde, and Roberta/Clyde finds acceptance and value as a stooge for the father's schemes.

For much of their adventure Roberta/Clyde acts as her father's partner and accomplice, going along with his scheme of staying in the horrible, peculiar town of Knocking Hammer while the father works out how to scam a lonely widow, Pammy. Clyde absorbs the lessons of the father, such as "Be the Unexpected" and use "dazzle camouflage" to blind your con. The father makes Clyde in his own image, and over time Roberta/Clyde so perfects the role of the father as to best him at his own game. When the father sends Roberta/Clyde crawling down into a cave at gunpoint to reclaim a suitcase of money which may or may not be there, Roberta/ Clyde waits for him; and when the father peers down to check on Clyde's progress, she slashes his throat with the father's own knife, "Sheila," "who had no problem with the idea of turning against him" (297). The father's goal was to create a perfect son in his own image, a violent boy who gets what he wants, regardless of others. The father succeeded in creating Clyde, for in this reflected image the protagonist takes on the qualities of the father and uses them against him, just as she uses Sheila to kill her father. Upon hearing the convoluted story of Clyde, Roberta's wise but ultimately doomed friend, "the Great Wesley," reflects, "The son shall bathe his hands in parent's blood, and in one act be both unjust and good" (299). And thus it was that Clyde became the father's greatest success and undoing. Roberta embraced the reflection and perfected it, taking control and turning the tables on her father.

As Roberta becomes Clyde, a warped reflection of the father, she also comes to reflect the twisted desires of a pedophile sheriff she encounters in her journey with her father as "Ee-gore," a mentally handicapped boy. The sheriff desires a boy incapable of understanding his advances and protecting himself, thus Roberta comes to reflect the sheriff's perversions. However, just as Roberta/Clyde ultimately embodies the reflection of the father and prevails against him, so too does Roberta/Ee-gore succeed in embracing the distortion to survive. While staying in the town of Knocking Hammer during a scam with the father as Clyde, Roberta attempts to keep a low profile and not irritate the father. The sheriff of the town, however, takes a definite interest in the new "boy."

> The sheriff tilted his head at me. "He's so damn ugly he's cute. You know who he reminds me of? That little humped over Ee-gore from that movie, what the hell was it, that horror one? Come on over here, Ee-gore."
> The father said, "He bites."
> "Haw," said the sheriff.
> "I'm telling you," the father said, "He bit our minister in the gonad one time. Talk about embarrassment."
> HAW HAW HAW
> The sheriff swept his hand over his privates. "Mine are so big he'd never get a grip." (176)

The sheriff indicates his affection for Clyde/Roberta by commenting on his/her "cuteness" and offering the name of Ee-gore after Igor from the horror movies. It is an appropriate moniker, alluding to the gothic origins of the story and the "gore" Ee-gore eventually creates. Furthermore, Igor as presented in the movies is the assistant for many a mad scientist or villain, just as Roberta/Clyde/Ee-gore assists the father, himself a criminal. The sheriff, however, sees Ee-gore as the reflection of his longing, an easy sexual conquest and someone he can control.

The sheriff further indicates his lust for Ee-gore when he jokes about the size of his genitals, and he later tries to force Ee-gore to perform oral sex and, prophetically, is "bitten," or slashed by the knife named "Little Debbie."

Indeed, Ee-gore eventually comes to accept the reflection, if only for a time, mimicking the horror movie counterpart and acting as a silent, handicapped boy. The sheriff, according to the father, is "tantalized" by Ee-gore and, as the narrator explains, attempts to "get me into his car with offers like, 'I'll let you blow the siren, Ee-gore, I got twenty six candy bars, Ee-gore.'" (207). Ee-gore extracts his ultimate revenge when the sheriff attempts to force him/her to perform oral sex. The father has signed Ee-gore/Clyde over to a rehabilitation home for handicapped youth and the sheriff is quick to offer a ride and "friendship," explaining, "Ee-gore, right now you need a friend in the worst way, don't you?" (225). The sheriff's notion of friendship involves sexual assault:

> He said, "We can make this easy or we can make this hard. If you try to bite me, you won't have a mouth left. Understood?"
> He wanted me to take a drink. He passed me the bottle. I took a glug and passed it back. I wanted him to know I was being cooperative. There was the sound of him unbuckling his belt, and the unzipping and the rearrangement of pants. He put his hand on the back of my neck and pushed my head downward. I didn't resist. I didn't hesitate. Never hesitate. Move fast, follow through, let the blade do the work.
> My first swipe was a reach-around. Little Debbie was so sharp I didn't know I truly cut him. I felt something like a knife passing through a hard-boiled egg but that was all. (226)

Ee-gore exploits the reflected image of desire the sheriff has placed upon him/her, acting compliant, "being cooperative," and playing along with the scene. Ee-gore drinks as directed, and even lets the sheriff push him into position, but Ee-gore is prepared. Ee-gore achieves "the unexpected" and maims and eventually kills the sheriff. Ee-gore utilizes the sheriff's own lust-induced myopia to destroy him. Ultimately, the hunchbacked "idiot" takes advantage of the sheriff's weakness and assumes dominance over her attacker.

In contrast with the violence of Clyde and Ee-gore, Roberta's most peaceful reflection is that of a victim known as a "Mystery Child" and "Michelle." After being found alone in the desert after murdering her father and the sheriff, a Christian Homes woman takes in Roberta as the "Mystery Child" and dubs her "Michelle," an innocent, amnesiac child. As the Mystery Child and later Michelle, Roberta enjoys a brief period of peace. In a picture of this reflection, she tilts her head to the side and gazes plaintively at the viewer (fig. 4.4). She does not appear angry as much as resigned as she holds tightly to a dog named Cookie. In the picture, Roberta as the Mystery Child looks bald and fragile, not so much female or male, resembling an androgynous newborn. In a sense she is reborn into this new world; apart from her father she is no longer Clyde, but she can't simply return to "normal" after her journey. The narrator explains the picture:

> We looked bad and crusty. The caption called me the Mystery Child and the story underneath told of my shocking condition and amnesia and asked did anyone recognize me, anyone in this world? The picture was of the olden me, my hair very very short, shaved like a boy's and my arms and legs so skinny and my expression very paralyzed, me holding Cookie in my breadstick arms. And even though most of the blood was washed off of us we were still very convincing because the newspaper photographer told the Christian Homes lady to please leave some of the blood, he did not want all of the blood showing, but please leave a little because blood was the drama and the interest but too much of it was an appetite wrecker and it was a morning paper. (14)

Mystery Child/Michelle thus reflects the reporter's idea of an eye-catching but not too upsetting picture for the paper, as well as the Christian Homes lady's desire to assist a frightened, blameless child. Roberta takes on the identity of this unassuming Mystery Child and uses her silence as protection; she admits nothing and lets others assume what has happened to her, rather than what she has done. The Mystery Child is a blank slate, a tabula rasa, and is remade by the good Christians who take her in as Michelle, the lost victim of some horrible crime spree that leaves "everyone else . . . laying around in hacked-up pieces" (13). As suggested by the picture, the Mystery Child Roberta is genderless, no longer male but not yet female.

The Christian Homes lady orders the Mystery Child into the backyard so she can hose off the blood and "when the reality of the nude version of me was revealed, she freaked totally. Because up until then, everybody thought I was a boy. When it turned out I was a girl, that was a surprise no one was suspecting" (14). Roberta sheds the trappings and deeds of her male reflections, Clyde and Ee-gore, and is renamed Michelle, a compliant girl who makes sock monkeys for underprivileged children. It was a "decent life" (140). The narrator asserts, "I enjoyed life as Michelle. I enjoyed making sock monkeys for the Christian Missionaries International Sock Monkey Drive. . . . I enjoyed the Jesus they prayed to, a very different-looking Jesus from the one I was used to" (140). This is another world, where Michelle could "eat green beans and scalloped potatoes and ham made in an electric

Figure 4.4. "Mystery Child." Lynda Barry, *Cruddy* (New York: Simon & Schuster, 2002), 12.

skillet and drink big glasses of milk and snarf down tapioca pudding and hear the reverend list me in the names of people to pray for" (142). This life is a stark contrast from her previous world, like the Lawrence Welk specials she watches with the Christians. In this reality Jesus is friendly, not vengeful, and children drink milk and eat pudding, rather than swilling Corpse Reviver moonshine and smoking cigarettes.

Roberta does not last long in this peaceful identity, but returns home with her mother, where she grows and eventually takes on her most mature identity, "Hillbilly Woman"; for in the eyes of her friends, sixteen-year-old Roberta becomes this "Hillbilly Woman," a learned, mature woman as christened by Turtle, a lost, wandering drug addict who takes a liking to her. When Roberta and her new friend Vicky Talluso skip school, they come upon Turtle, who offers them drugs and friendship. Upon meeting Roberta, he immediately dubs her "Hillbilly Woman." When Roberta asks him why, Turtle responds, "Because you are a hillbilly girl lost in a hillbilly world" (45).

Vicky Talluso agrees, exclaiming, "She is! She is!" (45). Her friends believe that Roberta/Hillbilly Woman has seen a great deal in her short life, often the *wrong* sorts of things. By nature of her gruesome past, she cannot fit in with others; her manners, dress, and appearance alienate her from others and herself. The hillbilly also suggests a rebel of sorts, a defiant yokel who refuses to conform to the larger culture. Despite Roberta's life on the boundaries, Turtle also sees her as a sexual object, a woman, not a girl, hence the designation as Hillbilly *Woman*.

The Turtle reveres Hillbilly Woman as a sexual object and as a caretaker. When he introduces her to his friend Monkey, he gushes, "Meet your Queen. You will love her" (154). Monkey, too, sees Hillbilly Woman as a sexual being and is determined to discover her "true" identity. Monkey asks, "Like I don't even know your name. What is it? Because I know it's not Hillbilly Woman" (159). But Roberta/Hillbilly Woman doesn't answer; at this moment, reflected in Turtle's and Monkey's gaze, she is a woman and an outsider. She is Hillbilly Woman.

Turtle, the Great Wesley, Vicky, and her brother, the Stick, see in Hillbilly Woman an active, aggressive leader. Acting in accordance with their image of her, Hillbilly Woman takes charge of these friends and takes them on a parallel journey, searching for the treasure she left behind and telling the story of her father. It is this journey and story that is described by Roberta in the diary. Not only is Hillbilly Woman a teller of tales, she is also active in her own destiny and the destinies of others. She drives the car, literally and figuratively. This represents a change from previous reflections; while Ee-gore, Clyde, and Michelle took control when they had to in order to survive, they were not leaders. Nor did these identities feel compelled to share their stories with others, following instead the father's dictum, "Loose lips sink ships."

Not only is Hillbilly Woman a sexual object, she also acts as a mother of sorts to the band of misfits. When Great Wesley's brother, known as the Sultan, uses Vicky for sex and quickly abandons her and then begins kicking Wesley, Hillbilly Woman does not hesitate: "The Sultan was about to kick him again but was stopped by a sudden cut on his arm, a slice, very clean and very deep and instantly gushing. Little Debbie gleamed in my hand" (264). Hillbilly Woman acts; she defends Wesley and Vicky against a bigger bully, then leads her friends on their own journey, driving away from the past. This is a horror story, and the band of misfits does not drive off into the glorious sunset. While Hillbilly Woman attempts to drive them to the site of the father's hidden money, she fails. Wesley, Turtle, and the Stick commit suicide. Vicky survives. But without the others and returned once more to the home of the mother, Hillbilly Woman reverts to Roberta again.

The Final Girl: Roberta as Author

At the conclusion of the book Roberta, the final girl,[13] comes to question the reflections imposed upon her and attempts to create her own. In fact, before the Stick passes away Roberta decides to rename herself. The Stick tells her, "I have a crush on you, Roberta" (302), and she replies, "I told him my name was no longer Roberta. I told him my name was Junior Bizarre" (302). The Stick, her ill-fated suitor, does not call her Hillbilly Woman or by any of her other names, indicating he sees Roberta and not his distorted reflection of her. Roberta, however, disassociates from her identity as Roberta, choosing the unusual moniker Junior Bizarre, perhaps referring to the legacy of the father. "Bizarre," however, seems appropriate, for Roberta has certainly lived a strange and unusual life. Bizarre also suggests living outside the norms and conventions of society, and Roberta definitely does not conform in appearance or attitude to stereotypes of young women. Perhaps "Junior" refers to her size and stature, a smaller version of the strange and unusual.

Just before the Stick slits his wrists, he points out the scar on Roberta/Junior Bizarre's arm, which reads, "*I'm sorry*." Who is this "I" engraved on Roberta's arm? Who is the "I" narrating the last few paragraphs?

> And so that is what I am about to do right now. Sneak out and meet Vicky by the Diggy's Dumpster. And then tomorrow night, after the concert she promised she will come with me to the train tracks. And she promised she will give me the little push I need unless something happens and she gets together with Neil Young.
>
> And so if you are reading this, if you are holding this book in your hands right now it means my plan worked completely, I am gone. I am gone. I got my happy ending.
>
> And so whoever you are, if you want the money, you can have it. My description of the location is decent and followable. But watch out for Dreamland. Beware of Air Force. Stay Navy all the way.
>
> That is all.
>
> This is the End.
>
> I dedicate this book to my sister, Julie. (304)

In the final lines Roberta reverts to her persona as the author and crafter of the next, the Roberta who pens the initial suicide note that reads "Roberta Rohbeson 1955–1971." The author incorporates a combination of all of the reflections imposed upon her: Roberta, Clyde, Ee-gore, Michelle, and the Mystery Child. The narrative ends from a definitive "I" perspective, yet it ends in death. Apparently, this is the only way out of the fun house and away from the reflections of others; her only immortality comes through her words.

It is Roberta's sister Julie, however, who has the final word, a handwritten scrawl at the bottom of the page that exclaims, "<u>fuck</u> you roberta!!! I <u>hate</u> you roberta!!! <u>Where are you</u>??" (305). It is as if Roberta has just at this moment disappeared and Julie has found the diary, not quite believing that Roberta is truly gone. In an initial reading it is difficult not to scrutinize the handwriting, wondering if someone has actually, physically inscribed this message. Is this really the end? Has some vandal defaced the book? Julie's final words add authenticity to the idea that this book is truly someone's diary, and the reader is simply peeking into her world.

Barry told Benny Shaboy that it was Roberta who concluded the book:

> Roberta stopped talking. She said the last words and they were so clearly the last words and it was very strange. On one hand I was overjoyed to be finished and that state lasted for a while. And then I felt funny, not sad really, but disoriented because she was gone and she'd been so alive in my head for so long and now she is totally gone. No where to be found.

Barry once again challenges her readers to participate in the story as Roberta invites the audience to take the money, and it is up to the reader to continue the story and decide what happens next. Did the author, Roberta, commit suicide after the Neil Young concert? The conclusion suggests, given that the reader is indeed holding the book in his or her hands, that the author has taken control of her life and death and that her "plan had worked" and she found her "happy ending" by ending her life, as her friends Turtle, Wesley, and the Stick did. While the conclusion remains open-ended and mysterious, in *Cruddy* Barry undoubtedly presents the image of a girl struggling to find her place amidst the reflections and identities foisted upon her by others. Roberta responds to her environment, embodying the images of others and using them to her advantage, fighting to survive. At the conclusion of *Cruddy* Roberta disappears, yet through her story she achieves the immortality she hoped to attain as well as a vessel for her many reflections. Roberta relishes her identity as the author, and though others gaze upon her, twisting her into versions of the self as filtered through their desires, Roberta's compulsion to write her story and create an identity as the author begins and ends the book.

Why did Lynda Barry choose to write this story as a novel, rather than creating a graphic novel or comic? One might argue that the novel form freed Barry in many ways—her loquaciousness was allowed free reign and her penchant for digression was indulged—but more importantly, Barry was released to roam widely with her characters, expanding their geography, and furthermore felt liberated to explore more sinister themes and ideas. The action of Barry's comic *Ernie Pook's Comeek* remains within a small radius, the neighborhood where the children live, and the events often transpire within rooms and inside homes. It is a very tight, very domestic sphere of influence. The novel and play *The Good Times Are Killing Me* similarly take place within a small vicinity, presenting an intimate look at race relations within a neighborhood. Barry's later works *One Hundred* Demons, *What It Is*, and *Picture This* move beyond the tight confines of a child's community, but barely, remaining for the most part within a particular locality close to the author's experience. *Cruddy*, however, travels far and wide, a rarity amidst Barry's oeuvre. While the book begins within the confines of Roberta's "cruddy" home, the narrative travels and moves rapidly and over long distances, from city to wasteland and back again. Unfettered and freed by the form of the novel, Barry allowed her characters to roam widely and with abandon.

When working with the novel form, Barry also indulged her interest in horror. Certainly, numerous comic artists have dealt with the dark and macabre in their work, so one might ask why Barry chose to rely primarily on a text-based novel rather than exploring darker themes in comic art.[14] For all of the gore of *Cruddy*, it is interesting to note that throughout her oeuvre, Barry chooses not to depict extreme violence through her own artistic renditions. In *One Hundred Demons* Barry only alludes to the molestation of a young girl, but refuses to create explicit artistic renditions of the act. In *Ernie Pook's Comeek*, Barry similarly avoids drawing pictures of the sexual assault of one of the characters. However, it seems that relying on text, as opposed to graphic imagery, freed Barry to explore the dark, the disgusting, and the violent. This approach limits Barry's accountability to some extent, for the pictures are crafted in the readers' minds, thus making the audience complicit in creating the mental images. In the essay "Lightning and Visuals," James Dickey speaks to the "infinitely valuable personal nature of the image" (12) evoked when reading:

> What each person sees in his head is the inevitable product of genes, chromosomes, heredity, environment, the past, the present, memory, fantasy, reality, dream, and many other factors which, when set in motion—or stillness—throw upon the screen the living picture. It is your *life* the picture lives with, your life and my life. (13)

Just as the characters in the book create images of Roberta based on their own desires, each reader creates an image of Roberta in his or her mind. A comic artist bears responsibility for drawing a picture, but a novelist drafts the words that the reader uses to form a unique depiction based on his or her life experiences. Although Barry incorporates some artistic renditions, the bulk of the picture making in *Cruddy* is left to the reader, and the reader thus becomes a part of the process of calling upon his or her own experiences to create an image and an identity for the girl known as Roberta.

What does *Cruddy* say about girls and girlhood? Does *Cruddy* reflect the reality of most girls' experience? Clearly not. This dark, disturbing text acts as a counter to overly optimistic conceptions of girlhood, offering a painful, exaggerated correction to idyllic myths. Yet apart from the gore and the hyperbole, Barry's text-based rendition of girlhood also posits a fragmented, illusory conception of self for young girls. When Roberta looks to others, she sees infinite, distorted reflections of the self based on the imperfections of others. Society, like a hall of mirrors in a fun house, reflects itself onto and over her, overwriting the image of the girl again and again. Both Roberta of *Cruddy* and Alice of *Wonderland* inquire as to their identities before setting off on remarkable adventures. Yet Alice ends her escapades confused, still wondering who she is and doubting her experiences as a dream, while Roberta takes control of the fun house, leaving behind a textual reflection for the reader to puzzle over. *Cruddy*, then, suggests that if there is an escape from the confusion for the girl, it is to be found in creating one's own text and one's own narrative, assuming control of representations of the self.

5

Girlhood under the Microscope in *Ernie Pook's Comeek*

Although she has worked in many forms, Lynda Barry is perhaps best known for creating the cult favorite comic strip *Ernie Pook's Comeek*. Marlys, Maybonne, and Fred Milton and the many popular characters from the strip have over time become synonymous with Barry. Throughout her oeuvre, Barry's vision of girlhood explores the lives of girls through many lenses and mediums, and in her comic *Ernie Pook* Barry puts girlhood under a microscope, magnifying and examining tiny slices of life, and even these small samples exhibit a multifaceted perspective on girlhood. Barry penned *Ernie Pook's Comeek* for nearly thirty years, and the long-running comic clearly spirals around all sorts of issues, returning to them time and again through her key characters. As a weekly strip, *Ernie Pook* resists resolution, moving from topic to topic and character to character, and the strip certainly does not demonstrate an ascendant trajectory from struggle to success. This is no Horatio Alger rags-to-riches fairy tale, nor is it a charmingly innocent slice-of-life like Barry's favorite comic strip, Bill Keane's *The Family Circus*. The children of *Ernie Pook* struggle and fail and struggle again. Given the many years, many themes, and many characters of *Ernie Pook,* the analysis here is necessarily limited. Very little has been written in general about Lynda Barry in scholarly circles, and *Ernie Pook's Comeek,* in particular, merits additional academic study as it offers a rich, layered portrayal of a family of characters over many years.[1] The art, the writing, and the many issues addressed in the strips, such as poverty, divorce, bullying, gay and lesbian relationships, gender stereotyping, sexual abuse, and the ties of family and friendship, to name but a few, provide much material to interest the scholarly community. It is likely that as Barry's strips are reprinted in their entirety and in the original format by Drawn and Quarterly Press over the coming years, there will be renewed interest and additional scholarship to follow.

For now, though, in this consideration of *Ernie Pook* within the context of Barry's fascination with girlhood over her entire career, the analysis will focus on several key issues. First, as an artist and author working in numerous genres, why and how does Barry use comics to examine girlhood? What does this genre add that other mediums do not? In answering these questions, the analysis examines the ways in which Barry, through the form of comic art, utilizes multiple focalizers, narrators, and aesthetic styles to create a stereoscopic, magnified vision of girlhood that mimics the unstable experience of the girls depicted within the strip itself. This section provides an analysis of *Ernie Pook's* structure and style, including the format, drawing style, narrators, and focalizers. The investigation further considers what *Ernie Pook's Comeek* reveals about Barry's perceptions of girls, scrutinizing some of the themes and ideas associated with the girls as presented in the strip. Ideas that come sharply into focus over the years of the run will be considered, such as the pressure for girls to appear attractive and embrace stereotypes of feminine beauty, the dangers as girls pass between childhood and adulthood, and the importance of actively celebrating the joys inherent in the everyday. Issues that remain beyond the depth of field will also be noted, such as the strip's reluctance to directly depict extreme violence or brutality. Finally, Barry's comic art from *Ernie Pook* will be contemplated in relation to several ongoing concerns apparent throughout Barry's oeuvre, for in *Ernie Pook* Barry argues that for the girls presented in the strip, happiness comes from self-acceptance and exuberance, despite critics, and embracing the optimism and joy of childhood, a philosophy frequently embodied by the character Marlys Mullens and maintained in Barry's later works, *One Hundred Demons*, *What It Is*, and *Picture This*. However, before delving into the specifics of the inquiry, a brief introduction to the early days of the strip provides context for analysis.

Overview of *Ernie Pook's Comeek*

When Bob Roth offered Barry a weekly strip with the *Chicago Reader* in 1979, he "came to the rescue," as Barry told Joe Garden, and this opportunity allowed her to make a living through her comics. The weekly strip, originally known as *Girls and Boys*, initially focused on relationships, sex, and dating. Children occasionally appeared, but the emphasis was on adult concerns. As noted in chapter 2, over time the name changed to *Ernie Pook's Comeek;* and as the title transformed, the subject matter of the strip also changed, for as Barry made the switch from pen to brush around 1984, she also began to focus on children.

    Ernie Pook's Comeek started in just a few papers, but it came to be carried in numerous alternative weeklies. However, by 2008 the strip was being carried in fewer and fewer papers until Barry finally decided to stop drawing the strip in October of 2008.[2] Early in her career, taking chances on content was welcomed, but over time Barry felt constrained by overly cautious and conservative newspapers. Barry explained that "in the early days," risks "would have been completely allowed,"[3] in contrast with contemporary standards. Therefore, in the early years Barry was allowed to follow her evolving interests, and eventually *Ernie Pook* would come to be known as a melancholy strip about childhood, leaving behind its origins as a strip focused on adult romance and relationships that ended with a clear punch line. *Ernie Pook* was not an uproarious strip full of chuckles at the idiosyncrasies of precious, perfect children, rather, it showed a winsome, often bittersweet obsession with recapturing childhood moments.

Ernie Pook follows brother and sister Arna and Arnold Arneson and their cousins Marlys, Maybonne, and Freddie Mullens (with occasional appearances by a talking poodle named Fred Milton, who sometimes breaks into the continuity of the strip and spouts beatnik poetry, often about current, real-world events).[4] Though they have aged little, if at all, over the twenty-five years since they appeared, they have encountered rape, incest, bullying, neglect, brutality, homophobia, and sometimes a modicum of joy as well. Though pinpointing the exact timeframe when *Ernie Pook* takes place is difficult, it seems to occur around the time of Barry's own childhood, in the late 1960s and early '70s, with occasional jumps to contemporary moments. In an online discussion group, Alan Lewis noted, "It seems like almost all of the popular culture references in the comic are to the 60s–70s. Fred Milton exists in the modern day, commenting about current events. And in the Marlys/Arna/ etc. storyline, they sometimes refer to things that are only known in the present." Although the strip seems generally rooted in the 1960s to '70s, Barry takes license as she deems appropriate. While the setting feels general enough to be relatable to a wide audience, there are Pacific Northwest references that suggest the action takes place in the town where Barry spent most of her youth, Seattle.

Analysis and Inspirations

In *One Hundred Demons* (2002) Barry explained that after discovering "only certain people were 'advanced' enough for writing and literature," she found solace "when [she] started making comic-strips. It's not something a person has to be very 'advanced' to do" (215). Despite any misgivings, Barry has delved into other forms of expression in addition to creating comic art, and with an artist who works in so many genres and utilizes so many ways of seeing, one might ask what comic art could offer Barry's vision of girl-hood. How does Barry use the medium to depict girls' lives, and what, in particular, does this genre offer? In exploring these questions, this analysis draws from multiple schools of thought, including the fields of photogra-phy, microscopy, art theory, literary theory (including narratology), and comic art theory. Comic art theorist Thierry Groensteen's ideas, as pre-sented in *The System of Comics,* provide helpful tools for interpretation, although Groensteen argues that a comic strip itself is not substantial enough for analysis, for "the strip, itself, appears like a transit zone, in-sufficiently homogeneous or isolated to be able to claim a true identity" (58). My analysis relies on individual strips, but does so within the wider context of hundreds of strips as presented over almost thirty years, a body of work which, although admittedly different from the carefully formatted and bound comic books singled out by Groensteen, merits extended schol-arly attention given its weighty themes and carefully crafted and extensive depiction of childhood. In contrast with a comic book or graphic novel that is published on a certain date, the weekly strips represent a publishing event occurring weekly, month after month and year after year. Utilizing a musical analogy, Groensteen argues, "The strip passes for a measure—but an irregular measure, given that the duration of the panels is not constant" (61). However, in reference to *Ernie Pook*, the shape and format of the pan-els does remain constant, like a measure in four-four time each week; and when examined together (as they are presented in an anthology, for ex-ample), I would argue that they do comprise a larger composition with a "true identity," albeit a different one from a comic book or graphic novel.[5]

Comic theorists, such as Derik Badman, Harry Morgan, Julia Round, Neil Cohn, and Ann Miller, working with theories of narratology bor-rowed from literature and film, primarily adapt these theories to longer-form comics. Although their work addresses lengthier comic projects, their theories, particularly on point of view, are especially valuable when analyz-ing *Ernie Pook*, specifically when the strip is examined over an extended span of time. The narratological approach is still fairly new within comics scholarship, and thus individual comic scholars apply terms of narratol-ogy differently, relying on their own adaptations and translations when employing ideas from narratological theory that were originally intended for text-based literature and film. Therefore, when using narratological terms, this analysis will define them within the scope of this project only, acknowledging that widely accepted, universal terms and definitions have yet to be delimited.

While comic strips and comic books and graphic novels have definite differences, they share a common trait in blending word and picture. According to Pascal LeFevre in his article "The Construction of Space in Comics," on the limitations of printed symbols on paper: "Objects that appear on a flat surface can never show the complete reality of such three-dimensional objects. The flat and unmoving image can only use monocular cues to suggest depth: interposition or overlapping, convergence, relative size, density gradient" (159). And while it is true that Barry cannot rely on mixed-media collages as she does in other artistic endeavors to add depth and dimension to her comic work, she instead depends on multiple points of view, multiple narrators, and multiple narratives (textual and pictorial) even within the comic itself to give the suggestion of dimensionality, or as Julia Round suggests, the "hyperreal" (323). In her article "Visual Perspective and Narrative Voice in Comics: Redefining Literary Terminology," Round suggests that "the evocation of the hyperreal can be described as a side effect of the multiple points of view that are created by juxtaposition" (324). As with a stereomicroscope, Barry's comics bring in more than one angle and way of seeing (or reading or "hearing") to offer a more comprehensive, more dimensional perspective.

Despite the art's aforementioned flat, singular appearance on the printed page, the blending of text and picture comic art invokes a more complicated language than text or picture alone, an approach that works particularly well for Barry's rendering of the complicated, multifarious lives of girls. In her article "Comics as Literature: Reading Graphic Narrative," Hillary Chute suggests that comics in general offer a sort of "double vision": "In one frame of comics, the images and the words may mean differently, and thus the works sends out double-coded narratives or semantics" (459). As will be discussed in more detail in the following analysis, Barry makes use of numerous narrators, sometimes contrasting their narration with the accompanying images. She further complicates the comic by altering the art style to suggest not just different narrators but different illustrators, creating a multifaceted, often contradictory narrative. Barry's work, in particular, and the complicated language of comics, in general, demand that readers reduce speed, reading text and picture, filling in the gaps both literal and figurative, as one might study a slide under a microscope. Chute further notes that reading comics "can require slowing down; the form can place a great demand on our cognitive skills " ("Comics" 460), and this measured, attentive type of reading reflects Barry's prolonged consideration of girlhood through small but densely packed moments.

Figure 5.1."Sure is a gloomy morning." Bill Keane, *Family Circus*, 2 March 1986. This image was taken from the Bill Keane website: http://www.familycircus.com/files/80/80b.htm, accessed 28 April 2011.

When a sample is viewed under a microscope, there is a limited field of view—what is within the range of vision. Barry's field of view within *Ernie Pook's Comeek* is similarly limited, for the most part to the confines of a child's room, home, school, and, at the broadest, neighborhood. Similar in scope to Barry's novel and play *The Good Times Are Killing Me*, *Ernie Pook* depicts a domestic, restricted scene. *Ernie Pook* provides a window into childhood, similar in subject but different in mood from Barry's favorite comic as a child, *The Family Circus*, by Bill Keane, which allowed Barry to see another type of family as a girl. Some might be surprised that Barry, having created such an irreverent and often troubling world for her characters, would draw inspiration from a cartoon that has been labeled wholesome to the point of insipid. But Barry explained in the introduction to *Best American Comics 2008* that the tiny circles of *Family Circus* afforded a window, a viewpoint into another type of home and family. For Barry, *Family Circus* "brought [her] a lot of comfort"("Introduction" xiii). Although it features the entire family rather than emphasizing girls as *Ernie Pook* does, *Family Circus* similarly remains centered on the domestic sphere, home, school, and neighborhood, showing a small perspective on family life. In this strip from 2 March 1986 Keane invites the audience into a warm, domestic environment (fig. 5.1). While the weather outside the family home is ominous—the clouds grey and the interior and exterior dark—the mother and father are still cozily domestic as the mother, clad in fluffy slippers and robe, prepares the morning coffee. In the final section the panel is awash in brilliant yellow and the mother's nightgown turns pink as she holds her baby, with rays of joy

Figure 5.2. "Family Pictures." Lynda Barry, *It's So Magic* (New York: Harper Perennial, 1994), 6–7.

radiating from the mother and child. Mother declares that the sun has come out as she cuddles her baby, walking toward the smiling father. There is no narrator, just a few speech bubbles from the mother and father. Given the serene depictions of the family, there is little left for a narrator to say. Keane typically chooses a single panel for his daily strip, but this Sunday strip is divided into four sections without borders and bears a resemblance to Barry's typical structure. The family pictured in Keane's creation is depicted with smooth, comforting roundness, and any sharp words or edges are softened and cleaned up to provide a sweetened image of domestic life.

The characters of *Ernie Pook* do not live within the safe sphere of Bill Keane's loving gaze, but in Barry's neighborhood and Barry's world; and according to the *Washington Post*, this "is no sentimental vision of children at play, it's the real thing—children telling tales on each other; children lying to impress their friends; children as victims of parents and other adults; children suffering through boring classes with boring teachers" (X12). Barry herself explained, "They're not bad kids, but they run into problems, things kids aren't supposed to run into" (Cooper G1). This distinction is important; Barry does not portray villainous, bad-seed children in her strip. These are ordinary kids, perhaps even akin to Dolly and Billy from *Family Circus*, but the world of *Ernie Pook* is much more dangerous and the children must react accordingly. In the 1993 strip "Family Pictures," "good kid" Maybonne Mullens introduces her family (fig. 5.2).

In "Family Pictures" Maybonne presents her family in response to a school assignment. As with *Family Circus*, the scene is a domestic one, introducing her sister, mother, brother, father, and grandmother. Unlike Keane, the sharp edges and blemishes have not been smoothed out, but are accentuated. The wrinkles and frown lines of the menacing mother are fierce, and the family members are depicted as incredibly flawed. While Barry cites Keane as an inspiration and their comics share a similar field of view, the worlds they create and examine in miniature are decidedly different.

Structure

Just as a specimen to be viewed under a microscope must be processed and formatted specifically for viewing, Barry captured the world of *Ernie Pook* through a structure that became standard over the years, and this layout functioned to give a compact yet dynamic insight into girlhood. Each weekly strip had four panels set in a square pattern. These panels were at times subdivided, but generally each panel told a section of the story and each panel was densely packed. No space was wasted, as each panel was crowded with narration, pictures, and speech balloons. This rigid structure suited Barry, who in other endeavors, such as her novella, novel, and play, demonstrates a tendency to digress. The comic is the most organized and structured of her favored mediums. The four-panel structure forced Barry to edit and shape each tiny vignette into a tightly focused, four-part composition.

The 1986 strip "The Night We All Got Sick" Barry follows a typical structure (fig. 5.3). In the first panel she introduces the characters and the situation as the narration explains, "It all started when . . ." The second and third panels show the developing issue as the children suffer from food poisoning, and the final panel introduces the resolution as each child holds a "secret weapon" of hated food over the others. The structure clearly and concisely

Figure 5.3. "The Night We All Got Sick." Lynda Barry, *The! Greatest! of! Marlys!* (Seattle: Sasquatch Books, 2000).

relates a humorous anecdote from the Mullens and Arkins families and introduces Barry's featured children.

In fact, four of the characters that would come to dominate *Ernie Pook* first appeared in "The Night We All Got Sick." The strip introduces the narrator, Arna, who tells the story of the night she, her brother Arnold, and cousins Freddie and Marlys got sick after eating their favorite foods at a parade. Arna and Arnold chose cotton candy, Marlys chose a hotdog ("a perfectly stupid pick" according to Arna), and Freddie, a blue Sno-Kone. Once they recovered, the children were able to use these sickening victuals as a sort of kryptonite or "secret weapon," taunting one another with the nausea-inducing food item. The panel also marks a turn from more autobiographical strips to fictional. Although Barry did, in fact, become ill after overindulg-

ing in cotton candy,[6] the narratives came to revolve around fictional characters Arna, Arnold, Marlys, Maybonne, and Freddie. Barry revealed to Thom
Powers, "It's funny, because when the characters came—when Marlys and
Arna and Arnold and Freddie made their appearance and let me know that
they were staying—it was a whole other thing. Then it became fiction" (67).
Barry also told interviewer Todd Olson that her characters "were always
there. Like books in the library that I finally got around to checking out. They
seem to have lives apart from me. I think the closest thing to what I experience is what people who have imaginary friends experience. I don't exactly
hear her, but when I'm drawing Marlys I know what she is saying." When
asked about the infamous "Night We All Got Sick" strip, Barry affirmed,
"That's when all the characters —that's the first strip that all those characters appeared in. They never existed before that strip and that was—prior
to that strip, I was just doing—I never had any repeating characters. Matt
would say, 'You should get repeating characters. It's a lot easier.'"[7] Initially
unable to take long-time friend Matt Groening's advice, Barry didn't have
repeating characters until she was ready, but once her "imaginary friends"
took center stage, they were loath to leave.

With her focus on childhood and cast of characters established, Barry
felt free to experiment with the format, utilizing the square-panel structure
more creatively, as she did in the 1990 strip "The Plastic Wall." This strip,
narrated by the eldest regular character, Maybonne Mullens, addresses
Maybonne's inferiority complex (fig. 5.4). The four-panel strip opens with
a close-up image of part of Maybonne's face, with dark horizontal stripes
lining the background. The second panel moves to the other side of her face,
and placed next to one another the two panels show a tight, magnified view
of a section of her face. The uncomfortably close perspective reveals every
freckle and blemish. Her nose is awkwardly shaped and divided. Her small,
marked hands clutch at her face and the dark, horizontal lines parallel the
harsh lines of her bangs. These first two panels suggest, apart from the narrative, that Maybonne is divided, alienated from herself. The audience sees
a reflection of Maybonne as through a divided mirror. The third panel pulls
away a bit, to the more distanced perspective, showing multiple images of a
pensive Maybonne, surrounded by more thick black lines that suggest cra-
ziness, despair, a warping of reality. The final panel is even more removed
and the figure of Maybonne diminishes in size. This figure clutches a mirror, which shows yet another reflection of Maybonne, a disembodied head
caught in the circle of the glass. Maybonne stares at her image in a mirror,
still surrounded by thick lines spiraling around her, the lines having taken
on a distinctive spiral pattern suggesting a convoluted, circuitous maze.

Figure 5.4. "The Plastic Wall." Lynda Barry, *My Perfect Life* (New York: Harper Perennial, 1992), 90–91.

Even divorced from the textual narration, the unfolding of each panel, working together and alone, reveals Maybonne's state of mind.

The narrative text further explicates the thick black lines of despair in a potent introduction, for, as Dave Eggers points out, Barry is "the master of the opening line" (10), and she proves just that with the beginning panel, stating, "Ever since I found out I have a inferiority complex I have been feeling so terrible. Also, more self-conscious than I have ever known." Maybonne's friends (though this term is used loosely) have informed her that she has an inferiority complex, which has, in fact, brought on an inferiority complex. Maybonne laments the "stupid" things she says and has "noticed I am ugly compared to all my friends. Out of everyone it turns out I am the dog. I'm not saying this only to get attention. I'm realizing facts."

Maybonne thus feels unattractive and assures any readers that she is not saying this for "attention." The pragmatic Maybonne is not fishing for compliments but simply "realizing facts," at least the facts as presented by her friends. Despite her doubts and insecurities, Maybonne is able to see some of her good qualities: "reading comprehension, artistic and not to sound conceited but good at poetry." Deep down Maybonne does believe she has some merits, though she fears voicing them for sounding "conceited." In the end, however, these good qualities don't matter, for "how much does that count when your face + body + whole personality sucks?" Ultimately, Maybonne wishes

for everything about me to change. And then I swear to God I would quit acting insecure and be myself, like in all the songs where people are being themselves. I would stop faking and be for real and act free like Sue Acker and them, because for right now I am only a plastic wall of illusion, which I hate. If I have a possibility to change, please God, let it happen.

Rather than reconciling with her image and simply choosing to "be herself" as her younger sister Marlys might counsel, Maybonne feels everything about her body is unacceptable. With help from Sue Acker, Maybonne has reached the conclusion that she is "fake," a "plastic wall of illusion," and somehow it never occurs to her that it is Sue Acker who is fake. When she looks in the mirror, Maybonne sees only the surface and yearns to change to a more acceptable appearance. She hopes for fakeness to stop being fake. If only "everything could change," then Maybonne would be at peace with herself. It seems Maybonne has rather blatantly missed the point of self-acceptance, and in this carefully controlled strip Barry expertly illustrates Maybonne's warped reflection of self. Barry's thoughtful structure, then, functions similarly to a carefully prepared slide. Each strip takes a tiny incident and shines a light through it, magnifying the moment and revealing its hidden contours. As a small blood sample might reveal broader ramifications for one's health when the cells are enlarged and examined, even the smallest happenings in a child's life have larger implications once magnified and presented with careful, thoughtful interest.

Narration and Representation

Barry's samples of girlhood draw from several narrators who, over the course of the strip, employ different styles and address different subjects, offering

Figure 5.5. "Maybonne's Room." Lynda Barry, *The! Greatest! of! Marlys!* (Seattle: Sasquatch Books, 2000).

several voices of girlhood. Barry is well known for her skills as a writer, and it is part of her trademark style to give equal space to textual narration and picture within each panel, making her a verbose anomaly in a genre in which pictures generally take precedence. While the identity of the narrators differs from strip to strip and the girls express themselves differently within the narrative text, they are generally homodiegetic or autodiegetic female characters within the stories featured in picture form. Several of the most frequent narrators of the strip have already been introduced, however, given their importance throughout the series, key narrators Arna Arkins and her cousins Marlys and Maybonne Mullens bear additional attention.

Arna Arkins, eight, frequently narrated the earliest youth- focused strips from the mid to late 1980s and returned to narrate more frequently after 2000. Arna, a kind and somewhat quiet girl, loves dogs and despises her brother Arnold. Arna keenly observes and narrates the trials of school and the playground. Arna generally wears a striped dress and has a bob haircut, usually held back by a barrette. Over time, Arna's hair grows a bit and she begins to favor somewhat more "tomboyish" clothing. Barry spots Arna with tiny freckles, emphasizing that she is not a perfect, pretty girl. Arna functions as something of an "every girl," not so conspicuously flamboyant as Marlys nor as self-absorbed as Maybonne. Unlike Maybonne and Marlys, Arna acts as a more detached reporter or observer, relating the events without making them about her own worries and concerns, as seen in her narration from "The Night We All Got Sick." Arna's narration is printed with straightforward block capital letters, and her language is the most unadorned; she is the least narcissistic girl and acts to relate stories, sometimes featuring herself, but often focusing on others.

Arna's cousin Maybonne also serves as a frequent narrator, and though only fourteen, she tries to leave the world of children behind, stepping into a new "adult" world, but in doing so she suffers from depression, low self-esteem, and the general angst of adolescence. To the younger children, such as Arna, who narrates the 1997 strip "Maybonne's Room," Maybonne appears glamorous (fig. 5.5). Though she, too, wears glasses and is riddled with freckles, she has short, styled hair and has pierced ears, frosted lipstick, white glasses, beads, a belt, and even a bra. Maybonne figured more prominently in *Ernie Pook* beginning in the late 1980s, acting as a "parallel character" for creator Barry, who uses the character to bring out information from her own life story. She told Powers, "I never had a sister, but I find she is definitely a parallel character to me. I use information about my life to help her tell her stories" (69). Maybonne grapples with the very adult world of sex as well as school and classes. Her perspective emphasizes the "cruddy" (to borrow one of her frequent phrases) over the magical.

Maybonne is featured in the collections *Come Over, Come Over* (1990), *My Perfect Life* (1992), and *It's So Magic* (1994), and she frequently narrated *Ernie Pook* during the late 1980s and early 1990s. Maybonne inhabits a liminal space, perched at the edge of the adult world. Darcy Sullivan notes of Maybonne: "At times her observations seem too wise, too philosophical, the straining voice of her author rather than her soul" (43). Sullivan's observations hint at Maybonne's alter ego as a "parallel character" of Barry's own experience, yet as Barry points out, Maybonne is "much more together" than Barry was at fourteen.[8] Despite her mature voice, Maybonne is thrust into an all-too-adult world early, seeing and doing more than most mature adults could imagine. Maybonne's narration accompanying the action in each panel often takes an epistolary form in letters to Maybonne's friend Brenda and

Figure 5.6. "The Carnival." Lynda Barry, *The! Greatest! of! Marlys!* (Seattle: Sasquatch Books, 2000).

assumes a more confessional tone when framed as diary entries. As seen in "The Plastic Wall" and "Family Pictures," the font utilized for Maybonne's narration almost always takes the shape of typical, straightforward capitals marching across (at least) the top half of each panel, although Maybonne occasionally scrawls a letter in cursive.

Eight-year-old Marlys Mullens also narrates from time to time, often with dramatic results, but features frequently in both Arna's and Maybonne's narration, as she does in "The Carnival," a 1986 strip narrated by Arna in which Marlys sets out to spoil the fun of the neighborhood (fig. 5.6).

Even-tempered Arna describes the scene in which the neighborhood kids set out to stage a "carnival show." Her narration, lettered in careful capitals, occupies one-third to over one-half of each panel, and much of the remaining panel space is taken up by speech balloons recording the children's dialogue. This is very typical of Barry and of *Ernie Pook*, where text generally takes up a great deal of space. The images are thus very limited, but depict the diverse, decidedly unattractive children as they attempt to woo Marlys to participate in their fun. While all of the children are unappealing, with pockmarks and misshapen, buck teeth, Marlys stands out as especially repellent, with her pinched face and sharp, angry eyebrows. The final panel does not depict Marlys's breakdown when treated as "one of the gang," only the children's shocked, frightened reaction to her outburst.

Although Marlys is now a cult favorite among fans, in early depictions she was represented as an antagonist of sorts. Rob Rodi commented, "If there is a villain in this series of strips, it's her cousin Marlys, who figures as a spoiler in just about every scheme Barry's gang devises; Marlys' face is like a mass of boils with pigtails. Ugly is as ugly does—as just about any kid knows instinctively" ("Repeat" 60). Early images of Marlys are rather gruesome; with her tense face and frown lines, Marlys resembles an unpleasant, disagreeable child. Her cat-eye glasses look like they belong to a much older person, perhaps a menacing old lady down the street. Marlys parts her hair in the middle and pulls it into two tight, short ponytails that perch on top of her head, leaving a tiny fringe of bangs. She generally wears a short dress like Arna, featuring slanted stripes or a flower print. Darcy Sullivan commented of Marlys:

> In strip after strip, Marlys dances on the sidelines, demanding that people notice her. She's a classic comic foil—an id in ponytails—aggressive, conceited and ruthless in her pursuit of attention. But unlike her zillions of forefathers, from Eddie Haskell to *Little Nemo*'s Flip to Calvin, we understand that she's not cocksure at all. (45)

Marlys, despite her bravado, is emotionally fragile. She longs for love and security in a world in which grown-ups are absent at best, violent and cruel at worst.

Over time Marlys mellows considerably, becoming less of a spoilsport and more of a boisterous freethinker, as seen in the 1997 strip "Marlys' Yoga." Her figure has softened, her face losing the bitter frown lines and her glasses becoming rounder and less intimidating. Her pigtails point upward exuberantly, and she smiles more often. Barry explained that since her first appearance, "Marlys is a lot bigger. . . . I still think of her as a nice round kid."[9] In action and appearance, over time Marlys evolved into a free-spirited, self-absorbed, and self-assured heroine. When Marlys narrates, she tends to speak to the audience directly, either by assuming creative control or by addressing them directly, albeit through Barry's drawing (fig.

Figure 5.7. "Marlys Yoga." Lynda Barry, *The! Greatest! of! Marlys!* (Seattle: Sasquatch Books, 2000).

5.7). Marlys narrates exclusively through speech balloons with the exception of one narrative box in the final panel; and the positioning of her figure, staring straight out at the reader, as well as the direct address, "Hello and welcome," suggest the reader as a secondary character. Marlys, through her speech balloons, invites the audience into conversation, breaking the fourth wall and engaging in a conversation. While she narrates less frequently than Arna or Maybonne, this is her preferred mode of narration—direct contact with the outside world. Marlys would rather look out on the world she is sure is watching and tell her story.

Marlys, Maybonne, and Arna share narration duties, creating a varied textual narration on girlhood.[10] Each girl contributes her own personality to the narration, offering a robust perspective. Each girl also acts as a character in the strip, their figures occupying space, confirming and contradicting their text-based personas. In "Graphic Shorthand: From Caricature to Narratology in Twentieth Century *Bande dessinée* and Comics," Harry Morgan argues that "comics rely above all on the presence of a re-occurring character who becomes a close friend of the reader" (22). These girls become close, familiar friends to regular readers, who recognize their textual voices and physical figures with only the slightest of clues.

At times Barry complicates depictions of the characters, for on occasion Marlys herself takes control of her own representation, ostensibly illustrating the strip herself, which merits a brief discussion of Barry's drawing style in order to differentiate Barry's typical aesthetic with the altered one suggested to be that of Marlys. As is evident even in the small examples "The Night We All Got Sick," "The Plastic Wall," "The Carnival," and "Marlys Yoga," in presenting these small slices of childhood through the square, four-panel format, Barry displays a distinctive drawing style that has become something of a trademark. Comic scholar Pascal Lefevre argues that a comic artist's drawing style conveys a visual ideology:

> A drawer does not only depict something, but expresses in his drawing at the same time a philosophy, a vision; implicitly in every drawing style is a visual ontology, i.e., a definition of the real in visual terms. . . . Consequently the form of the drawing does influence the manner [in which] the reader will experience and interpret the image: the viewer cannot look at the object-in-picture from another point of view than the one the picture offers; he is invited to share the maker's mode of seeing, not only in the literal, but also in the figurative sense. (159)

Barry's drawing style has undoubtedly changed over time. Her earliest, scattered drawings, as discussed in chapter 1, were much more representational, illustrating realistic-looking women addressing absurd situations, such as the woman pondering the merits of dating a cactus in *Spinal Comics*. This early approach created a compelling disjuncture, juxtaposing bizarre circumstances with authentic-looking figures. Later, Barry continued to address themes of dating and relationships but assumed a punk-inspired, more abstracted style. As her style became more New Wave, the scenes and topics of the strip gradually became more realistic. And, as Barry settled in with her recurring cast of children her style evolved still further, remaining somewhat abstract but more childlike than punk rock.

The drawing style of *Ernie Pook*, for which Barry is particularly known, is rough and unstudied, suggesting the loose, untutored drawings of childhood. Even as the figures are somewhat nonrepresentational, Barry takes care to fashion the characters to emphasize their flaws and blemishes. In the world of comic art, girls are often depicted as adorable, apple-cheeked children or gorgeous superhero sidekicks, but Barry draws unattractive girls, a fact that she believes contributes to her reputation for poor draftsmanship. Despite the evidence that a strip might have carefully rendered details, according to Barry, it "doesn't count, and I think it's because the girls are so odd and they have the freckles."[11] However, reviewing Barry's early, more representational work as well as her sketches and doodles from the "Notes on Notes" section of *What It Is* provides clear evidence that Barry can draw in many styles, ranging from abstract to highly realistic, and her characters like Marlys, Maybonne, and Arna simply are not comely, winsome little girls. As opposed to idealized beauties or even more abstract outlines of girls, Barry takes great pains to depict the freckles and blemishes, the funny hair, and bad teeth of the young women she features. Her depictions intentionally accentuate flaws and imperfections; in an appearance-obsessed culture Barry's girls remain unsightly, a fact long bemoaned by characters such as Maybonne, as she does in "The Plastic Wall."

At times the illustration of *Ernie Pook* devolves into an even more childlike style, when Marlys assumes control of the strip and the art devolves into the shaky lines and botched figures of a child. Once again Marlys directly addresses the reader through text and illustration, as she does in the self-illustrated guide to being happy in 1991s: "How to Groove on Life" (fig. 5.8). The strip appears coarser and more childlike than usual, and the font is not the typical straightforward capitals. Marlys stands to the left of the first panel to introduce the strip, a similar posture to her greeting in "Marlys Yoga." The figure of Marlys looks rougher than she does normally, but not quite so childish as the following panels—a hybrid figure located somewhere between the usual image of Marlys and her own drawings, suggesting a devolution from Barry's representation to that of Marlys. The Marlys figure explains in childlike, scrawled handwriting, "hi everybody and right on peace to all people!!! From the Great Marlys!! People are always asking Marlys how did you get to be an incredible #1 Groover on life !!!!!!!!! it's so cinchy! Here's my instructions!!!" Marlys identifies herself with her usual self-confidence as "the Great Marlys" and suggests that happiness or "grooving" on life is quite simple, or "cinchy." She sets out her first rule below, "don't go around being insulting!!!" and follows with her other rules in panels two through four. These panels are divided into sections in which Marlys prints out the rule and illustrates it. The images often illustrate what not to do, how one might violate her rule, as in rule number 6, "Don't make people listen to your

Figure 5.8. "How to Groove on Life." Lynda Barry, *The! Greatest! of! Marlys!* (Seattle: Sasquatch Books, 2000).

singing for too many songs though. Let everyone get a turn." In the accompanying drawing just below the rule, a figure stands in front of three stick people sitting in chairs and declares she will sing her "1,000,009th number." Obviously, the stick figure has not read Marlys's guidelines for grooving on life.

The last rule, number 9, is scrunched into the bottom of the final panel. There is no illustration, just text declaring, "IF you are in a bad mood it will always Go away. This is very bad news for people who like their bad moods but they are not the #1 Groovers!!!!!!!!!!" In sharp contrast to her sister's constant cynicism, in Marlys's world, things will always get better. This is too bad, she comments, for people like her sister, who seem to relish their bad moods, but that isn't Marlys's concern, for Marlys always looks on to better things. Marlys's comic art shares many similarities with Barry's. Both crowd a great deal of text into each panel and both utilize the vernacular in dialogue. Marlys's figures even have stripped down versions of the clothing Barry uses as visual shorthand to denote different characters. Marlys has an uncluttered confidence and enthusiasm in her words and images, arguing for a sense of self-confidence rarely seen in adulthood.

Who Sees: The Focalized Gaze

Though they are frequent narrators, Arna, Maybonne, and Marlys, except in rare circumstances, do not act as focalizers; the audience does not see through their eyes. Rather, their figures are the specimens of analysis under the spectator's gaze. Although they claim the words presented in the narrative box at the top of each panel, they are usually pictured rather than picturing. In "Subjective Narration in Comics," Joris Driest notes, "Focalization has commonly been defined as 'who sees,' opposed to the 'who speaks' of narration. . . . The reader accompanies the focalizer in the story, so to speak" (1.2).[12] While scholars differ on terminology,[13] *Ernie Pook* is usually depicted from the gaze of an observer guided by the narrator, a character (almost always) pictured in each strip. The focalizer operates at a distance, gazing at the girls as samples for examination, following them through the four panels; and this observer is frequently privy to the internal thoughts of the characters.[14] Based on her book *Reading Bande Desinée*, Ann Miller would term the gaze in *Ernie Pook* as "zero focalization" for the perspective gives "access to the knowledge of all characters" (11), while Harry Morgan, author of "Graphic Shorthand: From Caricature to Narratology," would most likely refer to the *"reflector"*(another term for focalizer) in *Ernie Pook*, who sees from an "external perspective" or *"from the outside"* (37, emphasis in original). To further complicate matters, scholar Derik Badman, author of "Points of View: 'First Person' in Comics," would probably characterize the gaze in *Ernie Pook* as "fixed internal focalization," a focalizer who fixes attention on a character, as the gaze is "completely controlled by" the narrator's "cognitive point of view." Regardless of the complexities of scholarly terminology, it can be said that most of the time the gaze, or "who sees" *Ernie Pook,* is a distanced observer who follows the actions of the characters and is frequently aware of the inner thoughts and fantasies of the characters. This juxtaposition gives the reader a position as both insider and outsider into the girls' world. While privy to the private, confessional voices of the girls' narration, the reader observes from a distance, like an ethnographer or scientist. The audience is guided by the autodiegetic narrator and distanced by the gaze. However, while this is the most common focalized stance in the strip, the focalizer in *Ernie* Pook is not constant, for Barry employs variable focalization, shifting the point of view from strip to strip, and sometimes within a single strip.

At times the focalizer becomes a participant in the scene when Marlys narrates, as she does in the previous examples "Marlys Yoga" and "How to Groove on Life." In "Marlys Yoga" Marlys narrates through speech balloons and one small narrative box and maintains a running dialogue that invites the readers to participate in her yoga practice. Marlys asks, "Are you someone who is lame at P.E.? Same here. . . . Maybe Marlys bogus yoga is for you." While the gaze remains distanced from Marlys, watching her performance, Marlys calls out the focalizer, inviting him or her into a dialogue, or rather a monologue in which Marlys supplies all the answers. The reader remains removed from the proceedings, but the fourth wall is broken. The focalizer continues to see from a distance, but now participates in a conversation of sorts with Marlys. Barry has broken down some of the expanse separating reader and character, involving the audience in the lives of the girls.

In "How to Groove on Life" Barry further complicates notions of who sees, who narrates, and who participates. As previously discussed, at times Marlys takes over this strip by direct address to the audience through her narration and illustration. In "How to Groove on Life," Marlys narrates in a dramatically different, childlike font not contained by a narrative box, as is usually the case. As with "Marlys Yoga," Marlys again breaks the fourth wall and directs her attention to the audience, sharing her tips for "Grooving on life." However, unlike "Marlys Yoga," the altered drawing style suggests a somewhat different point of view. While "who sees" is still at a distance, watching the narrating girl, this time the gaze is blurred and distorted by the lens of the draftsmanship, with the implication that the artist's hand is that of Marlys. The perspective, though still distanced, is now filtered as if through Marlys's glasses; the vision has once again shifted, drawing the audience further into the world of *Ernie Pook*. Not only is the reader engaged in conversation with the narrator, he or she now sees only through her representation.

Although a rare occasion, at times the focalizer in *Ernie Pook* enters into the scene, in effect "looking over the shoulder" (Morgan 37) of the characters in what Morgan terms "ocularisation" (37) and what Badman (in "Points of View") calls "primary internal ocularization," as is the case in the 1989 strip "Beyond the Earth" (fig. 5.9). The strip begins with a typed header, apparently from a homework assignment, that alerts the reader to the context of the

Figure 5.9. "Beyond the Earth." Lynda Barry, *The! Greatest! of! Marlys!* Seattle: Sasquatch Books, 2000.

strip, implying the focalizer might be Marlys or perhaps an observer peeking over Marlys's shoulder as she completes her homework. Marlys once again takes over the narration and illustration. Below the homework question, "If you could visit another planet, where would you like to go?" Marlys draws and writes her own response, creating "The planet! of! Marlys!!!!!!," which follows a parallel orbit to earth, but the planet itself is marked by a small heart. Marlys's handwritten commentary, a marked contrast to the usual capitalized, carefully printed narration, explicates, "On the planet Marlys anyone named Marlys is #1 But no Marlys starts acting all conceited Because of it." In the final panel, the point of view pulls back, and the focalizer shifts to that of an observer, albeit an observer within the scene, looking over Marlys shoulder, as Marlys is depicted working on the assignment that has been on display at close range. These shifts in drawing style and in point of view invite an alternative conception, a different rendering of the field of view as encompassed by *Ernie Pook,* and create an additional layer for interpretation.[15]

Although Darcy Sullivan does not address focalization or ocularization as such in his 1991 article "Kids at the Abyss: Lynda Barry's *Come Over, Come Over*," he does note that the conflict between picture and narration complicates the reader's understanding of the strip, suggesting the unreliability of the narration and perhaps causing internal conflict for the reader. Sullivan argues that the text "destabilizes our understanding of the stories' ontological status. Superficially, Maybonne is telling the story, and the pictures are further fleshing it out. But Maybonne's narratives are often compromised by the pictures and the dialogue that accompanies them, calling into question the relationship between the two" (44). The multivalent elements of narration, dialogue, and image obfuscate analysis and make defining one unassailable interpretation impossible. The reader has the challenge and the authority to fashion meaning amongst the multiple layers of message. Is Maybonne an unreliable narrator? How much should the audience trust her? What about Marlys and Arna?

Sullivan wonders:

> If Maybonne's captions are personal and subjective, revealing and untrustworthy, how much can we trust the pictures? Do they represent an unequivocal reality which can round out Maybonne's version, or make it suspect? Or are the pictures events a different, less censored . . . depiction of events from Maybonne's point of view? If so, do the pictures and dialogue comprise her image of the events as she writes about them, or her memory at some later time—days later, weeks, months, years? (45)

In the end it is not entirely clear whether the audience is to accept Maybonne's narration as truth, the images and dialogue (or focalization) as truth, or find the truth somewhere in the gaps. It is obvious that there are differences between narrative text and focalized images, and one can guess (though it is only a guess) that in her diary or letters, Maybonne will tell her best version of the truth. However, the pictures often contain ghosts, swirly thought bubbles, and psychedelic backgrounds, disrupting any interpretation of the picture as intended to represent unvarnished reality. In presenting these contradictory tellings, the reader is offered another version and vision and given the option of deciding who and what to believe. Ultimately, Sullivan concludes, "Different clues support different answers. . . . The reader must question whose 'truth' a story represents, and what other truths might live in the fissures between reality and memory, memory and myth" (45). Barry's technique of contradictory points of view, narrative and focalized, forces the reader to play an active role in the epistemological process. The images do not simply illustrate the text but also subvert it, challenging the audience to explore different truths in the text, picture, and the spaces between.

Barry changes narrators, changes drawing style, and changes the focalized point of view, resulting in an unsettled, off- balance experience, mirroring the lives of the girls in the strip. While Sullivan argues that veracity lies with the reader's interpretation of the gaps between picture and text, other scholars suggest that, contrary to many other genres, in comic art the picture assumes more authority than the text. Will Eisner posits, "In comics, body posture and gesture occupy a position of primacy over text. The manner in which these images are employed modifies and defines the intended meaning of the words" (*Comics* 103), and Thierry Groensteen argues for "the primacy of the image and, therefore, the necessity to accord a theoretical precedence to that which, provisionally, I designate under the generic term of 'visual codes'"(3). Eisner and Groensteen (although basing their work on longer-form comics) contend that veracity resides primarily in picture rather than text. In *Understanding Comics*, Scott McCloud offers seven types of relationships between words and pictures in comic art, with text and picture holding various weights. According to McCloud's terminology, Barry frequently utilizes several of these relationships, including "word specific combinations, where pictures illustrate, but don't significantly add to a largely complete text" (*Understanding* 153), such as the example "The Plastic Wall"; "duo-specific panels in which words and pictures send essentially the same message" (*Understanding* 153), as is the case in "The Night We All Got Sick"; "interdependent" situations, "where words and pictures go hand in hand to convey an idea that neither could convey alone" (*Understanding* 155), as they do in "Beyond the Earth"; and "parallel" relationships, in which "words and pictures seem to follow very different courses" (*Understanding* 154), as happens in the example "So They Trade" from 1991 (fig. 5.10). Barry, in utilizing these various interdependencies, creates a complex relationship between picture and text, a richness mirrored in others aspects of the structure. *Ernie Pook*, with its constantly varying narrators, focalizers, drawing styles, and relationships between text and image, thus suggests a more postmodern conception of truth, or the lack thereof, positing instead a more relative and

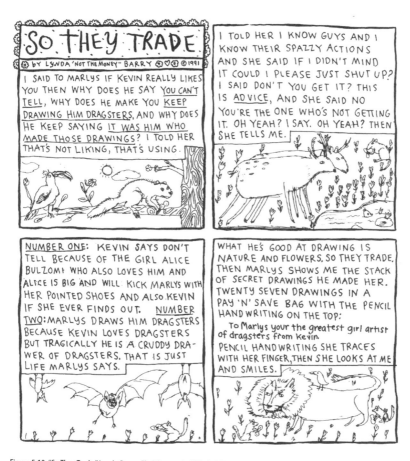

Figure 5.10. "So They Trade." Lynda Barry, *The! Greatest! of! Marlys!* (Seattle: Sasquatch Books, 2000).

more unpredictable sense of reality, a perspective well suited to girls finding their way in an uncertain, unreliable world.

The 1991 comic strip "So They Trade" exploits parallel interdependence, playing on the tension between picture and text, resisting easy interpretation, and complicating the notion that pictures convey a "truer" reality. Maybonne narrates the text-heavy strip, identifying herself quickly with "I said to Marlys," and her solid, capitalized text occupies over half of each panel as she attempts to advise her sister on the foibles of love, arguing that Marlys's crush, Kevin, is just using her. Maybonne uses underlining for emphasis, as well as a lowercase reproduction of Kevin's note within the narrative text box, and furthermore transcribes her dialogue with Marlys.

The focalizer is unclear in this strip; it could be from either the point of view of Marlys or Maybonne or an observer gazing over one of the girls' shoulders. And in a striking difference from many strips, rather than depicting a conversation, the pictures depict four panels of wildlife scenes rendered by what appears to be a child's hand. While the narrator is clear, the focalizer and illustrator of the strip remain dubious, the text playing out one story with the wildlife scenes seemingly contradicting the text. Is the truth in the text or the narration? The first panel features a squirrel eating a peanut on a tree branch, accompanied rather incongruously by a toucan. Flowers sprout from the tree branch and the sun shines overhead. The second panel shows a male and female deer surrounded by flowers. They are side by side, like lovers, facing a small pond, from which a small fish emerges. In the corner, the squirrel nibbles a peanut. The third panel depicts three bats perched above flowers; the ubiquitous squirrel nibbles his peanut in the bottom right corner. And in the final panel a lion dominates the space, once again surrounded by flowers. A bird sits on the lion's back, and this time two squirrels eat peanuts. Initially, it is unclear what these drawings have to do with Maybonne's warnings about boys and Marlys's sharp defense of Kevin, but in the final panel Marlys reveals that Kevin excels "at drawing nature and flowers" and exchanges pictures with Marlys. The readers have been viewing Kevin's secret drawings all along. Is Kevin using Marlys? He apparently gave her the drawings with the dedication, "To Marlys your the greatest girl artist of dragsters from Kevin," which is hardly a heart-wrenching declaration of love, particularly since Marlys is only the greatest *girl* artist of dragsters. Still, there is an innocence in the love Marlys feels for Kevin and in Maybonne's concern for her younger sister. Without the text the wildlife scenes would tell very little. However, by creating an ambiguous focalizer and scene, Barry produces in the reader the unsettled, confused quality of first (and subsequent) loves, wherein feelings and truths are unclear and one doesn't know what he or she is seeing or what to believe.

Barry teases out tensions between narrative text and focalized scene in the 1990 strip "Report on Love," which also addresses her frequent theme of love, and, in particular, love unrequited (fig. 5.11).

The narrator, Maybonne, is clear within the world of *Ernie Pook* but might prove confusing once removed from the context of the weekly strip. The focalizer and focalized are similarly perplexing, even for those readers immersed in the experience of following the strip each week. Although the focalizer is somewhat unclear in this scene, given Maybonne's narration, one might presume that the focalizer looking out on the busy street is Maybonne.[16] The first panel depicts a woman choking her son as strangers

Figure 5.11. "Report on Love." Lynda Barry, *My Perfect Life* (New York: Harper Perennial, 1992), 70–71.

hurry past, the dark lines of the background indicating a stark city land-scape. Maybonne as narrator philosophizes, "Love. What is it? It's supposed to be beautiful but love can be cruddy. Like loving someone who does not love you. Then you want to do a surgery on yourself to get rid of it." While Maybonne presumably references a long-running story arc concerning her infatuation with classmate Doug, the young child looks at the mother with an expression of love, despite the mother's angry expression and chokehold. The image suggests yet another example of the "cruddiness" of love not re-turned.

In the second panel a boy torments an older man while people wave goodbye, smoke, and talk on the telephone, ignoring the interaction of the boy and man. A couple in the foreground walks together in profile, though the man appears to be looking back at the woman. Maybonne's narration confesses that it is equally bad "if someone you just like starts being all in love," as Maybonne experienced with another boy, David. These words cast doubt on the relationship of the couple in the foreground. The third panel shows two seemingly happy couples, one in the foreground and one in the back left corner. A menacing figure in the lower right looks behind him while other people eat pizza, deliver packages, and carry on with life. The narration undercuts any happiness of the figures, speculating about "when you love them but all the things they do starts getting on your nerves." The text suggests that no complete happiness can exist; it is always eventually distorted.

In the final scene a couple argues in the center of the panel, while people yawn and continue their business. The narration concludes, "I had the gorgeous feeling of love but mainly I have had the cruddy feeling of love. All around the world I bet it is the same. Crud is the most normal feeling. They should write it in the sky so people will know and not feel so bad." The people going about their lives feel cruddy, but Maybonne assures us that that is the norm. She wants this sentiment inscribed across the heavens: happiness isn't standard; everyone is depressed. In knowing we are not alone and that the reality of love is cruddy, perhaps we will all feel a bit better. Of course, in realizing that cruddy is the prevailing sentiment, perhaps that sentiment will begin to shift. The focalized images offer no hope or alleviation for the narrator's depression, proposing only more bleakness within the contrasting scene.

While the focalizer remains at a distance in the "Report on Love," at times in *Ernie Pook* the focalizer enters into the scene and becomes a vicarious participant in the action, moving from observer to actor, and this point of view suggests a sense of the danger and fear of the situation. In a series of strips from 1991 Maybonne's friend Cindy Ludermyer is raped by several Catholic schoolboys. In the strip "It's Cool" the focalizer occupies an ambiguous position, behind and in front of Marlys as she witnesses the scene (fig. 5.12). The narrator, Maybonne, relates the story of Cindy's rape. Maybonne set out to "protect" Cindy when they go to meet some boys, but she arrives too late. Marlys follows, unbeknownst to Maybonne, and witnesses the scene. Maybonne describes the events in the narration, but the panels show the story as if the audience is part of the scene, hiding just behind Marlys. The focalizer has not assumed either Maybonne's or Marlys's point of view, but watches from his or her own perspective, not detached, but concealed within the bushes within the image. In the first panel the focalizer looks over Marlys's shoulder, the back of her head and her ponytails visible as she spies on the dark silhouette of Maybonne confronting the boys. The audi-

IT'S COOL

BY LYNDA "BACHELOR PARTY" BARRY © 1991

THERE'S JUST SOME THINGS THAT MEN HAVE TO KEEP TO THEMSELVES."IS WHAT THE BOY EDDIE DAVIS SAID WHEN I GOT TO THE SNEAK OUT PLACE WHERE I WAS SUPPOSED TO MEET CINDY LUDERMYER. IT WAS 1 AM AND SHE WASN'T THERE. ONLY EDDIE AND ANOTHER GUY VINCENT.

"SO SHE WAS ALREADY HERE THEN?" I ASK. EDDIE SAYS "MAYBE YES AND MAYBE NO." I GO, "QUIT BEING A SPAZ. WHERE IS SHE?" ON A ROCK I SEE HER SWEATER. THATS WHEN HE SAYS THE MEN THING AND WHEN VINCENT PUTS HIS ARM AROUND ME. "IT'S COOL." HE SAYS. "IT'S COOL. DON'T FREAK OUT." I GO "I'M NOT FREAKING OUT."

BUT I WAS FREAKING OUT. SLIGHTLY FREAKING OUT. FREAKING OUT FOR ME AND FREAKING OUT FOR CINDY WHO LOVES BOONES FARM APPLE WINE AND THERE'S THE BOTTLE EMPTY ON ITS SIDE BY THE ROCK. CINDY WHO I SAID I WOULD GUARD. "COME ON YOU GUYS TELL ME WHERE SHE'S AT." THEN A WALKING NOISE IN THE BUSHES. "CINDY?" I SAY. "CINDY?"

NO. IT'S DAN. THE ORIGINAL GUY OF THE CATHOLIC BOYS WHO CINDY LIKED. HE'S BRUSHING HIS PANTS OFF AND WIPING HIS MOUTH. "EDDIE." HE SAYS. "EDDIE." THEN HE POINTS INTO THE WOODS. "SHE'S ASKIN' FOR YOU." EDDIE GOES AND I TRY TO FOLLOW. "HEY." DAN SAYS. HE PUSHES HIS HANDS AGAINST MY SHOULDERS. "DON'T FREAK OUT, MAN. IT'S COOL. IT'S COOL."

Figure 5.12. "It's Cool." Lynda Barry, *It's So Magic* (New York: Harper Perennial, 1994), 60–61.

ence thus acts as another silent witness, peering out on the events from behind Marlys. The second panel shifts position to show Marlys's shocked face in the dark. The third panel outlines the black silhouette of the attacker, and the final panel shows the reflection of the boy grabbing Maybonne in the lenses of Marlys's glasses. This is, perhaps, one of the most horrifying moments in the history of the strip. A girl has been raped, possibly gang raped, and, unbeknownst to Maybonne, young Marlys witnessed it all. The perspective of the focalizer adds intensity to an already dramatic situation. While Maybonne's narration tells an appalling story, the focalizer's position within the drama forces the audience into the focalized images. The focalizer gazes out from a hidden position, then turns to see the horror of Marlys and sees the reflected image of violence within Marlys's gaze, as filtered through

Figure 5.13. "Stop Talking." Lynda Barry, *It's So Magic* (New York: Harper Perennial, 1994), 64–65.

her glasses. This masterful use of point of view provides an effective and poignant example of focalization.

Furthermore, this sequence presents an excellent example of depth of field—what is clear and what is muddled beneath the microscopic examination of *Ernie Pook*. When studying any subject beneath a magnifying lens, some elements come clearly into focus while others remain blurry and indistinct. In *Iconology*, W.J.T. Mitchell notes, "We can never understand a picture unless we grasp the ways in which it shows what cannot be seen" (39). The Ludermyer story arc addresses the very unsettling topic of the gang rape of a young girl, a topic unlikely to be addressed in most mainstream comics. However, Barry does so obliquely—the narration <u>and</u> the text both refer to the incident indirectly. There are no graphic depictions of the assault, and

Maybonne as narrator never states that a rape has occurred. Unlike other comic artists such as Debbie Drechsler, Phoebe Gloeckner, and Julie Doucet, all of whom also address sexual assault against females and choose to depict the violence with specific narration and pictures of genitalia and sex acts, Barry remains very chaste and opaque in her depictions of sexual brutality.

Even Barry's characters prefer not to speak of the violence. The 1991 strip "Stop Talking" discusses the girls' decision to remain silent about the attack, but makes no explanation for the strip's indirect referencing of "what happened in the woods" (fig. 5.13). The strip, narrated by Maybonne, explains how Cindy begs Maybonne not to say anything, and though Maybonne feels Cindy should report the incident to the police, she doesn't pursue the matter. The focalizer focuses on Marlys and her actions following the attack. Marlys does not tell, but she does prepare herself for battle, practicing her kung fu and wishing to be a boy. Though her voice has been silenced, Marlys refuses to be a victim.

In an intriguing shift, Marlys narrates and draws her own response to the incident in the 1991 strip "If You Want to Know Teenagers" (fig. 5.14). The focalizer for this comic is unclear; it might be Marlys or an external observer examining Marlys's work. The strip identifies Marlys as the creator, giving the perspective not as if seen necessarily through Marlys's eyes, but rather as filtered and processed through Marlys's experience, her eyes, and her hand. The narration, identified as that of Marlys both by the title and by the childlike scrawl, explains that this is Marlys's own poetry on teenagers and argues that the story is "made up." The four panels are divided and subdivided with various depictions of teenagers, and though Marlys emphasizes her representation is fiction, the names and scenes are very familiar. For example, the "Before" teenager calls out, "Hi Marlys Can you do me one favor." It is a polite request, but still a request for help, much like the request Maybonne and Cindy make of Marlys. Teenagers, according to the narration, "can look beautiful. Beautiful make up clothes handwriting," but Marlys's depiction of a lovely teenager comments, "I am so ugly Do you think so," a query most certainly posed by Maybonne many times. An attempt to draw a side view of a teenager is crossed through with a large *X*. In a note below the botched profile is the comment, "I messed up sorry it is ugly!" the narrative thus supplying an affirmative response to the teenager's question.

In the third panel the scrawled, handwritten narration reflects, "When they are riding on bummers you must watch out. Could be they want to talk to you. Could be they will yell in your face. But can you remember they are sad." Depicted immediately below are two teenagers under the caption

Figure 5.14. "If You Want to Know Teenagers." Lynda Barry, *The! Greatest! of! Marlys!* (Seattle: Sasquatch Books, 2000).

"Could Be." The teenagers pictured might feel hated or, in turn, hate you. The narrator, however, still tries to absolve the teenagers, being mindful of their sadness, and even hopes that "if its your sister who yells one good thing is sometimes she is sorry after." The accompanying illustration depicts Maybonne apologizing and Marlys assuring her "that is ok," but a note and arrow indicates that this is "me in the future"; thus Maybonne has not actually apologized, though Marlys has wished for the scene.

In the final panel Marlys tries to process what happened to Cindy. She narrates, "One main thing you got to know is they have secrets. You must not bust them on the secrets. Teenagers teenagers theres things that they do. And if you tell anyone they will cream you." Beneath this declaration there is no illustration, just a caption stating, "Sorry for no picture. I saw something I can't even draw it. Don't try to guess it. Just forget it." Marlys has glimpsed something horrible; she has spied a violent scene and is so horrified that she cannot, quite literally, picture it. There is no place for this act of violence in Marlys's drawing or in *Ernie Pook*'s depth of field. Marlys warns others away, urging them to forget it, even as she wishes she could. This breakdown in the illustrations has Marlys, as narrator and illustrator, abandoning pictures much as Barry does in rendering the incident; they are too dangerous, too real. She retreats behind the safety and ambiguity of the text that she hopes will bury the secret of the teenagers.

Beauty, "Knowing Things," and Exalting the Ordinary: Prominent Themes in *Ernie Pook's Comeek*

If sex and violence remain blurry and beyond the depth of field within *Ernie Pook's Comeek*, what issues and ideas come into focus? What themes does the strip address, and what do the comics reveal about Barry's understanding of girlhood? Barry's use of multiple perspectives, points of view, narrators, and techniques to show a multifaceted vision of girlhood over the extended time of the long-running strip has been discussed, as has her work challenging the reader with a perspective that is constantly in flux, mirroring the experience of the girls that must constantly shift and adapt to an ever-changing environment. *Ernie Pook* places the girls within a small sphere, an intimate world of neighborhood, school, and home, and in this environment the girls face several issues over and over. This section examines some of the key themes addressed through and by these girls, including struggles with beauty and appearance, the pressure to enter the adult world, and the joy and magic of the commonplace.

The girls of *Ernie Pook* are presented as flawed and unattractive, physically and as individuals. They are not cuddly and cute, but unattractive, damaged, and inconsistent. That is not to say the girls are all bad; they are neither completely cruel nor completely kind. The girls frequently struggle with the stereotypes of female beauty, a concern that reoccurs frequently throughout Barry's works. In the early strip *Girls and Boys* women frequently lamented their looks and dreamed of being skinnier and prettier. The young girl Lynda from *One Hundred Demons* demonstrates concern over her features, and even the tough girl Roberta from *Cruddy* mourns her "dog-like" appearance. As the girls of *Ernie Pook* consider physical appearance over the history of the strip, they come to no consensus or acceptance of their

Figure 5.15. "Perfect." Lynda Barry, *My Perfect Life* (New York: Harper Perennial, 1992), 24–25.

appearance, although it is an issue that the girls lament at length, often citing the pressures of pulchritude as females in a beauty-obsessed culture. Teenager Maybonne, in particular, is often shown gazing somberly into mirrors, bemoaning what she perceives as ugliness, as she does in the opening pages of the anthology *Come Over, Come Over* from 1990, in which she is depicted gazing into a handheld mirror with question marks surrounding her head. She asks, "Who am I?" Marlys stands close by and, showing none of her sister's ambivalence, answers definitively, "My sister!" Maybonne, in contrast to her sister's confidence, struggles with self-esteem (as well as her identity), and in the 1987 strip "Maybonne's Room" a vanity mirror dominates her bedroom. The mirror features sayings written in lipstick, and the table and drawers are covered with cosmetics to enhance her appearance.

In the strip Maybonne also acts "out songs in front of the mirror," and "if a sad song came on she'd get right up close to the mirror and try to see how she looked when she was crying. Other times she'd pull her shirt up and stare at her bra for no reason." Joan Jacob Brumberg comments in *The Body Project: An Intimate History of American Girls*, "Mirrors play a critical role in the way American girls have assessed their own faces and figures" (66), thus Maybonne's frequent mirror-gazing and fascination with her burgeoning womanhood are far from unusual and signal to the reader Maybonne's position on the verge of womanhood.

Maybonne's vanity mirror also emphasizes her border-crossing position as a child traversing the breach to adulthood. Her flowery decorations indicate general "girlness" and femininity, but the décor also suggests her ties to both the adult and child world. The sailor hat, gum wrapper chain, and teen magazines all hearken back to younger days, while the makeup, notes, and Maybelline cosmetics suggest budding womanhood. The door through which Marlys surreptitiously surveils her sister further signals the border between child and adult. The barrier physically divides the panel and the sisters. Marlys, on the outside looking in, dismisses her sister as "nothing but a fool" to fixate on breasts, a key marker of emergent sexuality. Maybonne, however, is in her own world, that of the mirror, and views the evidence of her incipient womanhood.

In her frequent self-studies, Maybonne indicates extreme dismay over her body, pointing out her main defects as "nose, lips, glasses, my whole face and entire body" in the strip "Maybonne World" from 1988. Faced with what she perceives as such overwhelming defects, Maybonne struggles with the current fad of "being yourself" in the 1990 strip "Perfect" (fig. 5.15).

Maybonne narrates the strip through the narrative boxes, while an external focalizer watches Maybonne as she gazes in the mirror, examining her appearance with glasses and without. Maybonne tries new expressions and poses as the narration suggests, "It's ok advice if yourself is beautiful but what do you do in case yourself really sucks?" Maybonne's sister Marlys, one might conjecture, would have little difficulty with the advice to "be yourself," for when she looks in the mirror she sees her strengths. Maybonne, however, wonders what to do when faced with the concrete evidence displayed in the mirror, which she believes reveals that she "sucks." What then? Do you "keep saying: in reality I am beautiful? Then what if you turn conceited?" She continues pondering how it can be beautiful to "be yourself" and then be rejected by a boy, or more specifically, Doug, who "frenched" her and now she is "invisible" to him. Maybonne, in revealing her "true self," has lost her image in the eyes of Doug. She searches for that self in the mirror, but in the final panel turns away, shedding copious tears. The reflection in the mirror, dry of tears, waves its hand frantically, as if trying to pat Maybonne's back soothingly, or perhaps attempting to draw her attention back to her own image in the mirror. Is the reflection trying to comfort Maybonne or turn her to face herself, as the "be yourself" mantra demands? The disconnect between Maybonne's body and her reflection is clear; she stands divided, her identity split, trying to accept herself because she is told to do so by the people she wants to be like, rather than through any true self-esteem. Maybonne tries to be like the others and ironically hopes that in conforming she will stand out enough to be noticed by Doug. Her reflection, however, tries to call Maybonne back to herself.

Maybonne's sister Marlys, on the other hand, has the utmost conviction that she is, despite her freckles and funny pigtails and glasses, utterly captivating, perfect even. If anything should change, it would be the world around her, not Marlys. Marlys is confident in her sense of self and her appearance. Marlys even rejoices with Maybonne's nemesis: the mirror. For Marlys, the mirror offers an opportunity to play and rejoice. In the 1987 strip "Found a Peanut," Marlys acts out a television show in the bathroom mirror while her cousins watch; and although Marlys end up slipping off the toilet seat and acquiring "some magic bruises" on "her magic arm," her joy in her reflected image remains undaunted, as evidenced in the 1993 strip "Family Pictures," in which Marlys is seen enthusiastically "standing on the closed toilet seat so she can watch herself sing in the mirror."

Throughout its run *Ernie Pook* focuses a great deal of attention on girls at the threshold of adulthood, like Maybonne, and girls pushed into the adult world too soon, as both Marlys and Maybonne discover, exploring the disastrous consequences of girls thrust into a violent and brutal world of adults. The dangerous, unhappy consequences of entering adulthood (generally marked as the transition into junior high) for girls is a theme reiterated in *The Good Times Are Killing Me, One Hundred Demons,* and *What It Is.* In *Ernie Pook*, this drama is played out in the relationship of sisters Marlys and Maybonne. The older Maybonne possesses greater knowledge of the adult world than Marlys, and perhaps it is this information that has paralyzed her and convinced her to bear witness to the ugliness of life, rather than the beauty. While Marlys remains firmly planted in the childhood realm, Maybonne teeters on the edge of maturity and thus faces pressures her sister does not.

Maybonne, for all her narcissism, feels for her sister's confrontation with the brutality of life. On the edge of the adult world, Maybonne can't go back to childhood and hopes her sister can remain hopeful in the inno-

Figure 5.16. "Knowing Things." Lynda Barry, *The! Greatest! of! Marlys!* (Seattle: Sasquatch Books, 2000).

cence of childhood just a little longer. Maybonne "knows things" about life, and it weighs on her, as in the strip "Knowing Things" from 1989 (fig. 5.16). Maybonne, in her block capital narration, explains that Marlys is "only 8 so she's still not sick of knowing things." The focalizer, a removed observer, focuses on the interactions of the two sisters. In the first panel Marlys tends to the many bean plants she has chosen to experiment on for a school assignment, while Maybonne chastises her. A close image in the second panel shows Marlys watering a bean plant with an eye dropper while singing, "I'm Milton your brand new son," the theme music to the 1965–1968 *Milton the Monster* cartoon. It is an appropriate choice of song, given that the cartoon revolves around a mad scientist, Professor Weirdo, who tried to create a monster. However, while creating the monster, the Professor added too much "tincture of tenderness" to the concoction, resulting in the kind and loveable Milton the Monster. Marlys, too, is trying to create a new life in her bean plants and is experimenting with the best methodology. According to Maybonne's narration, "She planted 30. She's trying KoolAid, milk, and Cragmont Root Beer. She rubbed one with Vicks. She put Milk Duds in the dirt of one. She says she's looking for the secret formula."

In the third panel Marlys cradles one of the plants protectively, while the other bean plants are perched on the window sill, growing, it would seem, just fine. But Maybonne tells her she's "Cracked" and comments in her narration that Marlys has been unduly influenced by "the books you keep reading with no reality in them. A magic tree starts talking and everything in the world can be magic." While Maybonne belittles Marlys, in the "you" she addresses the reader, chastising the reader for colluding with this fantasy.

Maybonne, however, is saddened by the inevitable, as she relates in the final panel, "I tried to explain to her the concept of reality and that reality is beautiful and she said her plants were reality and she was reality and her experiments were reality and I said the real reality was she was the torturer of plants and all the plants were going to die because of her and what I said came true. It came true. It came true. Marlys, I'm sorry it came true." Maybonne tries to tell her sister what reality is, and that there can be beauty in the way things really are (which seems strangely optimistic for Maybonne), but Marlys rejects this philosophy, saying that her truth, her belief in magic, is reality, not Maybonne's practical philosophy. Maybonne does not delight in the fact that her claim that "all the plants were going to die" came true. In fact, she seems deeply distraught by it, as if in stating the truth she aided in the inevitable. Maybonne's repetition of "it came true," suggests that she is slightly shocked that despite the immense willpower of Marlys, her prophecy eventually comes to pass. In the final panel Marlys sits at a table surrounded by her wilted bean plants in milk cartons, her head in her hands, small hash marks indicating that her head is moving, most likely rocking with tears. Her hands cover her eyes, suggesting she can't bear to look out on this reality of Maybonne's. Dark lines crosshatch around her, indicating Marlys sitting alone with darkness encroaching. Though Maybonne offers one version of reality, she feels saddened that in "knowing things" she has given up on magic. Marlys, who seems to have a touch too much of the "tincture of tenderness" as well, cannot bear a reality without magic. Despite any failures, Marlys refuses to be kept down for long. While Maybonne dwells in a reality of "cruddiness," Marlys offers something much brighter.

Figure 5.17 . "Marlys' Auto Bingo." Lynda Barry, *The! Greatest! of! Marlys!* (Seattle: Sasquatch Books, 2000).

Marlys represents one of the most addressed and clearest themes in the view of *Ernie Pook* as well as later works *One Hundred* Demons, *What It Is*, and *Picture This*, that of finding joy in the ordinary. Marlys, despite her glimpses of Maybonne's cruddy reality, is an eternal optimist. While Maybonne watches, observes, and philosophizes, Marlys *does* things. She experiments with plants; she dances in the mirror; she makes life fun. While Maybonne pines over the sad, dreariness of everyday life, Marlys finds ways to celebrate the small things in life, as she does in her many games, such as "Marlys' Auto Bingo" from 1989 (fig. 5.17).

Marlys stands up in the left side of the first panel to directly address the reader and introduce her creation, a game she invented in case "you are going on a long car trip to your Grandma's" and invites the readers to "cross off the ones you see!" The focalized gaze, though removed and watching Marlys from a distance, is called to join the fun and participate, playing the game in the strip loosely structured like a bingo card. It is, she explains, "another perfect game from the world of Marlys!" Thus in the "world of Marlys" even a long car trip, an event that would seem boring to most, is made into a fun adventure. The first panel is divided into five bingo squares beneath Marlys and her introduction, and each subsequent panel is subdivided into six bingo squares featuring an illustrated example of a common sight or event that occurs on long car trips, such as "Bad smell of cow farm" or "You wake up with pattern of carseat on your face." No one looks forward to the "scary rest stop bathrooms with no doors on stalls," but in Marlys's world, there is cause to rejoice. Of course, with the pattern of the squares in the panels, there is no clear way of winning according to traditional bingo, but perhaps that is the point—winning is playing the game.

Playing the game, or the importance of participating in life rather than simply observing, is a clear theme represented in *Ernie Pook*. Through the reiteration of Maybonne's sadness as an observer and Marlys's joy as an active participant over numerous strips, *Ernie Pook* suggests that magic is found in the ordinary and to enjoy that magic one must actively pursue it. Maybonne, the girl on the edge of adulthood, lets things happen to her, while Marlys, the girl standing intractably in childhood, makes things happen and, in doing so, frequently assumes control of the strip, often coming to the rescue of the other children and adults in the strip. In an interview with Joe Garden, Barry remembered, "In my own life, no one ever did come to the rescue for anything," but Barry creates her own hero, Marlys, who never hesitates to take on the role.

The 1991 strip "No Matter What" demonstrates Maybonne's passive lamentations and Marlys's energetic involvement as Maybonne escapes to the roof of her grade school to lament her life so she can "pray to keep on believing life is magical no matter what, this is my main goal in life, Dear God swear to God I will keep on believing it's magic it's magic it's still so magic" (fig. 5.18). Maybonne acts as narrator and as focalized object for the focalizer, who gazes as if sitting alongside Maybonne, looking out at the night and into the face of the moon. Maybonne as narrator declares, "seems like the whole world is skating on thin ice but at least we're skating." In the fourth panel the gaze looks down from the roof, as the face of Marlys appears in response to Maybonne's prayer. In the bottom of that last panel, almost eclipsed by the heavy rows of text, Marlys peeks up, calling, "Hey! Found ya! Help me up, Ok?" Marlys brings hope and magic and companionship to her sister, allowing her to believe and offering her another view of the world.

Figure 5.18. "No Matter What." Lynda Barry, *It's So Magic* (New York: Harper Perennial, 1994), 126–27.

In "The Falling Leaves" from 1995 Marlys takes over the narration through a homework assignment, demonstrating the importance of action and once again rescuing her sister, who sits passively waiting and watching (fig. 5.19). The narration is constructed as Marlys's response to a homework assignment to write about fall. The original assignment appears in a flowing cursive across the top of the first panel, below which a more juvenile scribble tells Marlys's story, with text dominating each of the panels and the images occupying less than half of each box. In the first panel, below her words, the focalizer sees Marlys wearing a winter coat and holding up two leaves, one in each hand, but it is unclear just who is seeing. In the background a squirrel perches on a fence and tree limbs hang down, with only a few leaves clinging to the branches. Marlys begins her homework with the fairly typical re-

Figure 5.19. "The Falling Leaves." Lynda Barry, *The! Greatest! of! Marlys!* (Seattle: Sasquatch Books, 2000).

sponse to a homework assignment about fall (aside from the punctuation): "Well, first, most obviously, is the leaves!"

The second panel continues the essay but takes a much more personal turn, with Marlys relating family events such as Maybonne "getting, busted, for, shoplifting!" and "getting, illegally drunk, on, ripple, or, Boone's Farm, and, barfing!" and her brother Freddie "getting, socked, in the face, on Halloween!" As the news gets more distressing and personal, the image closes in tighter on Marlys and the squirrel on the fence. Her eyes are opaque and unreadable behind her glasses and her teeth stick out in a small smile as she tugs a branch down, touching a leaf.

In the third panel the scene pulls out, and Maybonne is visible inside the house, pulling back printed curtains to watch her sister playing with the leaves on the branch outside. Maybonne's position suggests that the first two panels might have been focalized from her perspective as she watches Marlys through the window. Outside, Marlys blends the personal with larger issues in her text, commenting on "Thanksgiving! The pilgrims, and, Squanto!" as well as her sister's grounding and the school play (in which Marlys will play a broccoli). The final panel closes in on a weeping Maybonne, still watching Marlys through the window. Tears run down Maybonne's cheeks as she covers her smile with her hand. A segmented speech balloon suggests Maybonne's words are tearful, or perhaps whispered, as she exclaims, "Oh, Marlys." The text finally reveals what Marlys has been doing with the leaves: "My sister, says, she will, kill, herself, when, the, last, leaf, falls, from, the tree, outside, her, bedroom, window! So, I, glued, 79, of, the, leaves, on! That, is, all, I, can, think of, to, write! The, end? By, Marlys!" Continually depressed, Maybonne threatens suicide in a dramatic gesture, "when the last leaf falls." But Marlys, undaunted by Maybonne's ordinary, miserable reality, takes action, creating her own truth and fighting against the change of seasons and her sister's sadness. Ever the observer, Maybonne watches as her sister comes to the rescue once again. Marlys's actions prove that magic still exists. Of course, the adult world misses all of the drama, as indicated by the teacher's comments in a bubble between the essay and the image. "B+ Good story, Marlys, but watch those commas!" The adults will not come to the rescue. The teacher will not ask about Marlys's sister, her brother, or what is clearly a very serious situation at home. The teacher only comments on the use of commas, the overuse of which gives the narrative a stopping, hesitant quality, implying the narrator is stuttering or pausing between each word. Luckily, Marlys acts even as the adult world abandons the Mullens sisters. In her conclusion Marlys asks if this is "The, End?" The question mark is all the more noticeable in its difference from the copious commas.

Marlys further demonstrates the authority of action as well as the power of enjoying smaller pleasures, even reforming the adult world with her enthusiasm, when Marlys comes to the rescue of the grown-ups, as she does in the 1989 strip "Mom's Birthday," which brings into sharp focus the differing realities of the two sisters (fig. 5.20). Maybonne narrates the strip, in clear, sturdy capitals on horizontal lines at the top of the strip, giving the impression of a diary or notebook. The text occupies about half of the upper quadrant of each of the four panels, with a focalizer's vision occupying the lower half. The bottom half of the panels depicts the girls' party preparations as Maybonne's narration explains, "It was Marlys' idea to give her a party. I tried to tell her Mom doesn't want a party. All she wants is a clean

Figure 5.20. "Mom's Birthday." Lynda Barry, *Come Over, Come Over* (New York: Harper Perennial, 1990), 58–59.

house. But Marlys started mixing the Betty Crocker and the Jello 1-2-3 anyway." Maybonne, the pragmatist, argues that their mother just wants a clean house, while Marlys demands a party. Maybonne is pictured sitting at a table with a checkered tablecloth eating a sandwich while Marlys mixes the cake batter, stating, "You do your thing and I'll do mine. I am not in this world to live up to your expectations because I am a child of the universe," an idea Maybonne indicates Marlys "heard on the radio" with an arrow. Maybonne rejects this thought but grudgingly assists her sister nonetheless, pooling her money and helping Marlys reach a card at the supermarket. Maybonne stands to the side, watching and arguing that their mother won't play games. Marlys eschews Maybonne's practicality, asking, "How do you know? You don't got ESP." Maybonne is further drawn into the party planning in the third panel, in which she wears a party hat and skewers marshmallows with plastic swords (hardly practical fare) in the right portion of the scene. Centrally situated in the panel, a cake sits atop a table. A birthday banner hangs above the girls, and Marlys watches for her mother out the window. Maybonne's commentary indicates that "it looked good. Even I have to admit I was excited."

The final panel shows Marlys's triumph. She occupies the center of the panel, blindfolded in a party hat. She waves her arms, holding onto a tail for "Pin the Tail on the Donkey." She asks, "Am I cold or hot?" Her mother sits grinning in a chair in the background, wearing a party hat, drinking from a mug, and smoking. Maybonne's narration admits, "I turned out to be wrong. She did want a party. 'You kids, you kids' she said when she opened the door, and she picked Marlys up and started to cry. Then I started to cry. And I'll always remember that night as a perfect night. A perfect night when I saw her happy." The Mullens females find redemption in a fanciful party. Maybonne's choice to watch the world go by, finding fault with herself and others, isn't the only one. It is Marlys's active reality of celebrations and balloons that saves the family and offers one "perfect night."

Barry, who suggested that Maybonne was a sort of "parallel character" to her own life, offers Maybonne's point of view as the one most commonly accepted, the one most adults hold. The figure of Marlys, representative of hope and whimsy and magic, and even the brief moment of respite that a comic strip offers, proposes another way of seeing the world. Marlys tenders an expectation of escape by focusing on the joy of the ordinary, just as *The Family Circus* offered Barry a visualization of another possibility, a world of cheery, commonplace moments. Throughout the run of *Ernie Pook's Comeek,* Barry provides a focused, narrow view of girlhood, presenting small specimens of tiny moments in girls' lives for extended examination and inquiry. These offerings continually upset the reader's equilibrium, shifting narrators, shifting focalizers, shifting even the artistic rendering, creating a highly developed vision of the lives of girls, and positing the readers as outsiders studying these girls, as participants peering over the shoulders of the young women, and even, at times, as the girls themselves. This experience of the hyperreal puts the reader off balance and on guard, echoing the experience of the girls depicted within the strip. The reader studies the girls and is one of the studied. Through this experience some issues remain beyond the depth of field; graphic depictions of sex and violence remain oblique and out of focus, while through many iterations the strip suggests that for these girls power resides in active pursuit of joy in ordinary pleasures, themes which resonate in Barry's later works, particularly *One Hundred Demons* and *What It Is*.

6

Scrapbooking the Self

"AUTOBIFICTIONALOGRAPHY" IN *ONE HUNDRED DEMONS*

The strips are about as autobiographical as a dream.
—LYNDA BARRY, quoted in Melinda de Jesús, "Of Monsters and Mothers"

To tell the truth of her own experiences as a girl, Lynda Barry found she had to lie, at least a little bit. When Barry turned her focus to exploring her own girlhood, she created a new comic form and structure offering the neologism "autobifictionalography" as the term to describe her approach to rendering the self in comic form. In *One Hundred Demons* Barry creates intimate snapshots of her multiple selves, with the girl "Lynda" at the center. In these strips Barry works with a longer, full-color format and experiments with new media, initially publishing the pieces online. When collecting the strips for a book version, Barry fashions a scrapbook of sorts, employing this gendered, domestic form to frame her life stories with ephemera from childhood and artistic collages featuring glitter, ribbon, and trinkets. These shaped and constructed images of Barry's life focus on girlhood as mediated through her memory and her skills as a writer and artist, suggesting a vision that stresses an archival record of personal history as presented through the interposing lenses of time and technology. Barry frames and constructs her own life, and in particular her own girlhood, revealing her idea of a dark, disturbing childhood from which the narrator ultimately survives, utilizing her own creative impulses to emerge victorious over the demons. In *Demons* Barry limns multiple selves conversing with one another across boundaries of time, space, place, text, and image. The representations of self—child, teen, and adult—challenge notions of femininity and beauty, of race and passing, and of class and social dictates, exploring how the figure of "Lynda Barry" was constructed by and in opposition to these discourse communities.

As accomplished as she is in so many other forms, why did Barry choose this particular construct to render her own life experiences? For that matter, what does this mode reveal about Barry's perception of girlhood? This chapter examines Barry's comic form of "autobifictionalography," detailing the process that inspired the form and analyzing how the structure of the comics, including the layout, length, color, style, narration, and focalizers, underscores Barry's efforts to challenge notions of truth in storytelling by creating a series of selves in dialogue with one another. Further consideration is also given to the scrapbook form of the anthology version of *One Hundred Demons*, which allows Barry to juxtapose comics with collected artifacts and oddities that complicate notions of truth and history, simultaneously revealing and concealing the self. Finally, this chapter contemplates what this collection reveals about Barry's perception of girlhood, the anthology emphasizing Barry's frequent proposition that the transition from elementary school to junior high and into adolescence represents a tragic shift for most girls and that the path to happiness lies in reclaiming the joy and spontaneity found in exploring the creative pursuits often associated with the play of childhood. First, however, a brief discussion of the tradition of autobiographical comics provides a broader understanding of the field within which Barry's *One Hundred Demons* operates.

Autobiography and Comic Art

Lynda Barry is by no means the first comic artist to take on the task of documenting one's own life, and her commonalities with and differences from her colleagues bear further scrutiny before analyzing Barry's own distinctive contribution to the genre of autobiographical comics. Scholars such as Bart Beaty and Joseph Witek have examined autobiographical comics at length, noting that the trend toward documenting one's life emerged as an offshoot of the Underground comics movement, propelled by pivotal projects such as Justin Green's *Binky Brown Meets the Virgin Mary* (1972), R. Crumb's various autobiographical comics, and Harvey Pekar's *American Splendor* (1978–2010). Charles Hatfield writes about the challenges and advantages of rendering autobiography through comics in *Alternative Comics: An Emerging Literature*. Hatfield argues, "Underground comix and their alternative descendants have established a new type of graphic confessional, a defiantly working-class strain of autobiography" (111). Barry, with her background in the rougher neighborhoods of Seattle, would certainly fit within this "defiantly" proletariat breed of autobiography.

For many comic artists emerging from the Underground and Alternative movements, autobiography offered a chance for rendering and reflecting on the self, a way of coming to understand personal history. For Harvey Pekar, Hatfield comments, "Autobiography is a means of autodidactism, as his comics represent a struggle for an understanding both emotional and intellectual" (110). Pekar's work features a commitment to documenting the banal minutiae of everyday life as a means of assaying identity. Barry, too, emphasizes the ordinary, reveling in small talismans of childhood like security blankets and old photographs, though her everyday imaginings stray toward the fanciful, with monsters popping in and out of her strips, thus veering far from Pekar's pledge to remain true to his authentic, commonplace experiences.

Another trend amongst contemporary comic autobiographers influenced by the Underground and Alternative movements is a willingness (some might go so far as to say a compulsion) to expose the worst of themselves. In the article "Estranging the Familiar: 'East' and 'West' in Satrapi's *Persepolis*," Nimi Naghibi and Andrew O'Malley posit, "A common feature of autobiographical underground comics is an emphasis on the inadequacy or ineffectualness of their subjects" (240). Barry, as with many of her fellow comic creators, frequently engages in self-deprecatory humor as well as harsh criticism of her shortcomings, as she does in "Dogs," in which she depicts herself as a vociferous, bellowing woman, her brow furrowed and spit flying as she tries to tame her misbehaving pets (fig. 6.1). Furthermore, Barry often comments on her deficiencies and insecurities as a young child, and in the drawing of her various Lyndas, she accentuates her awkward neediness and unsightly appearance.

While several of the comic artists most associated with autobiography, such as Pekar and Crumb, focus on adult life, still others, particularly women, pay special attention to childhood. Trina Robbins remarks that women, in particular, have spent so much time on their unhappy childhoods as to become cliché: "big chunks of women's comix tend to be about the artist's dysfunctional family, miserable childhood, fat thighs, and boyfriend problems. Although Kominsky seems to have invented the form, the autobiographical comic actually harkens back to the confessional style of mainstream romance comics" (qtd. in Davis 268). The influence of romance comics can clearly be seen in the work of artists like Aline Kominsky-Crumb and Julie Doucet, both of whom chronicle their very adult, very amorous adventures from a critical, sometimes jaded perspective.

Other female comic artists working on autobiography, such as Debbie Drechsler, Alison Bechdel, Marjane Satrapi, and, more recently, Arial Schrag

Figure 6.1. Excerpt from "Dogs." Lynda Barry, *One Hundred Demons* (Seattle: Sasquatch Press, 2002), 172.

and Miss Lasko-Gross, defy easy categorization, focusing less on romance and more on exploring a wide range of girlhood experiences and doing so with diverse aesthetics and writing styles.[1] Bechdel and Satrapi explore their girlhoods in the longer, graphic novel form in their memoirs *Fun Home* (2006) and *Persepolis* (2000), respectively, creating lengthier (and widely acclaimed) accounts of their adolescence and young womanhood. The young artist Lasko-Gross also renders her adolescence in the books *Escape from Special* (2007) and *A Mess of Everything* (2009), with each of these memoirs comprised of numerous short graphic stories. Schrag presents an unusual understanding of girlhood as her chronicle was created during her adolescence rather than from the adult perspective looking back, with *Definition* (1997), *Awkward* (1999), *Potential* (2000), and *Likewise* (2009) drawn during Schrag's time during and directly after high school.

Barry's foray into autobiographical comics shares commonalities with these artists, yet Barry's *Demons* offers a collection of short comics on various autobiographical themes, rather than the longer, sustained narratives of memoirs like *Persepolis* by Satrapi and *Fun Home* by Bechdel. Perhaps most similar in style and substance is Debbie Drechsler, who cites Barry as an inspiration and similarly chooses to label her comic art creations addressing girlhood as semiautobiographical. Drechsler's books *Daddy's Girl* (1996) and *Summer of Love* (2002) deal with incest, alienation, and the difficulties of adolescence. Drechsler also works in short strips that were later collected into longer collections. However, while Drechsler focuses directly and painfully on the violence, illustrating in detail abuse of all sorts, including detailed depictions of genitalia and sex acts, Barry chooses a more oblique approach, suggesting the abuse without ever stating it explicitly, as she does in the strip "Resilience." Clearly, Barry is not the first female to examine girlhood in the comic form, and these comic artists addressing girlhood bear additional scholarly attention, both individually and in conversation with one another. However, Barry's take on girlhood, unique in form and content, immediately stands as its own creation, that of "autobifictionalography."

Process

Barry did not immediately set out to create a scrapbook of comics and collected artifacts from her life; the project began with an exploration of new and old technologies. Barry was initially inspired to explore her girlhood when experimenting with different mediums: sumi brush painting, online comics, and, eventually, collage. While working on *Cruddy* in the late 1990s, Barry began to experiment with sumi brush painting. As she began playing with the technique, often inspired by a single word or phrase, the demons of her life emerged. "At first they freaked her, but then she started to love watching them come out of her paint brush," explains a kindly looking monster in the introduction to *Demons*. The demons eventually took a more formal shape as seventeen strips (each with twenty panels) that appeared from 7 April 2000 to 15 January 2001 on the popular online magazine *Salon.com*. Online publishing allowed Barry the freedom to experiment with a longer format and to utilize color in her comics. Barry enjoyed the process of working with *Salon.com*, especially editor Jennifer Sweeney, and Barry later dedicated the book of collected strips to Sweeney. The anthologized print version of the comics was published by Seattle-based Sasquatch Books in 2002 and featured strips that were paired down to eighteen panels presented with two large panels per page. Barry further polished the strips and developed additional features for the printed collection. Working with Tom Greensfelder and Amie Z. Gleed, Barry designed an introduction, concluding "Do-it-Yourself" tutorial, and collages for the front and ending pages, as well as collages featured between each of the strips. Barry told Lev Grossman, "I really wanted to use every possible square inch. I wanted it to look like Fruit Loops and sparkle paint!" Barry had big ideas for the format of the book and, consequently, a big fight on her hands, as she explained in an online interview with *Independent Publisher:* "I do have to say it took a lot of crying, screaming, Mick Jagger–style posturing, James Brown–style begging, arm twisting, smoke-blowing and flaming e-mails to get the publisher to agree to the book looking the way it does."

In a personal interview Barry reflected that she is not "as attached to the comics in the book, but I love the collages and the pictures all over the outside and stuff."[2] Barry's favorite element of the book, the colorful collages, hearken back to her mixed-media portraits from the "Music Notebook" portion of the original printing of *The Good Times Are Killing Me* in 1988 and foreshadow the eccentric collages from *What It Is* in 2008 and *Picture This* in 2010. In fact, this multilayered anthology comes to resemble nothing so much as a scrapbook. Indeed, the collected artifacts and ephemera along with personal essays in comic form in *Demons* act as a scrapbook of selfhood. Although *Demons* might seem to violate the notion of scrapbook as private document, throughout history scrapbooks were created to share personal triumphs and accomplishments with guests and visitors, thus treading the boundary between public and private.[3] In this collection Barry assembles previously published texts and positions them artistically along with various objects, captions, and collages. In the introduction to *The Scrapbook in American Life*, Susan Tucker, Katherine Ott, and Patricia Buckler argue, "Scrapbooks are an autobiographical form but with a twist. The compiler envisions himself or herself through the images positioned on the page. . . . [T]he makers express themselves with every swipe of glue yet ultimately remain free, elusive, and hidden" (2–3). Barry thus assembles snapshots of herself through her comic art along with other materials, artistically presenting a vision of selfhood that incorporates artistic renditions of identity along with photographic evidence and mass-produced artifacts, blending an inner vision of character with historical documentation. Through this method the creator herself remains essentially obscure, revealing her soul while retaining some measure of privacy. Given the complex interaction between Barry's comics and the accompanying elements added to the anthology, the analysis presented here thus considers *One Hundred Demons* as a whole collection, complete with comic strips, collage pages, introduction, and conclusion, as published by Sasquatch Press in 2002, rather than as individual strips published at *Salon.com,* although important differences between the formats are noted and the impact of the initial online publication is discussed.

Novelist and critic Alice Sebold commented on the success of Barry's scrapbook project, arguing:

Each story begins with a collage painting, then works into a paneled strip, and the ultimate thing happens as you read these pieces: You see visually and read narratively, and because of her color choices and the collage elements, you feel both textually and texturally (!) the world the characters live in. It is a painful world, an honest world, a transcendent one. (26)

The blended text format of *Demons* thus offers another representation of girl-hood, in which Barry cuts and pastes her memories and integrates them with personal documents, commercial messages, and a fair bit of glitter and paste. This pastiche differs from that of other comic artist autobiographers, male and female, but reinforces Barry's insistence on the fractured identity of girl-hood. The editors of *The Scrapbook in American History* note, "If scrapbooks can be distilled to one overarching interpretive theme, it is that of rupture. Scrapbooks shuffle and recombine the coordinates of time, space, location, voice, and memory. What could be more emblematic of the fractured nar-ratives of modernity than scrapbooks?" (Tucker, Ott, and Buckler 16). The scrapbook genre therefore reveals the fissures, ruptures, and lacunae of girl-hood in Barry's *Demons* and, furthermore, illuminates the elements seaming an identity together through form and content. However, before considering the ways in which the elements of the scrapbook work together to show an-other vision of girlhood, it is necessary to examine the components in more detail. The first element examined, then, is the most prominent feature of the collection, Barry's comic art, created initially by brush and later pub-lished online at *Salon.com* before being published in book form.

The Comic Strips

Publishing online offered Barry another opportunity to experiment artisti-cally, liberating her from the small, black-and-white panels that she utilized to conform to the publishing guidelines for the weekly alternative papers. These new works were created by hand, not on a computer, but scanning and publishing the strips in the online environment accommodated a bolder, more colorful format and allowed Barry to develop longer narratives. At *Salon.com* each strip was comprised of twenty panels, but these were edited down to eighteen panels for the book form. This expanded length allowed Barry to indulge her penchant for extended written narration and allowed additional room for illustration, but still managed to constrain the artist-author's tendency to indulge in unstructured digressions (as evidenced by her text-only creations). Barry's drawing style in *Demons* bears a strong resemblance to her work in *Ernie Pook's Comeek*, but the use of the sumi brush results in a looser approach that appears more painterly and less con-strained. While still far from representational, Barry's conceptual method appears more polished and composed in *Demons* than in the weekly strip. The soft lines and washes of color suggest a calling up and rendering of self from memory, the ambiguity of recollection reinforced in the sinuous lines.

This format made it possible for Barry to work in color, and each panel is awash with bright, brilliant tones and soft strokes in vivid hues. In the article "Liminality and Mestiza Consciousness," Melinda de Jesús notes, "The full-color graphics of *One Hundred Demons* are an integral part of this process of self-creation. Barry's exquisite storytelling power lies in the potent mixture of her narrative and drawings: her comics enable the reader literally to 'see' Barry's world as she does and thus enter it even more fully" (223).[4] Readers thus see the stark contrast of the figure of Lynda's red hair and freckles beside her mother and grandmother's dark features. Without color, it would be far more difficult for readers to see Lynda's ability to "pass" in the white community, an issue immediately apparent in color. The bright colors also add to the feeling of veracity in the longer strips, while the muted black and white of *Ernie Pook's Comeek* suggests a distance in time and place, a flattening of experience. In contrast, the bright, vibrant colors of *Demons* offer a contemporary feel. This experience of temporality is underscored by the mediums through which the audience encounters the strips. In their original format, as presented through the technology of computers and the Internet, the strips suggest contemporaneity and immediacy. Even the book format, with its shiny pages and colorful binding, offers an impression of vitality and newness.

Reading *One Hundred Demons,* the audience enters into Barry's simulacrum of childhood and experiences it along with the narrator, who comments on the top half of the panels. The narrative text generally occupies a large portion of each panel, similar to Barry's work in *Ernie Pook*, and the writing is most often inked in straightforward capital lettering. Occasionally the font shifts, with one word or phrase lettered in a flowery cursive, adding emphasis to particular phrases; this technique slows the reader's comprehension as they must account for the differing fonts while reading. Based on the content, the narrative text further suggests the narrator is an older, wiser Lynda (as pictured in the opening introduction) reflecting back on her childhood. The narrator Lynda resides in a particular present, signaling her point in the present time with phrases such as "I wish." However, the narrative voice spends much more time in the past tense, relating what came before. This narrator Lynda intimates a wistfulness and nostalgia for the past, longing for people and objects long gone and lamenting mistakes uncorrected. Charles Hatfield notes of many comic autobiographers that this tension between narration and depiction adds "to a sense of distance between the 'naïve' self depicted in the autobiography and the older, more sophisticated self responsible for the depiction" (128). The narrator represents an older voice, remarking on the many images of Lynda and her

Figure 6.2. Excerpt from "Head Lice and My Worst Boyfriend." Lynda Barry, *One Hundred Demons* (Seattle: Sasquatch Books, 2002), 16.

life. The strips recounted by the narration take place at various places and times, all plucked from Barry's life. Much of the action takes place during Barry's childhood in Seattle, but Barry also jumps in time to her present life. The narrator suggested by the text boxes is autodiegetic and extradiegetic, and as Luc Herman and Bart Vervaeck note, the narrator "stands above the events he narrates, but he *has* experienced them" (85). The older, reflective "Lynda" who narrates is part of the action in the past but removed from the action by time.

The narrator remains relatively stable throughout the collection, as does the focalizer. While the gaze in *Ernie Pook's Comeek* shifts occasionally, creating an unpredictable, unstable point of view, in *Demons* the focalizer remains, with very few exceptions, fixed as an external perspective closely following the scenes as described by the textual narrative. In fact, a careful examination reveals that Barry takes fewer risks and pursues fewer innovative angles and viewpoints in these autobiographical strips than she does in her fictional ones. Perhaps the adventure and innovation is inherent in the content as *Demons* explores these snapshots of selfhood, rather than imagining fictional experiences from multiple points of view.

The strip entitled "Head Lice and My Worst Boyfriend" that opens the collection follows a typical pattern, indicative of the common form Barry employs throughout *Demons* (fig. 6.2). The textual narration introduces the subject matter, with the pictures illustrating. While many comic art scholars argue for the primacy of the image, in *Demons* (and in her other comics) Barry frequently inverts this idea, relying on text as the primary source of information, with the illustration providing additional exegesis. In this example and in much of Barry's work, text "anchors" the image, the text thus being "necessary for the comprehension of the situation" (Groensteen 130). In the introduction to "Head Lice" the narrator announces the subject of the strip, lice, an idea not clear from the action pictured in the first panel. A tiny nit adorns the embellished letter *A* that opens the narration, playfully echoing an ancient, sacred text. Looping cursive occasionally disrupts the standard capitalized lettering, emphasizing key words and phrases such as "head lice," "Neanderthal," "smoking," and "house flies." The narrative text crowds the images, with speech bubbles taking up even more room for words. The speech balloons also follow the same lettering style, while incorporating the vernacular of Barry's Filipino heritage. The focalizer watches from a distance, following the story of a young Lynda in her neighborhood. The panels depict a girl eating and sharing three-year-old candy and spraying bug spray while her grandmother encourages her to use a flyswatter.

In "Head Lice" and for most of the strips the focalizer does not enter into the interiors of the scenes and participate as a character or witness, but rather remains a distanced spectator. Rare exceptions do occur, with a few panels ocularized from the perspective of one of the Lynda figures, such as a panel looking at the "Lucky" sign in "The Visitor" (fig. 6.3). The narrator opens "The Visitor" explaining, "Lucky's Foods was a grocery store with a pale blue neon sign that looked good in the rain. It was in a bad part of town where police sirens were often blaring" (112). Below the narrative text is an illustration of the glowing neon sign in blue and yellow, with the darkened night skyline in the background. The signs in the window of the grocery store below tout the specials for "cantaloupe" and "pork roast." In the sequence that follows, the narration tells of Lynda as a teenager falling for a bagger at Lucky's and tripping on acid with him. They end up in Chinatown, where they encounter Lynda's mother and various other relatives. Lynda's Filipino heritage is not immediately apparent to the bagboy, nor is it telegraphed to the reader, for she is depicted as pale with red hair. Lynda struggles with passing and hiding her background: "I didn't tell him I spent a lot of time in Chinatown when I was little, that my relatives hung out in a Filipino restaurant on the next block, that my uncle was cutting hair in the barbershop we just passed and that my mother could be right around the corner parking the car" (116). The boy interprets Lynda's ease in Chinatown to an adventurous spirit, but after Lynda's mother makes an appearance, swearing at her daughter from a car window, Lynda opens up to the boy about her background and ethnicity, after which he hastily departs. In "Liminality and Mestiza Consciousness," Melinda de Jesús argues, "Whiteness distances Lynda from colorism and

Figure 6.3. Excerpt from "The Visitor." Lynda Barry, *One Hundred Demons* (Seattle: Sasquatch Books, 2002), 112.

racism but also from her family and culture" (231). Lynda thus stands as an outsider in both worlds, unable to connect with her family or the bagboy.

Barry underscores this sense of loneliness and isolation with the final panel of the strip, yet she also creates a connection between the reader and Lynda, as they share the same point of view. The last panel features a view of the same Lucky sign, this time with darker colors and a tighter point of view. The narration comments on the bagboy's leaving: "He nodded and said the Lucky's sign looked beautiful in the rain but he was quitting. And there was this girl he was in love with who he talked about until his bus finally came. I sat on the bench for a long time afterwards. I was cool. Very cool. It wasn't like I had never been robbed before" (120). While the identity of the focalizer is not entirely clear, the lack of figures within the panel as well as the narrative text suggests Lynda sitting on the bench gazing at the sign, long after the boy departs. The text of the Lucky sign, internalized within the scene, opens and closes the strip, pulling the reader into another point of view and thus the action, remarking on the scene from within. Ann Miller notes, "The only text which can be fully integrated into the diegesis is that which occurs on decors or objects within the fiction" (98); and this particular example of ocularized text thus stands as a rare example in *Demons* as the object of the first-person point of view, as well as an example of meta-text, ironically commenting on Lynda's luck. Barry thus makes a rare use of shifting point of view within *Demons* to create a bond between audience and character, transcending barriers of race and the politics of passing. Barry also disrupts the distance and focus of the external focalizer's gaze on occasion when incorporating bits of real objects and recreated artifacts into the strips, such as a photograph of Lynda with a friend and an artistic re-creation of a security blanket. These objects argue for the veracity of the strips, providing evidence of Barry's remembrances and creating links between the strips themselves and the interstitial collages.

Truth, Fiction, and a Series of Selves

Various incarnations of Lynda stand as the most frequent objects of the focalizer's gaze, suggesting a heteroglossic sense of self, an approach often utilized by many contemporary comic artists, certainly influenced by post-structuralist theory. Bart Beaty argues, "Post-structuralism in particular has deposed the unified subject of autobiography by positing discourse as preceding and exceeding the subject, calling the very basis of the genre's distinctiveness into question" (141). Hatfield also points out that the medium of comics itself deconstructs the notion of a unified self: "The interaction of word and picture—that basic tension between codes—allows for ongoing intertextual or metatextual commentary, a possibility that threatens the very idea of a unified self" (127). Thus the rendering of a narrative voice along with a constructed picture of the self calls into question the idea of a singular identity, a concept exploited by Barry throughout *Demons*. Hatfield also points to R. Crumb and the Hernandez brothers as other creators who feature "the self as successive selves" and "carry us to the vanishing point where imagination and claims to truth collide. Yet these pieces still demand and play on the readers trust: *they still purport to tell truths*" (124, emphasis in original). Barry alleges an undeniable although unreliable authority in telling her story through these multiple selves, playing with the creator's vision of herself and with the visions others have of her. While Barry's *Demons* argues against a unified speaking subject, in bringing this collection together, including the strips, collages, and tutorials, Barry also manages to create an exceptional vision of "Lynda Barry." This image surely remains a fictionalized, heteroglossic self-representation, yet this created identity gives the impression of distinctiveness and coherence as well as probity.

In a review for the *Filipino Express*, Marcelline Santos-Taylor expresses the feedback of many readers of *One Hundred Demons*, arguing that even with full knowledge of the somewhat fictionalized nature of the text, "you get the feeling that the whole book is nothing but honest." Perhaps this should not surprise, given that Barry, in rejecting the notion of any authentic, uncomplicated truth residing in the text and choosing to depict (textually and visually) her numerous selves, engages in what Hatfield calls "ironic

Figure 6.4. Excerpt from "Introduction." Lynda Barry, *One Hundred Demons* (Seattle: Sasquatch Press, 2002), 6.

authentication," thereby reinforcing the impression of truth-telling. Hatfield explains, "We might call this strategy, then, authentication through artifice, or more simply *ironic authentication:* the implicit reinforcement of truth claims through their explicit rejection. In brief, ironic authentication makes a show of honesty by denying the very possibility of being honest" (125–26, emphasis in original). Through her self-representation as unattractive and awkward (at all ages and to varying degrees), Barry's self-deprecation argues for such ironic authentication. Barry furthermore underscores authenticity through the frequent meta-moments in which she pictures herself shaping and creating the project that is *Demons*, drawing attention to the conspicuously crafted nature of autobifictionalography.

Barry almost immediately undermines her own credibility in the collection by prefacing the table of contents with the warning, "Please Note: This is a work of autobifictionalography," and follows the warning with an introduction that pictures Barry at a drafting table, joined by a garrulous demon (fig. 6.4). The introduction is painted on legal paper turned on its side, with vertical lines running throughout. The choice of paper underscores the homespun, "found" notion of the text; when the introduction is painted on cast-off paper, it is clear that this is not high or unattainable art, but a medium accessible to the masses.

A multi-eyed demon arises from the waves to help launch the book, explaining the autobifictionalographic process while the adult/creator Lynda demonstrates. Despite the numerous, all-seeing eyes, this is not a menacing demon. A monkey with a very familiar looking headscarf is emblazoned

Figure 6.5. Excerpt from "Introduction." Lynda Barry, *One Hundred Demons* (Seattle: Sasquatch Books, 2002), 7.

across his chest and a little bird perches on his head. The juxtaposition of woman and monster demonstrates Barry's concept of autobifictionalography even as the text continues on to define it. The circles of fatigue under Lynda's eyes, the messy hair and headband, and the carefully labeled everyday arti-facts, "coffee," "water," "birdie," and "author," stress the mundane, ordinary part of "auto-" or self-storying. The cheerful monster, however, embodies the fictive nature of the comic. In the following panels the figure of an adult "Lynda Barry" sits at a drafting table painting with her brush and ink stone (fig. 6.5). She wears the ubiquitous headband tied into a bow on top of her head and her eyes are hidden behind glasses (much like *Ernie Pook* characters Marlys and Maybonne). The figure looks weary, with grey and brown lines radiating from her eyes and forehead. In swirling cursive font, the narra-tion wonders, "Is it autobiography if parts of it are not true?" In the next panel, Lynda stares down at her drawing, a tiny version of the last panel, and wonders, "Is it fiction if parts of it are?" This scene calls attention to the creative process of self-invention through art and argues for Hatfield's idea of ironic authentication. These self-reflexive, meta-fictional panels underscore the composed nature of the book itself; the *mise en abyme* leaves no doubt for the audience that what follows has been shaped by an artist.

Though the ramifications of Barry's direct challenge to notions of fiction and autobiography may resonate as truthfulness, or ironic authentication, Barry suggests a lighter reason for emphasizing the ambiguous, autobific-tionalographic nature of the text in a conversation with Whitney Matheson: "I guess the reason is because there are people in the stories I've told who really do exist. And if they want to say, 'THAT NEVER HAPPENED!' I'd like to have them be able to do so" (7d). Barry further clarified: "The strips are about as autobiographical as a dream. Which is to say, all of the elements are from my life, but the arrangement of them in a story, the condensing and the story line is more intuitive. Nothing in the stories are untrue, but nothing in the stories are presented as unassailable fact" (qtd. in de Jesús, "Of Monsters" 23). Heather Meek recounts that Barry "describes how one may replay a conversation over in one's mind many times. One may imagine and fixate upon the things one might have said until the fictional, idealized version becomes so real that when one retells the story the way it should have happened, 'you're not lying!' The imagined truth, the better truth becomes the only truth one wants to believe in." The strips in *Demons* reveal the "better" truth, the truth shaped and tailored to the author's taste. Some comic art autobiographers stress fealty to the mundane truths as evidence of accuracy. Hatfield cites Harvey Pekar as an example of a creator who believes "that persuasiveness resides in literal accuracy, in minute fidelity to 'mundane events' as they happen," while other creators "have recognized that the genre isn't about literal but rather about *emotional* truths" (Hatfield 11, emphasis in original). As previously discussed, though Barry, like Pekar, obsessively chronicles small happenings in her life and painstakingly re-creates scenes from her childhood, her approach differs greatly in its elevation of the fanciful, emotional truth of the experiences over direct representation of events.

Medieval audiences might find much to admire in Barry's notion of autobifictionalography, for at that time there was also a rebellious movement to affirm the "better truth" over literal proceedings. Writers in the Middle Ages experimented with composing in the vernacular, English, and in taking on this revolutionary task, according to Nicholas Watson, stressed *sapientia* or "heart knowledge" over *scientia* or "head knowledge" (339). Watson notes that expressing and identifying the truth of the experience, or heart knowledge, didn't require special training or even intellect, but "was available to all" (339). Gillian Rudd further explains:

> The basic contrast between *sapientia* and *scientia* is obvious from the roots of the two words. *Scientia* comes from a verb (*scio*) and so is associated with active acquisition of knowledge and learning. One enacts a verb, one deduces knowledge and may put it into practice; what one learns tends to be abstract, a theory, which can be understood fully, or proved, only when applied. In contrast *sapientia* comes from a noun—*sapor* (taste)—which summons up the world of the senses and trusts to the reality of experience rather than theory. (19)

For Barry, the "idealized," re-imagined version that expresses what should have happened trumps either a prose-laden traditional autobiography or a comic that professes to authenticity. While the neologism "autobifiction-alography" reflects Barry's quirky humor, the merit of a genre that acknowledges the fiction inherent in all forms of self-representation seems clear. Obviously, individuals immersed in the work of composing life stories realize that the quotidian minutiae that make up one's life do not fit into tidy little narratives with a clear beginning, middle, and ending. The shaping done by the artist involves a twisting or distortion of the experience, seen as it is through the lens of the subject and translated for the observer. The reader will never know the "real" truth, yet given the origins of the narratives in life experience, neither are they altogether invented. Barry continually disrupts any master narrative or identity, instead choosing to represent the self as multiple and fragmented, as is the case with her other heroines.

Barry depicts numerous "Lyndas" in the comic strips: the aforementioned narrator, who "speaks" through the text; the very young Lynda clutching her doll in "Resilience"; the girl playing kickball in "Lost Worlds"; and many versions of an adolescent Lynda on the border between child and adult, as in "Dancing," "Common Scents," "Hate," and "The Visitor." A young woman Lynda also appears, fending off boyfriend problems in "Head Lice and My Worst Boyfriend." The most common Lyndas present in the collection, perhaps not surprisingly, are the girl Lynda, the slightly older adolescent Lynda, and the artist Lynda seen painting and drawing.

The youngest Lynda stands as a striking example of Barry's oblique approach to trauma in the strip "Resilience." The strip is prefaced by a collage featuring a photograph of a very young girl, greatly resembling the youngest, drawn depiction of Lynda, with bright curly hair and a translucent orange band covering her eyes (fig. 6.6). The girl smiles brightly, her chin resting in her hand, a finger coyly posed on her cheek. The masking of the eyes suggests blindness, a veiling or suppression of vision. The orange bar remains somewhat transparent, implying that some of the truth and the horror seep through. In a chapter on Barry entitled "Materializing Memory" from the book *Graphic Women*, Hillary Chute suggests that the orange paper is "filtering our ability to see her—and also, at least graphically, filtering the subject's own outward gaze at us" (116).

The photo is juxtaposed with the girl Lynda figure who opens the strip as she ponders her past and growing up too quickly. Various drawings, bits of fabric, stamps, and pieces of tape surround the photo and drawing. A menacing demon is placed next to the photograph, its head that of an alligator and its body that of a man. The demon is smeared with red, sug-

Figure 6.6. Collage page. Lynda Barry, *One Hundred Demons* (Seattle: Sasquatch Press, 2002), 62.

gesting blood, while a bit of fabric covers its genitals. Another squat, black demon is placed upside-down directly below the other monster. A photo of a black-and-white teddy bear is inverted between the photograph of Lynda and the illustrated Lynda, a reminder of a childhood turned topsy-turvy. The inscription "Can't Forget" covers a reddish-orange flower in the right corner and is echoed in the windowpanes at which the drawn Lynda stares, which are inscribed, "Can't remember/Can't forget." On the opposing right-hand collage page, the word "Forgot" is lettered on a starburst on a blue sheet of paper, contrasting with the orange flower's "Can't Forget." The title panel features three demons holding a sign that reads: "Today's Demon: Resilience." Beneath the demons a doll rests amongst red and orange flowers. In her reading, Chute argues that the doll represents both the girl Lynda and the doll clutched by Lynda in the final panel of the strip. Chute remarks, "This wounded figure stands in for her" and thus the entire piece "is set up, then, so that the very end of the story circles back to the collage; it defies linearity" (*Graphic Women* 117). Indeed, the opening photo of the girl from the collage is also reiterated in the final image of the strip, in which the figure of a young Lynda sits in a field of red flowers (echoing the flower from the collage), wearing a little dress and clutching her doll to her chest while an adult male figure asks, "Hey there, Sweetheart. Do you and your dolly want to go for a ride" (72). The man is pictured from the waist down, his head severed, his crotch and a lit cigarette level with the young

Figure 6.7. Excerpt from "Resilience." Lynda Barry, *One Hundred Demons* (Seattle: Sasquatch Press, 2002), 66.

girl, creating an ominous parallel between the object of his attention and the alligator monster from the opening collage.

The strip opens with the image of an adolescent Lynda sitting at a table, her chin in her hands, staring out a darkened window. The narrator asks, "When did I become a teenager? It doesn't happen in a day. It wasn't when I turned thirteen and stared out the window at the rain waiting for a feeling" (64). The narration continues to say she did not become a teenager after her "first kiss," but rather was forced to grow up quickly, for "when I was little, bad things had gone on, things too awful to remember but impossible to forget. When you put something out of your mind, where does it go? Dark ghosts in limbo moved me around. I didn't know how to fight them" (65). As the narrator alludes to a dark childhood experience, young Lynda's mother lectures her, pointing an accusing finger and shouting, chastising her, "God watches you! N'ako, he knows what you are. He <u>saw</u> you" (65), as Lynda quivers. The panels continue on, rendering Lynda's unwelcome knowledge of sex (fig. 6.7). Apparently, this was common knowledge, for "nearly every kid in my neighborhood knew too much too soon. Some people call it 'growing up too fast' but actually it made some of us unable to grow up at all" (66). This unbidden information and pressure does not allow Lynda to grow naturally into the next stage of maturation, intimacy, but instead forces a sexualized identity of mature womanhood upon her far too early.

The thirteen-year-old Lynda figure rests in bed, wondering what to do about a boy's invitation to "get together" in a "more comfortable" spot. Still very much an unattractive figure, Lynda covers her eyes, as if unable to witness the scene to come. Ilana Nash notes in the book *American Sweethearts*, "Standing at the crossroads between childhood and womanhood, the teen girl faces Janus-like in both directions, a liminal figure who combines two identities that incite pleasure and anxiety in the adult male" (3). This Lynda struggles amidst the competing identities placed upon her. Society and the male gaze, in particular, objectify her as a child and as a woman, leaving the figure paralyzed and hiding in bed, unable to move forward.

As the strip progresses, Lynda is relieved when her first kiss, the paper boy, leaves her for a more sexually experienced girl in her home economics class, but it is not this boy or his kiss that has shattered her sense of self. This event occurred earlier and is something Lynda cannot outrun, no matter how hard she tries to "be good" (70). Later, the young Lynda tries desperately to find a place with the "good girls" at school and calls out after the "Asian clique," hoping they will wait for her, but they have already left the frame. "I'd be good and the dark ghosts would vanish. When your inner life is a place you have to stay out of, having an identity is impossible. Remembering not to remember fractures you. But what is the alternative? Tell me" (70). Lynda tried to "be good," to avoid the adult world of sex, but as a result of her past abuse she was doomed. She had to always remember not to remember and doing so broke her, making any sense of self out of the question. The pressure of repressing past abuse divides Lynda, thus denying her the ability to establish an identity. The narration directly addresses the readers with the predicament, inviting them to offer her an alternative, another way of being in light of her past.

In the fourteenth panel Lynda returns to her bed, begging God for death while the narration above argues, "This ability to exist in pieces is what some adults call resilience. And I suppose in some way it is a kind of resilience, a horrible resilience that makes adults believe children forget trauma" (70). In this way Lynda cannot achieve an identity, instead reaching physical maturity while the psyche remains in pieces. Society, the strip contends, applauds the ability of children to survive into adulthood while maintaining the façade of an identity in the wake of abuse as "resilience." In compiling these strips from her life, remembering that which she could not bear to recall and rendering the pieces of self that endured such identity-shattering trauma, the author attempts to reassemble a fractured psyche, creating a self—not a homogeneous, unified self, but a heteroglossic one, composed of many voices speaking to one another across time and space.

Eventually, Lynda uncovers her eyes, leaves the safety of her bed, begins wearing more feminine clothing, and catches "up with the home ec girl's way of being, doing things that scared me but made me feel exhilaratingly

Figure 6.8. Final panels from "Resilience." Lynda Barry, *One Hundred Demons* (Seattle: Sasquatch Press, 2002), 72.

whole. I know this may be hard to understand, this compulsion to repeat the situations that harmed you" (71). The young Lynda pictured in panels fifteen and sixteen, though still wearing short hair and maintaining a tomboy-ish appearance, now shows off a sleeveless flower-print dress as she stumbles in the dark, throwing up on a boy and wondering, "Why do you keep <u>doing</u> this?" as the caption explains, "2am, very drunk, no ride home" (71).

The next to last panel reflects, "You can't remember that time, you can't forget it but you do remember never to remember it, the time when the shattering into pieces became a way of life" (72), while a still young but now noticeably tired and sickened Lynda is lectured by her mother who calls her a "prostitute," defining her daughter as a purveyor of sex (fig. 6.8). The final panel answers the questions of the very first: "I became a teenager when I discovered how to give myself that feeling of wholeness, even if it lasted only for a moment, even if it got me into huge trouble, it was the closest I could come to . . . to . . . I don't remember" (72). Lynda thus crossed into adulthood when she began chasing that feeling of wholeness that would bind all of the fractured pieces of herself together—the narrator further implying that the pursuit was often through abusive sexual relations. Just as Marlys was unable to remember and depict Cindy Ludermyer's rape in *Ernie Pook's Comeek* in 1991, the narrator cannot speak aloud the horror, although the last picture shows a hint of what happened.

The final panel echoes the photograph in the opening collage, linking the artifact of identity with the re-imagined self. Unlike many contemporary comic autobiographers, Barry chooses to address abuse indirectly in this strip, asking the reader to draw conclusions based on these self-images as well as the narrator's text, which poses the question, "When I was still little, bad things had gone on, things too awful to remember but impossible to forget. When you put something out of your mind, where does it go?" (65). This young Lynda is the most vulnerable self-depiction in the book; the other, older Lyndas are survivors, no longer innocent. Much of what follows in the collection centers on the aftermath of these events, the destruction of a pure, trusting little girl. This tiny girl is drawn just once, a fleeting glimpse of a child, the photograph verifying the truth that she once existed, not just in the creator's imagination.

Two frequent Lyndas featured in *Demons* are the girls positioned on either sides of the juncture between childhood and adulthood, one a girl who plays kickball and covets her friend's dolls, another who drinks and does drugs. The younger girl Lynda appears to be about eight or nine years old, with short, spiky red hair and conspicuously tomboyish clothing. She struggles with femininity and class in "Girlness," with racism in "Common Scents," and with her mother in "Hate" and "The Aswang." Barry also frequently depicts herself on the verge of adulthood, a change she suggests starts with junior high in strips such as "Magic" and "San Francisco." In both of these strips the liminal Lynda leaves friends behind, commenting, "Once I turned 13 and started junior high and realized how lame I really was, there was no way I could have an 11-year old best friend" (103). The teenager Lynda of "Resilience," "First Job," "Dancing," and "The Visitor" struggles with boys and drugs and anxiety over appearance. An older, middle-aged Lynda also appears in "Election," "Dogs," "Lost Worlds," and "Girlness." This older Lynda attempts to make peace with her past and is also frequently depicted as an artist and author. It is this more mature Lynda who achieves some sense of wholeness and happiness through art, which allows her to reconcile with her past selves as she does in the strip "Lost and Found."

The multifarious Lyndas are juxtaposed against one another, crossing the boundaries of time and location to question identity. Much as the collages bring together various ephemera that work against and with one another to form an artistic whole, these Lyndas converse across the strips, questioning, consoling, and challenging one another to compose a self. For example, in the strip "Lost Worlds," Barry contrasts scenes of young girl Lynda participating in a neighborhood kickball game with an older, adult Lynda looking down from an airplane. The strip confounds time, reaching across the chronological divide as the young Lynda waves at an airplane just as the older Lynda gazes out the window at the world below. The narration explains, "I believed the people in airplanes could see us and thought we looked cool," but continues on, "This was long before I grew up and found

Figure 6.9. Excerpt from "Lost Worlds." Lynda Barry, *One Hundred Demons* (Seattle: Sasquatch Press, 2002), 36.

out you can't see very much from an airplane window. Big things, yes, but the little things are lost" (32). The action of the strip itself contradicts the voice of the narrator, for even from a distance, the audience does see the little things, from the freckles on young Lynda's legs to the "grasshopper that fell in the storm drain" (35); and young Lynda doesn't give up hope of being noticed despite the warnings of others, continuing to wave just in case she is seen. The narration asks, "What would I give to have just one more ups. What would I give to see them all again. Chuckie, roll the ball this way. Chuckie, roll me a good one" (36); and the figure of Chuckie appears, Band-Aids and all, and the narrator's wish is granted through the re-creation of the scene in the strip (fig. 6.9). It would seem that the narrator does go back in time, returning to the places and the selves left behind. The narrative text asks, "Who knows which moments make us who we are? Some of them? All of them? The ones we never really thought of as anything special?" (36). This strip and this book attempt to answer the query of the narration as it revisits some of these moments, thus making them special; and in choosing them, they are marked as the moments that make up a self.

The strip "Common Scents" demonstrates a similar sense of nostalgia, this time setting the young Lynda in opposition to the unseen Lynda of the narrative text, exploring Barry's racial heritage. In the strip the narrator notes, "I have always noticed the smell of other people's houses, but when I was a kid I was fascinated by it" (52), as a young Lynda (with freckles, pale skin, red hair, and tiny bow) investigates the smells of various neighbors' houses. This young Lynda can't smell her own home, although the neighbor girl states, "My mom says your people fry weird food and save the grease and

Figure 6.10. Excerpt from "Girlness." Lynda Barry, *One Hundred Demons* (Seattle: Sasquatch Press, 2002), 184.

also that you boil pig's blood which is the reason for the smell" (54). Young Lynda is "shocked" by the idea that "your people," or Filipinos, have a particularly bad smell and takes this news to her grandmother, a "philosophical sort of person," who explains, "God has made every people! And every people makes ta-ee! And every ta-ee smells bad!" (57). Young Lynda looks unconvinced, but the narration reconciles with the past, remembering, "Our house smelled like grease and fish and cigs, like Jade East and pork and dogs, like all the wild food my Grandma boiled and fried. And if they could get <u>that</u> into a spray can I'd buy it" (60). In the article "A Graphic Self," Rocio Davis notes that in comics "the process of memory often involves the symbolic interrogation of particular artifacts, sensory details like the taste of specific food or the smell of a childhood home, brief conversations or episodes that resound emotionally in the author's memory" (268). This distinction certainly holds true for Barry's reminiscences in *One Hundred Demons*, which dwell at length on the smells of Barry's home, the taste of her favorite foods, and the smallest details of her youth.

"Common Scents" once again shows a young Lynda moving within the Filipino home community as well as the neighborhood white community. This is another instance in which Lynda "passes," a result of her light skin and red hair, thus giving her access to racism she might not otherwise encounter. There are then two more representations of Lynda, two more selves—the white Lynda as perceived by the neighbor girl and the Filipina Lynda as understood by her family. Lynda assumes the white identity to bond with the other children and hide from her ethnic identity. Lynda's grandmother, however, serves as the voice of reason, and the narrator with the wisdom of age now comes to accept her heritage, fondly recalling the scent of her home and wishing it could be bottled like the white community's pre-packaged air fresheners.

Barry juxtaposes multiple Lyndas, young and of middle age, to puzzle out her tangled relationships with femininity, race, and class in the strip "Girlness" (fig. 6.10). The initial panels contrast the tomboys on Lynda's street, a multi-ethnic group of girls with short hair, freckles, and Band-Aids who wear shorts and T-shirts as they scowl in front of their dark, tightly packed houses surrounded by telephone poles, with the "girlish girls" who lived "up where the houses were nicer" (184). These mostly white girls have long flowing hair and pretty flowered dresses and clutch pretty princess dolls as they pose, smiling, in front of a bright, well-tended home.

The images argue that class and race confer femininity, a notion confirmed by the next two panels, when a tomboy Lynda attempts to trade an empty Band-Aid box for a "super tressy doll" while the narration wonders, "If I had these things, would I have been a girlish girl too?" (185). Barry also links her ambivalence over girlness to the legacy of her mother, who was "quite feminine" and is depicted brushing her long black hair, with conspicuous red fingernails and a flower-print dress. The narration explains that Lynda's mother "loved girlish things but when she saw actual little girls with all the girlish accessories, it made her furious. It made me furious too. Furious envy exploded inside of me" (186). The older, adult narrator speculates that her mother must also have been jealous, particularly since her childhood in the Philippines was so "miserable." Lynda's mother is half Filipina, for her mother was Filipina but "her father was an American who died before" (187) the war began; thus, like her daughter, she experienced a mixed racial heritage. The narration wonders if it was the war that made her mother deny Lynda the luxury of enjoying girlish things, or whether it was simply her personality.

The tenth panel introduces Mariko, the only "girlish girl" on Lynda's street: "Her mother was from Japan. Her father was from Mexico. She was beautiful" (188). Mariko, like Lynda, comes from a diverse family, yet instead of denying her femininity, Mariko's mother forces her to become an extremely girlish girl, to the point when "mud on her pink tennis shoes" (189) makes her cry. The narration wonders, "Which was worse? Girlness that was insisted upon or girlness that was forbidden?" (190). Melinda de Jesús argues, "Maternal enforcement of narrowly defined gender identities hurts both Lynda and Mariko because it denies them the chance to construct their own versions of girlishness" ("Of Monsters" 17). Lynda and Mariko thus cannot claim their own gendered identity and unwillingly act out the tropes forced upon them by the dominant narratives of race and class as well as the power structures within their own families.

The adult Lynda does eventually reclaim her girlness from the control of others with help from a surrogate mother figure, an unlikely hero named Norabelle, a thirteen-year-old girl who rescues the adult Lynda, telling her she can reclaim her "girlness." Norabelle is depicted as a hybrid tomboy/girly girl. She wears her longish hair in a high ponytail and favors sporty striped T-shirts along with her bracelets and earrings. The adult Lynda takes Norabelle shopping, showering her with the girly items she once desired. When Norabelle tries to convince Lynda to buy herself the feminine "Super Monkey Head" stationery, she argues, "It was too frivolous, too girlish, too late" (192). But Norabelle will not be swayed, noting that "Super Monkey Head doesn't have an age limit. It's for everybody" (192). The narration contemplates, "Thank God the powerpuff girl was there to bring me to my senses, to remind me that the war was over, and that it's never too late for Super Monkey Head and her pals" (192). Now, removed from the class- and race-based narratives of femininity, as well as her mother's influence, Lynda finally crafts her own sense of what it is to be a girl, in the process acting as a mother and a daughter and finding a maternal role model in a teenage girl.

Barry ends the collection with yet another self-depiction, this time a photograph that pulls the reader out of the world of the comic and offers a metatextual commentary from the creator. As Roz Ivanic suggests in *Writing and Identity*, "Discussing the writer's identity places an act of writing in the context of the writer's past history, of their position in relation to their social context, and of their role in possible futures" (338). These photographs posit yet another identity for "Lynda Barry," anchoring the work in a simulacrum of the real. In the final pages the photographed version of the older, artist Lynda demonstrates how the readers can draw their own demons. This photographed Lynda looks much like the painted one; she sits at her drawing table surrounded by brushes, ink, ink stone, and other tools of the trade. She wears her trademark red bandana tied into a bow at the top of her head and can be seen drawing a demon, apparently *the* demon on the facing page; and the remnants of other sections, such as the panda bear from the strip "Lost and Found," are scattered around her. Light illuminates this small workspace and the rest of the space disappears. What follows is a photographed tutorial on how to paint one's personal demons. Heidi Benson contends, "Barry is not just a storyteller, she's an evangelist who urges people to pick up a pen—or a brush . . . and look at their own lives with fresh, forgiving eyes" (D1). This evangelist ends her lesson in demonology with a photograph of Barry painting another monster. But this time Lynda's face is bisected; the emphasis here is on the drawing of the demon on the work-table, not on the author herself. Although her image starts and ends the collection, in her final picture the attention shifts to the work and away from the autobiography of the woman and artist. Chute remarks that this photo indicates Barry's "refusal to perform the role of 'objective' correlate to her drawn self in order to authenticate the autobiographical subject" (*Graphic Women* 125). Through this photograph Barry disrupts the self-depiction to point the reader back into the fictionalized world, simultaneously inviting the audience to create their own scrapbook of selfhood and shifting the focus from her persona. The editors of *The Scrapbook in American Life* argue that

> scrapbooks, then, are a material manifestation of memory—the memory of the compiler and the memory of the cultural moment in which they were made. . . . [T]hey are but partial, coded, account—very small tellings of memory. Scrapbooks contain abundant hieroglyphics for the researchers who can decipher them, yet their often-enigmatic contents can stymie even the most patient scholar. (Tucker, Ott, and Buckler 3)

In *One Hundred Demons* Barry offers a personal, autobiographical project; but in assembling her work into a scrapbook of comic strips, collages, and tutorials, she remains elusive through these "small tellings of memory" that resist simple conclusions.

Demons and the Scrapbook

Why did Barry choose this scrapbook of strips, collages, and tutorials for her first foray into semiautobiographical comic art? *One Hundred Demons* allows Barry absolute control over her depiction of self as a girl. In her play *The Good Times Are Killing Me* Barry created a scene of girlhood through a play, but had to turn the script over to a director and actors who added their own thoughts and physical selves in order to embody her vision of girlhood. *Cruddy*, Barry's illustrated novel, focuses on a textual rendering of girlhood through the fictional heroine Roberta Rohbeson, but relies primarily on an image created in the reader's imagination that draws from his or her own lived experience and knowledge, thus limiting Barry's power of presentation. *Ernie Pook's Comeek*, her long-running weekly strip, was constrained by limits of print, space, time, and color, as well as the editorial influence of the newspapers themselves. With the help of new technology and an old

Figure 6.11. Collage page. Lynda Barry, *One Hundred Demons* (Seattle: Sasquatch Press, 2002), 50.

form, Barry finally turned to her own experiences of girlhood and chose to represent them with a pastiche incorporating her favored form of comics along with collected artifacts of her identity, all assembled in an artistic, multi-layered manner, stressing her many ways of seeing life as a girl.

Barry followed a long tradition in creating a scrapbook form to show-case her autobiographical work focusing on girlhood. For as Susan Tucker, Katherine Ott, and Patricia Buckler note, in recent years in particular "scrapbook and album making was considered a female activity, linked to traditional female concerns of holding families together and preserving nostalgic items" (10). Thus Barry's concentration on girlhood, preserving the small moments of childhood and surveying her family history, par-ticularly the females in her life, finds a reflection in the female-identified genre of the scrapbook. Barry seems to play with the gendered idea of the scrapbook in the collages, bringing in bits of ribbons, lace, flowers, and sparkly paint along with black demons, skulls smoking cigarettes, and vari-ous monsters (fig. 6.11). Furthermore, this format allows Barry to depict simultaneous selves in conversation through picture, word, and ephemera and forces the reader to make sense of these dialogues. This postmodern approach challenges a singular, unified identity much as comic artists like R. Crumb do, but Barry pushes this patchwork of selves into numerous incarnations—text based, comic-art based, photographed—as evidenced through supporting historical documents.

The final incarnation of *Demons* as scrapbook permits Barry, unlike many of her contemporaries in the comic art world, to frame her life and girlhood from numerous points of view and through different mediums simultaneously. While this approach suggests chaos or ataxia, and indeed this disorderly vision mirrors the confusion felt by the Lyndas, the resulting book itself is clearly the creation of an artist and author—though a multimedia, multifaceted portrayal of self, it is nonetheless an aesthetically pleasing one, shaped and formed into art.

When taken as a whole what does *One Hundred Demons* reveal about Barry's view of girlhood? The collection features a great many similarities with Barry's other works like *Ernie Pook's Comeek*, *The Good Times Are Killing Me*, and *Cruddy*, noting that the pivotal turning point for most girls is the juncture between grade school and junior high. For all of her heroines, the transition into junior high is the bridge to adulthood. Even the youngest of Barry's heroines, including the many young Lyndas of *Demons*, face adult concerns at an early age; they confront rape, incest, and violence well before junior high. The struggles of the young Lyndas suggest that Barry's ideas of the trials girls must meet stem from her own life experience and are not entirely fictive in nature. As with her other works, *Demons* suggests that adults are unreliable and cannot be counted on for help.

In fact, for the Lyndas the book argues that the best hope for a way out and happiness is to create another reality. In the final strip of the collection, "Lost and Found," Barry argues that happiness can be found in the creative process, a theme emphasized here and throughout Barry's works. The prefatory collage to the strip jumbles actual classifieds together with ribbon, stamps, a photo, and images from the strip into a colorful pastiche of found objects implying veracity and more fanciful objects calling attention to the created nature of the piece. The first four panels of the strip picture an adolescent Lynda (with the usual red hair, unflattering haircut, and multitudinous freckles) lying on her stomach, reading the classified ads in the newspaper. The narration explains, "After I learned to read, I loved getting home from school and waiting for the afternoon paper. . . . The first section I turned to was the classifieds. I always read the 'Lost and Found' ads . . . [and] each quarter-inch ad was like a chapter in a book" (208–9). In each of these ads the young Lynda was able to "fill in the blanks," inserting her own image into the vacant spaces, imagining dangerous situations that only she could resolve. An ad for a crypt conjures up the story of a vampire luring unsuspecting victims into his lair, while an ad for a wedding dress brings to mind innocent maidens being sacrificed. The ninth panel depicts a teenaged Lynda sitting at a desk writing in a diary—the flowery cursive transcript of the diary floats above her, "I thought Bill liked me but turns out he doesn't" (212). The narration reveals:

> When I read about writer's lives, there are usually stories about writing from the time they were little. I never wrote anything until I was a teenager, and then it was only a diary that said the same thing over and over. Writers talk about all the books they loved when they were children. Classic stories I never read, but I lied about because I was scared it was proof I wasn't really a writer. (212)

An older Lynda with glasses and a bow holds her hands in a prayer-like position while speaking to another women who is, according to an arrow, "super dramatically educated. Knows about 'story structure' and 'arc' and 'plot points'" (212). Lynda, who pretends to have read *Wind in the Willows*, is marked by an arrow indicating she is a "jive-ass faker who can't spell and has no idea what 'story structure' means" (212). The narration suggests that she loved reading *Reader's Digest* and especially "Hints from Heloise" as the panels flash back to a girl Lynda writing her own tip for Heloise. A flashforward in the fourteenth panel returns to teenager Lynda, who is denied entry into a creative writing class that is only for "advanced" students by Mrs. Snobaroo. The fifteenth panel jumps forward a bit more, depicting a college-aged Lynda writing a paper on *The Bell Jar* as the narration continues, "But only certain people were 'advanced' enough for writing and literature. In college it got even worse. I loved the wrong kind of writing and I never could break a story down to find the symbolic meaning, although I sure tried to fake it" (215).

This struggle to find voice, however, comes to an end, the narration argues, "when I started making comic-strips. It's not something a person has to be very 'advanced' to do. At least not in the minds of literary types" (215); and though the narrator suggests that she has found an outlet composing comics, there is also censure that this type of writing isn't valued by the literary community, as emphasized by the image of an adult Lynda holding a glass of wine and chatting with a couple who exclaim, "So you're a cartoonist! How adorable!" (215). Despite the condescension of the academic, literary community, as represented by Mrs. Snobaroo and the couple who find her profession "adorable," Lynda finally finds an outlet for her creativity that feels comfortable for her.

The narrator attempts to make peace with the lack of credibility in the next-to-last panel (fig. 6.12), noting, "Nobody feels the need to provide deep critical insight to something written by hand. Mostly they keep it as short

Figure 6.12. Excerpt from "Lost and Found." Lynda Barry, *One Hundred Demons* (Seattle: Sasquatch Press, 2002), 216.

as a want ad. The worst I get is, 'Too many words. Not funny. Don't get the joke.' I can live with that" (216).

Barry points to the commonly held idea of comics as humorous gag strips—a genre rather than a medium for representing a variety of forms including memoir, novel, instructional manual, and history, as well as humor. Still, the narrator decides she can accept the ignorance as long as she can keep doing her work. Below the narration an adult Lynda sits at her desk, pencil in hand, as an overhead light shines down on her, looking very much like the photograph of the actual Lynda Barry at the end of the book. Her text floats above the desk: "GALS, Ever felt so intimidated by the idea of writing that you've never even given it a try? Think writing is only for 'writers'? Sure is common!" (216). This bit of text directly addresses women, challenging the idea that writing is for someone else, such as the "super-dramatically" educated or the "advanced" students. In the final panel of the strip, and the book, the narration states, "Especially because I'm sure that the nine-year-old version of me who made up all those 'classified stories' would think that this one had a very happy ending" (216). The image returns to that of the nine-year-old Lynda, head in hands, lying on her stomach, reading the classifieds. She says, "Lost. Somewhere around puberty. Ability to make up stories. Happiness depends on it. Please write" (216). Thus the young Lynda speaks in the voice of the adult Lynda, decrying the loss of creativity of youth as it was drained by a society that told her she was not good enough. However, the act of the book and the author creating it from the fifteenth panel show the audience that the author has regained her "ability to make up stories" and that this is a happy ending. A little note in the same font as adult Lynda's text floats above the young Lynda, further commenting, "And Yes, Gals—the first thing I read in the paper is still the 'lost and found'" (216). In "Lost and Found" an older, wiser Lynda reconciles with her younger selves and promises hope for the future, a fulfilling life gained through self-expression.

This final strip reaffirms several of Barry's key views on girlhood expressed throughout *Demons* and in *Ernie Pook's Comeek*: escape through creativity and a celebration of ordinary moments. Even as the strips expose the trials of existing on the borders, as a Filipino Norwegian Irish girl who passes as white and as a girl who wears jeans and fears "super tressy" dolls, the scrapbook format itself celebrates the imagination and the reclamation of tiny, lost moments from life. Scrapbook scholars Tucker, Ott, and Buckler note, "The collage of the scrapbook more overtly juxtaposed the scraps of found or used objects with the memories of the compiler. The viewer must seek the hidden rhyme that connects the elements on the page" (17). The reader of *Demons* is thus challenged with finding the "rhyme," the creator piecing her identity together and thus reconciling with the girl of her past. Novelist Mary McCarthy once explained, "You really must *make* the self. It's absolutely useless to look for it, you won't find it, but it's possible in some sense to make it. . . . [Y]ou finally begin in some sense to make and to choose the self you want" (qtd. in Plimpton 241). Lynda Barry makes herself through the scrapbook of *One Hundred Demons*, reveling in this boundary-crossing artistic expression, creating an identity, and presenting her most personal representation of girlhood. This self, this voice, is certainly one constructed through invention, imagination, and remembrance, but it is also shaped through recalling and rendering the past, reassembling images of the self, and re-envisioning the story of a life.

Mirror, Mirror

REFLECTIONS ON GIRLHOOD AND GROWING UP

Tis' certain, the greatest magnifying glasses in the world are a man's own eyes, when they look upon his own person.
—ALEXANDER POPE, *The Works of Alexander Pope, Esq.*

After a turbulent, up and down career, Lynda Barry seems poised for a renaissance in popularity and critical acclaim. *Chicago Tribune* reporter Christopher Borrelli noted the important and underappreciated role Barry has played within the comics world in his 2009 article "Being Lynda Barry," citing as evidence the words of renowned contemporary comic artist Chris Ware, who believes "Lynda was the first cartoonist to write fiction from the inside out—she trusted herself to close her eyes and dive down within herself and see what she came up with. We'd still be trying to find ways into stories with pictures if she hadn't"; and scholar Ivan Brunetti, who posited, "She's become one of the most important cartoonists we have—however quietly people are recognizing it. She was first to do fictional comics that felt autobiographical, which is the draw today with graphic novels, and she was the first strong female voice in comics" (both qtd. in Borrelli). Barry, it would seem, is on the verge of resurgence, a revival her old friend Matt Groening says is "long overdue." (qtd. in Borrelli).

Indicative of her rising popularity, Drawn and Quarterly Press published Barry's visual Künstlerroman/writing workbook/philosophy text *What It Is* in 2008, followed by the companion drawing workbook entitled *Picture This* in 2010. In the do-it-yourself writing book *What It Is*, Barry begins with a reflection of her own development from young girl to artist and author through a loose, dreamy comic painted on legal paper without panels or borders. This amorphous representation of self showcases another way of seeing, one freed from the boundaries of a small comic strip or the confines of a text-based novel. Rather, this dreamlike form brings found artifacts together with Barry's words and self-portrait, offering another glimpse of Barry as a girl. Upon completion of her demonstration of the creative process through narrative and illustration, Barry then invites the reader to look in the mirror of his or her own experience, writing and creating personal images. *What It Is* is a curious collection, and Barry's representation of her growth from girl to artist offers a narrow, magnified autobiography along with a writing instruction manual. This hybrid Künstlerroman comic proselytizes the power of Barry's creative process, her young life bearing witness to the perils of not heeding one's artistic inclinations.

Barry followed the success of *What It Is* with the complementary text *Picture This*. If *What It Is* is a Künstlerroman, *Picture This* is the product of that artist's development, an art book that further shifts attention from the creator to the creative process. While a few loosely structured autobiographical comics do appear, depictions of the self are rare, and there is much less of a focus on educational materials or a structured course of study. Rather, *Picture This* introduces new fictional characters such as the "Near Sighted Monkey," as well as bringing back returning players, such as *Ernie Pook* characters Marlys, Maybonne, and Arna. As with her previous works, images of girls imagined and autobiographical appear throughout the text, representing moments of doubt and loss. While there is a sense of momentum and progression over the course of the book, *Picture This* is not constrained by a formal agenda or strict linear development, instead flowing and meandering from idea to idea while showcasing the creator's gorgeous paintings and lush collages.

Despite some differences, *What It Is* and *Picture This* both foreground many of the continuing themes and concerns that pervade Barry's entire oeuvre, and thus the works serve as a useful point from which to launch a consideration of Barry's diverse ways of seeing girlhood throughout her various projects and over her long career. After examining her latest works, the attention turns to an exploration of Barry's oeuvre thus far. What does Barry say about girlhood, and how do these multiple lenses reinforce her vision? This chapter concludes by considering Barry's many texts and genres focusing on girlhood, pondering the commonalities and lingering questions highlighted by her career.

Far different from the hand-stapled and collated books of Barry's early career, *What It Is* is a large, sturdy book; the 208-page hardcover measures just over eight and a half by eleven inches, and the cover features a colorful pastiche of images such as monkeys and monsters, as well as hand-printed text asking questions such as "Do you wish you could write?" and "What is an image?" The book is roughly divided into four sections, demarcated by variously colored borders. The blue-bordered opening section, entitled "What It Is," poses a series of questions such as "What is an idea made of?" handwritten on yellow legal paper with a patchwork of images surrounding the query. The collages surrounding the handwritten questions do not offer definitive answers, yet the collection of found images, paintings, and scrapbook pictures certainly meditates on the questions, sometimes suggesting a response or yet another line of inquiry.

The question pages rely heavily on scraps from vintage children's books and classroom textbooks, suggesting a nostalgic, melancholy return to youth. In a discussion with Sean Rogers for *Walrus Magazine*, Barry revealed that she found inspiration in the papers of Doris Mitchell, a grade-school teacher who saved her students' work over the years. Barry inherited Mitchell's papers and was particularly drawn to the scribbled work of the children, a great deal of which appears in the collages. These question collages reflect back to the interstitial scrapbook collages in *Demons*, which featured tiny artifacts from Barry's life such as photographs, forms and receipts, and found objects such as buttons and toys, juxtaposed with comic art. The collages from *What It Is*, though similar in aesthetics, feature more universal objects, such as pages from old textbooks, discarded letters, and a great deal of Doris Mitchell's stash of abandoned homework and lessons. These collages imply a broader story, rather than an individual one, and utilize the remains of childhood, in particular, to build a connection, rather than to shine insight into one individual's experience.

A narrative comic interrupts these free-form puzzles with the story of the author's life as an artist. Though not bound by the conventional comic panel format, the wordy narration coupled with images of childhood connects with Barry's enduring hallmarks. This visual Künstlerroman comic also expands on Barry's trademark style; the text and image are no longer divided by the traditional thick black line, nor is she limited by the strict confines of small panels. There is no need to crowd the images to the bottom of each box to make room for Barry's admittedly wordy style. Rather, the text and pictures mingle and mix, creating a relaxed, dreamy feeling. The blue-bordered section focuses on the girl's development as an artist as a way of establishing identity and instructing others in the importance of finding voice. This Lynda is no longer bound and isolated by panels or fictional warnings; rather, her story is told as a lesson and a cautionary tale.

The narrative comic chronicles the story of Barry's development as an artist. Barry opens with several images of herself as a young girl with red hair, freckles, and a bandage on her knee, reminiscent of the small self-depictions from *One Hundred Demons*. Lynda stares into space and is surrounded by fanciful figures—rabbits, butterflies, and sea creatures. The narration recalls, "When I was little, I played a certain staring game that seemed to have invented itself. I would hold as still as I could and make my eyes like a toy's eyes that don't move—and I would wait" (9). The narration explains that Lynda "believed there was another world that would show itself to [her] in the smallest ways. The gray kitten in the picture by my bed would accidentally blink his eyes. The girl in the picture would breathe. I believed there was another world—but I only noticed it when it became harder to get to" (11). Interestingly enough, for an artist and author who returns again and again to images of girls, the young Lynda finds a passageway into a magical world through the subtle, imagined breathing emanating from the picture of a girl.

The narration, interrupted with frequent questions and collages, recounts Lynda's search for imaginary friends and her fascination with television, a mechanism that provided her with both the solace of ready-made images of contentment and mind-numbing entertainment (53). The television also introduced Lynda to monsters that seemed very familiar, particularly the Gorgon, whose image turned anyone who gazed upon it into stone. She concludes, "That I had a very Gorgon-like mother never occurred to me, and if it had, I would have been lost. Did the Gorgon help me love my mother? I think she helped me very much" (66). The mother who appears in *One Hundred Demons* is similarly terrifying, but this is perhaps the author's most pointed and most straightforward commentary on their relationship.

As she grew, Lynda searched for the "aliveness" she felt as a child, copying the art of others, but "by the 5th grade most of us knew it was already too late" (80). Lynda continued to search for what she lost as a young girl, the magical reality she sensed in the picture of the cat that blinked and the young girl who exhaled: "There had been a time when a toy elephant was as alive as a real rabbit in the grass. I didn't know there were different kinds of aliveness, and two worlds contained by each other" (11). It was Marilyn Frasca, Barry's professor at Evergreen State College, who helped Barry return to her childlike perspective. The narration explains that as Frasca observed Lynda's many paintings, she said very little, but what Frasca was doing was "closer to the staring game I played in the trailer when I was little. . . . What is an image? It's the pull-toy that pulls you, takes you from one place to another. The capacity to roll seems to be what Marilyn's way of working brings back. . . . I would remember and forget about this for the next 30 years" (122). The narration implies that though Frasca gave her the tools to return to a childlike state of play, the narrator did not completely embrace the message at the time, instead "remembering and forgetting" the lesson for thirty years. Given this admission, *What It Is* can be seen as a performance designed in part to help others, but also to bear witness to past mistakes and self-doubt, creating a written record to defend against amnesia.

The next section, a didactic "Activity Book" bordered in peach, shifts the focus from her own experience to that of the audience, expounding on Barry's process for remembering the thrill of creation and promising to help anyone feel "the aliveness of images" (136) through the method Barry also espouses in the "Writing the Unthinkable" writing workshops she teaches around the country. After establishing the import of following one's creative impulses and not forgetting the joy of play through the Lynda figure from her own girlhood, Barry transfers her gaze to the audience. This is not necessarily an easy transition, for, as critics indicate,[1] much of the drama and interest in the book spring from the travails of Lynda's journey; but Barry's passion to the cause of educating the reader is very much in evidence in this section, a great deal of which was previously published as a mini-comic for "Free Comic Book Day" in 2007. Pascal Lefèvre notes, "The extradiegetic world can never be directly represented in the comic—except when a real mirror is pasted on the page" (161); but aside from pasting an actual mirror, Barry makes a clever attempt to shift the locus of control and vision to the reader. The audience is guided by Sea-ma, a friendly but rather dogmatic sea monster, and other guides, such as the Magic Cephalopod, who present a workbook designed to inspire others to write and find their own images. The next section, entitled "Let's Make a (Free/Do It Yourself) Writing Kit," is bordered in green and builds on the workbook, inviting readers to expand on the tutorials of the previous section, with Sea-ma guiding readers to develop their own tools to spark creativity and inspire writing about images.

The final section, bordered in orange, offers Barry's "Notes on Notes," a glimpse into her process for creating the book, a postscript to the work that compiles an assemblage of artifacts from the artist. It features cartoons, sketches, quotes and thoughts, and a peek into some of her successes and failures, such as the rejected cover for a new Penguin edition of *Little Women*, which was turned down because it was not "Lynda Barry enough—the art director says it doesn't look like my work which makes me laugh a little and also cry a little" (200). Clearly, even an accomplished cartoonist like Barry suffers rejection and misunderstanding; she has become victim to her own popularity and is punished for not producing work in the same style. By including this disappointment, Barry makes it clear that she proselytizes this process not for commercial gain, obviously uncertain even for recognized artists and authors, but for more personal satisfaction.

While audience interaction remains a theme throughout Barry's works, *What It Is* represents her most rousing and direct call to action. In past comic art projects Barry carefully distanced herself with disclaimers of "autobific-tionalography." This time, however, the version of Lynda represented in the text is an autobiographical version of the self. There is no distancing through a fictional lens, and this unabashed representation of the author is offered as a point of connection with readers, a way of inspiring the reader to learn from "Lynda Barry's" life and to set out on his or her own creative journey. *What It Is* thus marked new territory for Barry, a project which purports to authenticity (or at least doesn't deny the possibility) in depicting her own journey as an artist and does so with the expressed intention of setting the audience on a similar path. This life story is told for a reason; she is a lesson to all readers that they must embrace creativity in their own lives through Barry's method. Bart Beaty argues that "autobiography in comics holds the possibility of giving the author birth for the first time" (144), and it would seem that Barry aspires to birth not only for herself (or an image of herself) but for the audience as well.

In *What It Is* the figure of a young Lynda Barry stands as a locus of loss, the point at which Lynda lost hope. What happened? The narration comments, "No one told me the print on the wall was just ink and paper and had no life of its own. At some point the cat stopped blinking, and I stopped thinking it could" (12). What is clear is that for this particular girl, "Lynda Barry," growing up is presented, as scholar Charlotte White perceives of most girls in literature, as "overwhelmingly negative" (197). The Lynda of *What It Is* has a terrible home life, a Gorgon of a mother, an unforgiving school, and not even an imaginary friend to confide in. She thus calls upon words and images to save her. "Thanks to a supermarket give-away" (27), the girl received four books, "*Tales by the Brothers Grimm,* and *Hans Christian Andersen, The Arabian Nights,* and *Heidi*" (27). These books allowed her to endure because "paper and ink have conjuring abilities of their own. Arrangements of lines and shapes, of letters and words on a series of pages make a world we can dwell and travel in" (38). This conjuring, this magic of sorts, did not provide an escape for Lynda, but a way to carry on. The narration argues that stories "can't transform your actual situation, but they can transform your experience of it. We don't create a fantasy world to escape reality, we create it to be able to stay" (40). The young girl from *What It Is* learns to find another world that makes her reality bearable through the power of images. Furthermore, in the book, Barry as narrator and shaper of the text chases the magic that is lost to the adult world, and she invites her reader to join with her, following the images and hopefully setting out on his or her own journey. The key to happiness, Barry seems to say, is to return to the innocence and expectation she felt as a young girl before she lost the ability to imagine.

Barry followed up on her enthusiastic call for personal expression through writing as presented in *What It Is* with another invitation to readers, this time to reclaim artistic pursuits in 2010's *Picture This*, an activity book that asks, "Why do we stop drawing?" and encourages readers to experiment with various artistic styles. Although similar in its heuristic nature to *What It Is*, *Picture This* differs in meaningful ways. *What It Is* loosely follows the format of Barry's "Writing the Unthinkable" workshops and features the collage question pages and the autobiographical comics in addition to the step-by-step, how-to writing workbook exercises that guide the reader through her writing process. *Picture This* is more of a meta-cognitive book, a picture of Barry's process laid bare and meditated upon by a cast of new and returning characters. The result is a less structured, even dreamier quality than *What It Is*. *Ernie Pook* characters Marlys, Arna, and Maybonne return, along with some of the figures from *What It Is*, like the Magic Cephalopod and the Meditating Monkey. The Near Sighted Monkey, a muse and trickster figure wearing a red bandanna very similar to one frequently worn by the actual Lynda Barry, arrives with a pet chicken and is depicted with bright watercolors on various discarded scraps of paper, getting into trouble and urging the audience to have fun and get messy. Fan favorite character Marlys is frequently depicted throughout the book as an exuberant paper doll to play with or as a picture the reader can color. Following the philosophy of the precursor *What It Is*, the audience is invited to engage with the figure of the girl, playing with her and reclaiming creativity.

Picture This is divided into four "magazines," one devoted to each of the seasons. The book opens with "Winter" (bordered in blue), which asks readers to try various art exercises, including collecting odds and ends and making scrap collages, creating cotton-ball chickens, covering pictures in dots, and working with various brushes. In the "Spring" magazine (bordered in green) Barry introduces mood doodles and the joy of painting with cotton swabs while exploring her own history when she "realized " she "couldn't draw" as a girl (102) and explaining how her famous characters from *Ernie Pook* came to be and "quickly took over" her comic strip (116). The "Summer" magazine (bordered in peach) focuses on using colors, while the "Fall" section (bordered in brown) expounds on the power of handwriting and the importance of drawing not only pictures, but also words, as Barry did to draft her illustrated novel *Cruddy*.

There are snippets of comics and scraps of autobiographical sequences interspersed across the magazines, but there are fewer autobiographical comics in *Picture This* than in *What It Is*. Lynda the girl appears again, once more at the moment she loses the ability to draw and create. This time the figure of Lynda as a girl is joined by other fictional girls, *Ernie Pook* characters Arna and Marlys, and these young women also struggle with the desire to explore artistic pursuits. In fact, one of the opening comics suggests that Arna has picked up *Picture This* at the local library and is struggling with expressing herself through art, an example of *mise en abyme* as Arna mirrors the readers' experience of reading the text within the text itself. In the comic Marlys wants to depart the library and urges Arna to leave the book behind, and when the two girls return to the library at the end of the *Picture This*, the branch has closed and Arna cannot get the book again. Although Marlys and Arna are shown drawing and coloring and trying some of Barry's techniques throughout the text, in the conclusion there is a sense of loss and closure, a dead end of sorts, as it becomes clear that they have lost the world of ideas as represented by the library and have entered the moment of adulthood when they realize they cannot draw.

Barry underscores the dark forces that discourage creativity in the frequent faux advertisements from "Don't Cigarettes." Barry thus links the negative influences and naysayers to a product widely disparaged as damaging and unhealthy; and many of the adults dissuading any type of artistic endeavor, such as Lynda's mother and the almost-adult Maybonne, are portrayed smoking. In one tiny advertisement the copy reads, "You're about to make a picture. Have a Don't instead. It's Safer. You're not any good. You waste time" (212). However, many of the creative gurus of the book, including Mr. Beak, the Near Sighted Monkey, and even the Meditating Monkey, also smoke, yet these characters frequently draw and create for pleasure. Perhaps these figures have conquered the "Don't's," the disapproving voices, and choose to create in spite of any fears or doubts.

While *What It Is* draws heavily on school papers such as old homework, textbooks, and teacher notes, giving the book an educational sheen and underscoring the didactic nature of the text, *Picture This* pulls from more diffuse sources and has a broader, less specific feel. However, both books expand the boundaries of comic art as instructional manuals, as evidenced by the difficulty many stores have in shelving the books. Are they graphic novels? Self-help books? Autobiography? Barry has created yet another interdisciplinary and category-crossing genre to showcase her talents in these two works. Certainly, the different sections, styles, and formats contained within *What It Is* and *Picture This* demonstrate Barry continuing to explore and create and extend her artistic endeavors, evolving and changing her approach and illustrating different ways of seeing. As an artist and author Barry constantly expands and diversifies, experimenting with new methods and genres. Yet figures of girls remain at the center across her works. From *What It Is* in 2008 and *Picture This* in 2010 all the way back to the early *Two Sisters Comeek* from 1979, the image that recurs throughout Barry's oeuvre is that of the girl.

Some authors write novels about girls. Others draw pictures about girls. Still others create comics about girls. Barry does all of these things, not content to settle in just one genre or style. Barry's work ranges from primarily picture-based, such as the portraits in *Naked Ladies!,* to her text-based essays and articles, with her comic art, featuring both text and picture, falling somewhere along the middle of the spectrum. Barry also plays with notions of truth and fiction, creating the highly fictional, extremely hyperbolic horror novel *Cruddy* and writing straightforward, matter-of-fact essays for the newspaper. Barry further experiments with style and artistic rendering, trying her hand at painting, collage, comics, and pen-and-ink drawings. Barry even ventures into drama, dabbling with motion and sound and expanding her idea for *The Good Times Are Killing Me* into a play. Barry's oeuvre offers many genres, many lenses, many girls, and many ways of seeing, creating a multidimensional perception and a superlative perspective on girlhood. Barry's approach places images of girls in contrast with one another: an embodied performer enacting a girl on the stage, as opposed to a word-based description of a girl in a novel, juxtaposed against a visual illustration of a girl, compared with the complex interaction of text and image that depicts a girl in a comic strip. Barry expertly explores the divergences and points of connection amongst these many images of the girl, utilizing complementary modes of representation to reveal a polyscopic ontology of girlhood. Throughout Barry's extensive, multivalent representation of the lives of girls, what ideas and themes predominate?

Barry's girls reflect the world they live in, which is collectively represented as a dark and dangerous place. Countering any idealized representations of idyllic childhoods, Barry unerringly portrays society as a destructive, punishing force and adulthood as a stultifying burden. Race, class, and misogyny conspire to pull people apart, and girls should be aware and afraid of a brutal culture that rapes and molests young females. Racism taints the friendship of Edna and Bonna in *The Good Times Are Killing Me*, creeping in and poisoning their bond, altering their relationship, and polluting the adolescent girls who eventually choose to accept and play out their parts in a racist society. Violence reigns when a faceless man molests a little Lynda in

One Hundred Demons and on a dark night when a gang of boys rape a young woman in *Ernie Pook's Comeek* while Marlys and Maybonne watch in terror. In *Cruddy*, Roberta Rohbeson witnesses a litany of horrors including murder, decapitation, and sexual violation, not to mention unceasing physical and mental abuse. In Barry's creations, girls occupy a very perilous position.

Unfortunately, these girls cannot look to adults for any kind of assistance. With a few exceptions, the adult contingent is either absent or malicious and vindictive. Adults continually abuse and assault the girls, taking advantage of them and using them for their own pursuits and pleasures. Parents, the adults in roles generally assumed to provide protection and guidance in a hazardous environment, are often the most appalling of the lot. From Roberta's murderous, vindictive parents, so terrible as to only be known as "the Mother" and "the Father," to Lynda's own absent father and Gorgon-like mother in *Demons*, *What It Is*, and *Picture This*, adults, especially one's own parents, are best feared and avoided.

As to the young women themselves, Barry creates an uncompromising and multifaceted depiction of girls, freckles and all. Throughout her many genres and mediums Barry utilizes various techniques, from harrowing textual descriptions to terrifying visual portraits, to depict a bleak, dangerous, and ultimately destructive landscape to be maneuvered with skill and care by her heroines. These girls stand out amidst the darkness, a striking contrast in their complexity and grittiness, in character and representation. These are not pretty girls. In *Cruddy*, Roberta offers the self-representation, "I'm what people might call a dog" (60), and in *Ernie Pook's Comeek*, Maybonne also refers to herself as a "dog." Readers conjure up images of girls based on Barry's words, forced to fashion and identify with unbecoming heroines. While in the world of comic art girls are often portrayed as sweet and lovely in appearance and disposition, Barry steadfastly illustrates unattractive girls and, in her opinion, is therefore labeled a poor draftsman. Barry explained in a personal interview that despite evidence to the contrary, "people think if you make homely characters, particularly girl characters, if you make homely girl characters, it must be because you can't draw."[2] Given their appearance, the girls across the genres challenge notions of femininity and beauty in a culture in which a girl's worth, even that of comic strip character, is often judged primarily by appearance. In a society rife with beauty pageants for prepubescent girls and even the seemingly innocuous but always attractive *American Girls* dolls, these girls represent a reality rarely seen in popular culture: real-looking girls. For some readers and critics this reality is so incomprehensible it must be indicative of a mistake or lack of skill on the part of the artist. Barry also challenges society's preoccupation with beauty through the content of strips like "Girlness" from *One Hundred Demons*, which tackles the trap of femininity, and through the obsessive preoccupation with appearance from figures like Maybonne Mullens in *Ernie Pook*. These girls never stop feeling inferior based on their appearance. Barry reinforces the value of all girls by continuing to illustrate them as imperfect and unattractive and refusing the ever-popular makeover montage, instead focusing on the struggles of young females in a beauty-obsessed culture.

While the girls of Barry's universe are not made of "everything nice," nor do they please the eye with their attractiveness, despite their harsh environs the girls are represented as capable. Each of the girls featured in Barry's works faces a cruel and unforgiving society and must make her way the best she can. The girls endure and at times even find some measure of happiness. However, some clearly reach greater heights than others. Some, like *The Good Times Are Killing Me*'s Edna and Bonna, manage to maintain the status quo but find no happiness in the outcome. Others, like *Ernie Pook*'s Maybonne Mullens, make do only to dwell in dreary melancholy. In *Cruddy*, Roberta Rohbeson carries on through unspeakable horrors until such time as she chooses to live through her words rather than deeds. Exuberant Marlys Mullens obviously succeeds in achieving a great deal of self-fulfillment, never accepting negative criticism and remaining ever hopeful. The multiple Lyndas as depicted in *One Hundred Demons*, *What It Is*, and *Picture This*, following Marlys's lead, also find satisfaction in returning to a childlike state of play and take strides to create an identity through personal history and self-expression.

Action seems to be key in the advancement of Barry's girls, perhaps not surprising since Barry encourages her audience to actively participate in making meaning from her strips, sometimes by coloring in *Naked Ladies*, or perhaps by filling in the blanks as requested in *Ernie Pook*, or even by drawing their own monsters in *One Hundred Demons*. In order to thrive or in some cases manage to survive, the girls must act. Maybonne Mullens, the resident melancholy teenager of *Ernie Pook*, watches the world passively, bemoaning her fate. She consequently suffers from depression and seems to have only spurious friends and very few triumphs. Maybonne's sister Marlys, however, acts swiftly and decisively, barreling into every situation and making her presence known. Marlys chooses to dive in regardless of the situation. Edna Arkins, the lead in *The Good Times Are Killing Me*, much like Maybonne, reacts to events around her but rarely takes action. When she witnesses racism and the slighting of her friend Bonna Willis, Edna fails to take a stand, instead rationalizing the events so as not to take action. Edna thus watches passively as her friendship with Bonna falls apart, resigned that this is simply the way things have to happen.

Action is required of Barry's girls, but simply engaging with the world is not enough to flourish. The girls must also act in such a way as to lead themselves away from the corruption and disillusionment of adulthood and back toward the hope and magic of childhood. Edna eventually does make some choices, deciding to ignore racism and pursue a friendship with the more popular girls, thus setting her on the path to separation. Her friend Bonna Willis also makes bad choices, denigrating Edna and mocking her, which ultimately leads to a violent slap and the utter dissolution of their bond. The two girls have clearly stepped actively into the adult world of racism, violence, and ugliness. Roberta Rohbeson, the girl featured in *Cruddy*, is perhaps Barry's most active heroine, but can certainly not be deemed a rousing success. Roberta learns to adapt to the horror and brutality of the world, boldly killing those who wish to do her harm and carefully preparing for the future with the help of her favorite knife, Little Debbie. Roberta, however, cannot live in this warped world; and though she survives through engagement rather than submission, it is only so that she can make the choice to kill herself. Action in and of itself is not enough.

Barry's heroines are most successful when they pursue their childlike exuberance and return to a state of imaginative play. For Barry's girls, crossing the border into adulthood brings inescapable angst and anxiety; and to return to, or continue to dwell in, a younger, more hopeful and imaginative place brings fulfillment. Again and again, Barry points to the juncture of junior high as a pivotal moment, in which the girls lose an essential element of naïve hope and whimsy that is replaced by an adult's concerns and expectations. Bonna and Edna can no longer be friends when they go to junior high; as Edna explains, "We all automatically split into groups of who was alike" (*Good Times* 100). Lynda from *Demons* "realized how lame [she] really was" (103) upon entering junior high, and the contrast between the older Maybonne's moping and depression and Marlys's joy and bliss in *Ernie Pook* clearly illustrates the effects of junior high in indoctrinating girls into the harsh constraints of adulthood.

Barry depicts the girls achieving some measure of happiness when they shake off the bonds of adulthood and revel in imagination. Barry contends that play allows one to handle the angst of the world and, as she explained to Sean Rogers, "to manage anxiety." For these girls and for Barry, this sort of play is necessary for survival. Bonna and Edna come together through a shared love of music, dancing and singing together and cementing their bond, and Barry posits that music is one way to access a childlike state of earnest play.[3] Edna wonders "why just hearing a certain song can make a whole entire time of your life suddenly just rise up and stick in your brain" (*Good Times* 9), and for Edna and Bonna it is through music that they find a positive connection. Roberta enjoys the simple creativity of making sock monkeys while eating pudding as a change from her sojourn in the corruption of the adult world. In the strip "Girlness," the character of Lynda realizes the delights of youthful whimsy, deciding that it is not too late to embrace her playful side, concluding that "it's never too late for Supermonkeyhead and her pals" (192). Norabelle, a thirteen-year-old girl and "<u>true</u> powerpuff girl" leads the adult Lynda to a sense of wholeness, inviting her to finally embrace "girlness," buying silly Super Monkey Head stationery and accepting the young, feminine side of herself. This time it is a young girl, Norabelle, who actively campaigns on behalf of fantasy and fun, becoming the hero who saves the adult.

Barry's most successful or at least happiest heroine, Marlys Mullens, fully delights in wonder, actively pursuing her own agenda of general self-aggrandizement and indulging in imaginative play. Marlys suffers disappointments and brushes with the stark realities of life but chooses instead to never abandon hope, always believing in her own worth and in the possibility of the fantastic in everyday life. In her final comments in *The Best of Marlys,* Barry states, "[Marlys] helped me make some sense of things that I never had words for before. She became the imaginary friend I'd always wanted." Marlys appears as the girl who stands out amidst the backdrop of bleak adulthood to show another way. She illustrates her philosophy in "Valentine," a 2000 comic from *Ernie Pook's Comeek*, in which she creates a secret valentine, despite her cousin Arnold's teasing (fig. 7.1). Arnold says that "nobody wants her home-made valentine, a heart sent by anonymous is going in the trash," and taunts Marlys with the news that everyone believes her to be a "spaz." But Marlys continues on, unconcerned, responding, "If they throw it away, <u>no big,</u> *it still counts*. It still <u>totally</u> counts." Marlys's cousin Arna observes the careful construction of the valentine and narrates the strip. Marlys gives her heart, covered with "glitter sparkles," freely and anonymously, knowing that it does "count" and will make a difference. In spite of the pessimism of the outside world, as so ably demonstrated by Arnold, Marlys takes the valentine and "waves it so that the sparkles catch the light, says if her heart lands in the garbage, well, it won't be there for long." Marlys refuses to be dissuaded from her goal; she carefully crafts an emblem of her love and decorates it with glitter and sparkles and offers it up to the world. She has an unassailable knowledge that her gesture will be

Figure 7.1. "Valentine." Lynda Barry, *The! Greatest! of! Marlys!* (Seattle: Sasquatch Books, 2000).

received, and should either her literal or metaphorical heart be discarded, it will not remain there long. Who is this mystery valentine for? In the final panel Marlys turns the valentine over, revealing a letter *A*. The valentine is for Arna. Marlys will always rebound and continually, actively sends her love (decorated in sparkles, of course) out to her cousin and out into the world.

In *What It Is* and *Picture This* Lynda Barry follows Marlys's lead, reclaiming her belief in possibility—a picture of a cat might blink and the image of a girl might exhale if she waits for it to happen. In *Demons* and the two workbooks Barry also demonstrates another key to success for several of her girls, particularly those autobiographical ones—the power to author oneself through creative pursuits. Roberta achieves a melding of identities and a degree of immortality through shaping her narrative *Cruddy*, though given her past she feels unable to continue on in the physical world. And while the various incarnations of girlhood Lynda Barrys cannot actually re-experience childhood, in embracing the unwavering optimism of Marlys, the author can revisit her childhood and for that matter her entire life, making peace with her mistakes and authoring her own identity. In *One Hundred Demons* Barry returns to the monsters and trials of her life to find the truth of the experience and embrace the person she has become. In the book the figure of Lynda creates her own happy ending through the creative process, writing and illustrating an escape from her monsters and a way back to the hope and imagination of her youngest self. In *What It Is* and *Picture This* Barry asks her readers to join her, returning to the images of the girls (and boys) they once were. In a personal interview Barry posited that she is an "image wrangler. Yeah, that's what I am. I'm the image whisperer," and she finds great joy when she gets to "see the aliveness" in people when they follow their images.[4] Barry has become an ambassador of sorts, proselytizing the power of her creative process. But behind this technique and behind her many young girls there is a message from the cartoonist often noted for her expert skill in depicting childhood: Life is tough, and the only way to not just endure but to prosper is to be a girl who still believes in *and* makes her own magic.

NOTES

Preface

1. Lynda Barry, personal interview with author, Rhinebeck, NY, 19 July 2006.

2. In *Iconology* Mitchell suggests that "image" can be a very slippery term, since a "wide variety of things . . . go by this name" (9). Mitchell also points out that "image" means different things in different disciplines, for "each branch of this family tree designates a type of imagery that is central to the discourse of some intellectual discipline" (10).

3. See Melinda de Jesús, "Liminality and Mestiza Consciousness in Lynda Barry's *One Hundred Demons*," *MELUS* 29.1 (Spring 2004): 219–52, and "Of Monsters and Mothers: Filipina American Identity and Maternal Legacies in Lynda Barry's *One Hundred Demons*," *Meridians: Feminism, Race, Transnationalism* 5.1 (2004): 1–26; as well as Theresa Tensuan, "Comic Visions and Revisions in the Work of Lynda Barry and Marjane Satrapi," *Modern Fiction Studies.* 52.4 (Winter 2006): 948–64; Miriam Harris, "Cartoonists as Matchmakers: The Vibrant Relationship of Text and Image in the Work of Lynda Barry," in *Elective Affinities: Testing Word and Image Relationships,* ed. Catriona MacLeod, Véronique Plesh, and Charlotte Schoell-Glass (Amsterdam: Rodopi Press, 2009), 129–43; and Hillary Chute's chapter on Barry in *Graphic Women* (New York: Columbia, 2010).

Chapter 1

1. Lynda Barry, personal interview with author, Rhinebeck, NY, 19 July 2006.

2. Ibid.

3. Scholars differ on the most appropriate terminology when discussing comics; Lynda Barry prefers to designate her work as "drawing with words," rather than the more frequently utilized terms like *comics, comic art,* or *cartoons.* In a personal interview she explicated: "The only reason I called it drawings with words was because the word *comics* isn't the right word. *Graphic novel* isn't the right word either. I don't know if there's a right word for it. *Children's book* isn't the right word, but that's what they usually call something that has pictures with words. I don't know that there's a word for it. At least there hasn't been a word that satisfies me." While acknowledg-

ing the slipperiness of terminology in the comics field and recognizing Barry's own preferences, for simplicity this study uses the term *comics* to refer to both the short forms, such as the comic strip, and long forms, such as the graphic novel and comic book. Although these differing forms entail special needs and requirements, for this more general discussion the broader terminology is utilized.

4. Barry, personal interview.

5. Ibid.

6. Interview with Joe Garden, 8 December 1999, http://www.avclub.com/content/node/24257, accessed March 2008.

7. Barry, personal interview.

8. Ibid.

9. Ibid.

Chapter 2

1. Lynda Barry, personal interview with author, Rhinebeck, NY, 19 July 2006.

2. Ibid.

3. All quotes from Marilyn Frasca are from a personal e-mail communication of 26 August 2007.

4. Barry, personal interview.

5. Frasca, e-mail.

6. Ibid.

7. Ibid.

8. Ibid.

9. Lynda Barry, e-mail communication, 9 July 2007.

10. Ibid.

11. Robert Roth, phone interview with author, 19 July 2007.

12. Barry, personal interview.

13. Barry, e-mail.

14. Barry, personal interview.

15. The *Naked Ladies!* coloring book is not paginated, thus quotations from the text do not indicate page number.

16. As Hillary Chute points out in *Graphic Women*, Barry's spoken-word compact disc *The Lynda Barry Experience* recounts the opening scene in a piece entitled "Naked Ladies" in much the same language as the coloring book (104). However, in the "Warning" on the CD, Barry suggests that "the stories you are about to hear are true, except for the ones that are big honking lies," thus blurring the lines of fiction and autobiography.

17. Barry, personal interview.

18. Ibid.

19. Ibid.

20. David Astor, "Fewer Cartons in *Village Voice*," *Editor & Publisher Magazine* 19 July 1997: 64.

21. Barry, personal interview.

Chapter 3

1. Analysis of the pictures is based on the reproductions included under the title "Music Notebook" at the end of the 1988 version of *The Good Times Are Killing Me*, published by Real Comet Press. Later editions of the novel feature different black-and-white pictures illustrating the characters and situations featured in the narration and do not include the portraits that inspired the novel. Readers can only speculate on the experience of viewing the pictures as a collection in a gallery/coffeehouse setting, as the works are now held in private collections. While the experience of viewing the art in a gallery is transient, the pictures themselves endure.

2. "Time and Place" notes from the 1991 version of *The Good Times Are Killing Me*, published by Samuel French.

3. Ibid.

4. Lynda Barry, personal interview, Rhinebeck, NY, 19 July 2006.

5. Unfortunately, this analysis is forced to rely on the text of the play, only imagining the experience of the performance.

6. In the book *Picture This* (2010) Barry creates faux advertisements for "Don't Cigarettes," which come to represent negative impulses and inclinations.

Chapter 4

1. See Nick Hornby, "Draw What You Know," *New York Times* 22 December 2002: F10; and Alice Sebold, "Writing Outside," *LA Weekly* 30 May 2003: 26. Barry noted Spiegelman's dismay over her wordiness in a personal interview with the author in Rhinebeck, NY, on July 19, 2006.

2. Lewis Carroll, *Alice in Wonderland* (New York: Samuel Gabriel Sons & Company, 1916), Project Gutenberg Ebook, 12 August 2006.

3. Lynda Barry, personal interview with author, Rhinebeck, NY, 19 July 2006.

4. Ibid.

5. Ibid. Barry expressed that one chapter from the fourth draft of the manuscript "didn't quite ring" and was ultimately cut from the book.

6. When *Cruddy* was published, some critics had difficulty accepting Barry as a novelist rather than a comic artist. Benjamin Weissman argued:

> *Cruddy*, a work of serious fiction, has been met with some skepticism; the literary world appears to have little interest in a person whose primary mission is drawing pictures and writing dialogue in word balloons for little made-up characters published in the back pages of a fish wrap. . . . But Barry is one of the most amusing, character-driven comic artists in America, and *Cruddy* is a brilliant illustrated novel that deserves attention and praise. (55)

Some critics were willing to look at the book without prejudice, including Alanna Nash of the venerable *New York Times*, who wrote:

"Cruddy" can be an uncomfortable read—Barry spares no repulsive description of the dark doings here, and a rotting stench and the swarming of flies seem to follow everywhere. But the author's ability to capture the paralyzing bleakness of despair, and her uncanny ear for dialogue, make this first novel a work of terrible beauty.

Like Nash, many critics struggled with the discomfiting darkness of the work, including one reviewer from *Entertainment Weekly* who felt "her story is so heartbreakingly macabre that it can actually be painful to read" (review of *Cruddy*).

7. Barry struggled to convince Simon & Schuster to include the illustrations. Barry told Carrie Rickey that she "met with tremendous resistance from the publisher. . . . I was told that people would take the book less seriously if there were pictures in it." Barry remained stalwart and the illustrations remained.

8. In an interview with Benny Shaboy, Barry explained the process of creating the images, a procedure that included finger painting with watercolors and sumi ink, followed by line work.

9. The point of view for a few of the images, such as that on the cover, is unclear. They might be from another perspective or, as is suggested by the framing, are from Roberta's perspective as she looks at a mirrored reflection.

10. This analysis draws from William F. Edmiston, "Focalization and the First-Person Narrator: A Revision of the Theory," *Poetics Today* 10:4 (Winter 1989): 729–44; and Luc Herman and Bart Vervaeck, *Handbook of Narrative Analysis* (Lincoln: U of Nebraska P, 2005).

11. The following sections thus identify the main character's primary identity as "Roberta," while acknowledging the multiplicity of her identities.

12. There are no illustrations of Clyde, though many of the illustrations are from his/her perspective.

13. Roberta bears interesting similarities to what Carol Clover calls the "Final Girl" in horror films, as the last main character alive to tell the story.

14. Phoebe Gloeckner's 2002 book, *The Diary of a Teenage Girl*, shares many commonalities with *Cruddy*. Gloeckner's book, labeled "An Account in Word and Pictures," features a "Note of Caution to the Reader" similar to Roberta's initial address to the readers and follows a diary-like format reminiscent of *Cruddy*. While *The Diary of a Teenage Girl* is not as violent as *Cruddy*, the book also depicts the dark, disturbing trials of growing up as a girl.

Chapter 5

1. Although academic analysis of *Ernie Pook's Comeek* is rare, there are a few scholarly studies addressing the weekly strip, including "Selfhood and Trauma in Lynda Barry's Autobifictionalography," a chapter from Emma Tinker's 2008 thesis available at http://emmatinker.oxalto.co.uk/thesis, accessed November 28, 2010; and "Maybonne and Me," a chapter from *Seeking Passage: Post-Structuralism, Pedagogy,*

Ethics, by Rebecca A. Martusewicz (New York: Teachers College Press, 2001); as well as Darcy Sullivan's "Kids at the Abyss: Lynda Barry's *Come Over, Come Over,*" *The Comics Journal,* 140 (February 1991): 43–45.

2. Christopher Borrelli, "Being Lynda Barry," *Chicago Tribune* 8 March 2009.

3. Lynda Barry, personal interview, Rhinebeck, NY, 19 July 2006.

4. The political diatribes of Fred Milton, beat poet poodle, would make for an interesting analysis. Freddie Mullens also presents an intriguing representation of a boy's life, particularly in the collection *The Freddie Stories* from 1999.

5. This project draws from original comics as seen in various newspapers as well as the strips as presented in anthologies. While the anthologies have the advantage of grouping strips with similar themes, many of them break up the original four-panel-square format, putting two panels on each page.

6. Barry, personal interview.

7. Ibid.

8. Ibid.

9. Ibid.

10. Marlys, Maybonne, and Arna are the most frequent narrators, but not the only ones. Freddie Mullens and Fred Milton and occasional guests also narrate intermittently.

11. Barry, personal interview.

12. The ideas of "focalization" and "ocularization" become particularly tricky as they are defined and employed differently from scholar to scholar. Adapted from literary theory and film theory, these terms seem to be utilized with varying meanings from article to article amongst comic scholars. Their use is further complicated by differing definitions of "internal" and "external" focalization and ocularization. This analysis will attempt to define usage within the context of this particular examination, while acknowledging the disparate notions of the concepts and the confusion surrounding these contested terms.

13. See Driest, Morgan, Badman, Parent, Shamoon, Groensteen, and A. Miller. While all of these scholars utilize narratological theory, they differ on definitions of key terms such as focalization and ocularization.

14. According to his article "Points of View: 'First Person' in Comics," Derik Badman would call this "fixed internal focalization" because the narrative is controlled by the narrator's "cognitive point of view," while the panels are also in "zero ocularization," as the literal point of view is not from any one character's point of view. Harry Morgan, however, would most likely argue for a simple external focalization, an external point of view, and most other comic scholars ignore ocularization altogether.

15. Interestingly enough, Bill Keane also utilized this strategy in Barry's beloved *Family Circus,* with Billy occasionally "taking over" for Keane and illustrating the strip with a childlike manner.

16. Derik Badman calls this "secondary internal ocularization," which shows "the character/viewer's point of view" ("Points of View").

Chapter 6

1. Hillary Chute's book *Graphic Women: Life Narrative and Contemporary Comics* (New York: Columbia UP, 2010) provides extended analysis of selected works of five female comic artists, Aline Kominsky-Crumb, Phoebe Gloeckner, Lynda Barry, Marjane Satrapi, and Alison Bechdel.

2. Lynda Barry, personal interview, Rhinebeck, NY, 19 July 2006.

3. See Susan Tucker, Katherine Ott, and Patricia P. Buckler, eds., *The Scrapbook in American Life* (Philadelphia: Temple UP, 2006).

4. *One Hundred Demons* enjoys more scholarly attention than Barry's other works. In particular, see Melinda de Jesús, "Liminality and Mestiza Consciousness in Lynda Barry's *One Hundred Demons*," *MELUS* 29.1 (Spring 2004): 219–52, and "Of Monsters and Mothers: Filipina American Identity and Maternal Legacies in Lynda Barry's *One Hundred Demons*," *Meridians: Feminism, Race, Transnationalism* 5.1 (2004): 1–26; as well as Theresa Tensuan, "Comic Visions and Revisions in the Work of Lynda Barry and Marjane Satrapi," *Modern Fiction Studies* 52.4 (Winter 2006): 948–64; and the aforementioned *Graphic Women* by Hillary Chute.

Chapter 7

1. Critic Juliet Waters indicates frustration with the format, reflecting, "I felt some of the buzzing, bitter irritation that accompanies this question, 'Excuse me, but when do these formless things turn into monkeys?' What kept me reading were the autobiographical sections interspersed with cartoons of mean, smoking mothers, rigidly stupid teachers and perfect, taunting classmates." A *Time Out New York* review by Ariel Schrag concurred, noting that the narrative comic portions held their attention, while the question collages felt irksome:

> The book suffers a little from the frequent shifts between mediums: The comics themselves are a mesmerizing Disneyland ride, but looking at the collages is often more like just walking around the park. The various sections also contain quite a bit of repetition. Still, Barry composes with such urgency—you need to break free and start creating now or it will be too late—that it builds into an inspirational chant. And to answer the most important question: Does this book make you want to sit down and start creating? Absolutely. ("What It Is")

The immediacy and sincerity of *What It Is* seemed to strike a chord with reviewers, despite any frustrations, and most followed Wayne Allan Brenner, applauding "Barry at her enthusiastic best, her most sincerely encouraging, urging readers toward journeys of self-discovery and the joy of making, of appreciating, art."

2. Lynda Barry, personal interview, Rhinebeck, NY, 19 July 2006.

3. Lynda Barry, "Writing the Unthinkable" workshop, Rhinebeck, NY, 2006.

4. Barry, personal interview.

BIBLIOGRAPHY

Primary Texts

Barry, Lynda. "1619 East Crowley." *Mother Jones* February/March 1989–May/June 1991.

———. "Automatic Timer." *My Father's Daughter: Stories by Women*. Ed. Irene Zahava. Freedom, CA: Crossing Press, 1990. 94–97.

———. *Big Ideas*. Seattle: Real Comet Press, 1983.

———. *Come Over, Come Over*. New York: Harper Perennial, 1990.

———. *Cruddy: An Illustrated Novel*. New York: Scribner's, 2000.

———. *Girls and Boys*. Seattle: Sasquatch Books, 1999.

———. "Divine Teeth." *Body*. Ed. Sharon Sloan Fiffer and Steve Fiffer. New York: Avon Books, 1999. 55–59.

———. *Down the Street*. New York: Harper and Row, 1989.

———. "Ernie Pook's Comics." *University of Washington Daily*. 5 May 1978.

———. *Everything in the World*. New York: Harper and Row, 1986.

———. *The Freddie Stories*. New York: Harper Perennial, 1999.

———. *The Fun House*. New York: Harper and Row, 1987.

———. "Getting Saved." *1619 East Crowley. Mother Jones* 14.4 (May 1989): 60.

———. *Girls and Boys*. Seattle: Real Comet Press, 1981.

———. *The Good Times Are Killing Me*. New York: Harper Perennial, 1988.

———. *The! Greatest! of! Marlys!* Seattle: Sasquatch Books, 2000.

———. "Guardian Neighbor." *The Armless Maiden and Other Tales of Childhood's Survivors*. Ed. Terri Windling. New York: Tom Doherty Associates, 1995. 275–78.

———. "The Home Front/Modern Romance." *Esquire Magazine* August 1983–December 1988.

———. "Introduction." *Best American Comics 2008*. Ed. Lynda Barry. Boston: Houghton Mifflin, 2008. xi–xx.

———. *It's So Magic*. New York: Harper Perennial, 1994.

———. "Kids Extra Totally Happy Halloween." *Entertainment Weekly* 21 October 1994: 78.

———. *The Lynda Barry Experience*. Chicago: BMG, 1993.

———. *My Perfect Life*. New York: Harper Perennial, 1992.

———. *Naked Ladies! Naked Ladies! Naked Ladies!* Seattle: Real Comet Press, 1984.

———. "Oh Darling." *Crème de la Femme*. Ed. Nancy Davis. New York: Random House, 1997. 332–35.

———. *One Hundred Demons*. Seattle: Sasquatch Books, 2002.

———. "Picturing Happiness." *Life* 1 September 1991: 87.

———. *Picture This: The Near-Sighted Monkey Book*. Edmonton: Drawn & Quarterly, 2010.

———. "Pork Memories." *Los Angeles Times* 3 August 1995: H1–8.

———. "Sanctuary of School." *The Essay Connection: Readings for Writers*. Ed. Lynn Bloom. Boston: Houghton Mifflin, 1998. 647–52.

———. "She's Come for an Abortion. What Do You Say?" *Harpers* 285.1710 (1992): 43–55.

———. "Take My Advice." *Take My Advice: Letters to the Next Generation from People Who Know a Thing or Two*. Ed. James L. Harmon. New York: Simon and Schuster, 2001. 109.

———. "The Teenage Bedroom." *Home: American Writers Remember Rooms of Their Own*. Ed. Sharon Sloan Fiffer and Steve Fiffer. New York: Pantheon Books, 1996. 153–57.

———. "What Pop Fly Gave His Daughter." *Home Field: Nine Writers at Bat*. Ed. John Douglas Marshall. Seattle: Sasquatch Books, 1997. 71–82.

———. *What It Is*. Edmonton: Drawn & Quarterly, 2008.

———. "When Grandma Discovered Hotdogs." *Los Angeles Times* 18 October 1990: H13.

Secondary Sources

Acornplanet. "A Great Cartoonist Who Uses Ink Brush Painting." 4 February 2002. http://www.acornplanet.com/webhtml/lynda_barry.htm. Accessed 20 July 2008.

Armitage, Shelley. *Kewpies and Beyond: The World of Rose O'Neill*. Jackson: UP of Mississippi, 1994.

Badman, Derek A. "Panels & Pictures: Definition." *Comixtalk*. February 2008. http://comixtalk.com/content/panels_pictures_definition. Accessed May 2009.

———. "Points of View: 'First Person' in Comics." http://madinkbeard.com/ar chives/points-of-view-first-person-in-comics. Accessed 3 February 2010.

Beaty, Bart. *Unpopular Culture: Transforming the European Comic Book in the 1990s*. Studies in Book and Print Culture. Toronto: U of Toronto P, 2007.

Bechdel, Alison. *The Essential Dykes to Watch Out For*. New York: Houghton Mifflin, 2008.

———. *Fun Home*. New York: Houghton Mifflin, 2006.

Berlatsky, Noah. "Senior Moment: An Interview with Ariel Schrag." *Bitch Magazine*. 4 May 2009. http://bitchmagazine.org/post/ariel-schrag-interview. Accessed May 2009.

Bird, Stephanie Rose. *Sticks, Stones, Roots & Bones: Hoodoo, Mojo & Conjuring with Herbs*. St. Paul: Llewellyn Publications, 2004.

Bobo, Jacqueline. *Black Women as Cultural Readers*. New York: Columbia UP, 1995.

Brenner, Wayne Alan. "Your Library Wants These Bad: Four Graphic Volumes for Your Entertainment and Edification." *Austin Chronicle* 1 May 2008. http://www.austinchronicle.com/arts/2008-05-02/618790/. Accessed 28 November 2010.

Brumberg, Joan Jacobs. *The Body Project: An Intimate History of American Girls*. New York: Random House, 1997.

Buckler, Patricia P. "A Personalized Version of the Mexican War, 1846–1848." *The Scrapbook in American Life*. Ed. Susan Tucker, Katherine Ott, and Patricia P. Buckler. Philadelphia: Temple UP, 2006. 60–78.

C. R. "D & Q Grabs New Lynda Barry Title." *Publisher's Weekly* 8 January 2007: 8.

Callahan, Bob. "Let It Bleed: An Introduction to the New Comics Anthology." *The New Alternative Comics*. Ed. Bob Callahan. New York: Collier, 1991. 6–14.

Carrier, David. *The Aesthetics of Comics*. University Park: Pennsylvania State University, 2002.

Carroll, Lewis. *Alice in Wonderland*. New York: Samuel Gabriel Sons & Company, 1916. Project Gutenberg Ebook. 12 August 2006.

———. *Through the Looking Glass and What Alice Found There*. Millenium Fulcrum Edition 1.7. Project Gutenberg Ebook. 29 December 2008.

Chute, Hillary. "Comics as Literature? Reading Graphic Narrative." *PMLA* 123.2 (2008): 452–65.

———. *Graphic Women: Life Narrative and Contemporary Comics*. New York: Columbia, 2010.

Clover, Carol J. *Men, Women and Chain Saws: Gender in the Modern Horror Film*. Princeton, NJ: Princeton UP, 1992.

Cohn, Neil. *Early Writings on Visual Language*. Berkeley, CA: Emaki Productions, 2003.

Current Biography Yearbook. "Barry, Lynda." New York: Thomson Gale, 1994. 40–44.

Davis, Rocio. "A Graphic Self: Comics as Autobiography in Marjane Satrapi's *Persepolis*," *Prose Studies* 27.3 (2007): 264–79.

de Jesús, Melinda. "Liminality and Mestiza Consciousness in Lynda Barry's *One Hundred Demons*." *MELUS* 29.1 (Spring 2004): 219–52.

———. "Of Monsters and Mothers: Filipina American Identity and Maternal Legacies in Lynda Barry's *One Hundred Demons*." *Meridians: Feminism, Race, Transnationalism* 5.1 (2004): 1–26.

Deggans, Eric. "Minority Cartoonists: Don't Lump Us Together." *St. Petersburg Times* 14 January 2008. http://www.sptimes.com/2008/01/14/Entertainment/Minority_cartoonists_.shtml. Accessed 2 February 2008.

Di Liddo, Annalisa. *Alan Moore: Comics as Performance, Fiction as Scalpel*. Jackson: UP of Mississippi, 2009.

Dickey, James. "Lightnings or Visual." *South Atlantic Review* 57 (1992): 1–14.

Doucet, Julie. *My Most Secret Diary*. Montreal: Drawn & Quarterly, 2006.

———. *My New York Diary*. Montreal: Drawn & Quarterly, 2004.

Drechsler, Debbie. *Daddy's Girl*. Seattle: Fantagraphics, 2008.

———. *Summer of Love*. Montreal: Drawn & Quarterly, 2003.

Driest, Joris. "Subjective Narration in Comics." http://www.secretacres.com/ce/ce8.html. Accessed May 2009.

Edmiston, William. "Focalization and the First-Person Narrator: A Revision of the Theory." *Poetics Today* 10.4 (1989) 729–44.

Eggers, Dave. "After Wham! Pow! Shazam!" *New York Times*. 26 November 2000: Section 7:10.

Eisner, Will. *Comics and Sequential Art: Principles and Practice of the World's Most Popular Art Form*. Tamarac: Poorhouse Press, 1985.

———. *Graphic Storytelling and Visual Narrative*. Tamarac: Poorhouse Press, 1996.

Epstein, Daniel. "Miss Lasko-Gross on *Escape from Special*." *Newsarama*. 17 May 2007. http://forum.newsarama.com/showthread.php?t=113008. Accessed May 2009.

Fiedler, Leslie. "The Middle against Both Ends." *Arguing Comics: Literary Masters on a Popular Medium*. Ed. Jeet Heer and Kent Worcester. Jackson: UP of Mississippi, 2004.

Fleener, Mary. *Life of the Party*. Seattle: Fantagraphics, 1996.

Frasca, Marilyn. E-mail communication. 26 August 2007.

Garrity, Shaenon K. "All the Comics in the World #4." *Comixology*. 6 December 2007. www.comixology.com/articles/10/All-the-Comics-in-the-World-44. Accessed 2 January 2008.

Genette, Gérard. *Narrative Discourse: An Essay in Method*. Trans. Jane E. Lewin. Ithaca, NY: Cornell UP, 1972.

Geyh, Paula, Fred G. Leebron, and Andrew Levy, eds. *Postmodern American Fiction*. New York: W. W. Norton & Co., 1997.

Gewertz, Dan. "Little Lulu Comes to Harvard." 2 November 2006. http://www.hno.harvard.edu/gazette/2006/11.02/16-lulu.html. Accessed 3 December 2007.

Gloeckner, Phoebe. *A Child's Life and Other Stories*. Berkeley: Frog Books, 2000.

———. *The Diary of a Teenage Girl: An Account in Words and Pictures*. Berkeley: Frog, Ltd., 2002.

Groening, Matt. "Life in Hell." 2000. As printed in marlysmagazine.com. Accessed 13 April 2011.

Groensteen, Thierry. *The System of Comics*. Trans. Bart Beaty and Nick Nguyen. Jackson: UP of Mississippi, 2007.

Grossman, Lev. "Beyond the Funny Pages." *Time* 160.10 (2 September 2002).

Groth, Gary. "Debbie Drechsler Interview." *Comics Journal* 249. http://archives.tcj.com/249/i_drechsler.html. Accessed May 2009.

———. "Matt Groening Interview." *Comics Journal* 141 (April 1991): 78–95.

———. "Phoebe Gloeckner Interview." *Comics Journal* 261. http://archives.tcj.com/261/i_gloeckner.html. Accessed May 2009.

Harris, Miriam. "Cartoonists as Matchmakers: The Vibrant Relationship of Text and Image in the Work of Lynda Barry." *Elective Affinities: Testing Word and Image Relationships*. Ed. C. MacLeod and V. Plesch. Amsterdam: Rodopi Press, 2009. 129–43.

Harvey, Robert C. *The Art of the Comic Book*. Jackson: UP of Mississippi, 1996.

————. *The Art of the Funnies, An Aesthetic History.* Jackson: UP of Mississippi, 1994.

————. "Comedy at the Juncture of Word and Image." *The Language of Comics: Word and Image.* Ed. Robin Varnum and Christina T. Gibbons. Jackson: UP of Mississippi, 2001. 75–96.

Hatfield, Charles. *Alternative Comics: An Emerging Literature.* Jackson: UP of Mississippi, 2005.

Heer, Jeet, and Kent Worcester, eds. *Arguing Comics: Literary Masters on a Popular Medium.* Jackson: UP of Mississippi, 2004.

————. *A Comics Studies Reader.* Jackson: UP of Mississippi, 2009.

Herman, Luc, and Bart Vervaeck. *Handbook of Narrative Analysis.* Lincoln: U of Nebraska P, 2005.

Higonnet, Anne. *Pictures of Innocence: The History and Crisis of Ideal Childhood.* London: Thames & Hudson, 1998.

Hunter, Jane. *How Young Ladies Became Girls: The Victorian Origins of American Girlhood.* New Haven: Yale UP, 2002.

Inge, M. Thomas. *Comics as Culture.* Jackson: UP of Mississippi, 1990.

Inness, Sherrie, ed. *Delinquents and Debutantes: Twentieth-Century American Girls' Cultures.* New York: New York UP, 1998.

Ivanic, Roz. *Writing and Identity: The Discoursal Construction of Identity in Academic Writing.* Philadelphia: John Benjamins Publishing Co., 1998.

Johnson, Steve. "Lynda Barry Now Home in Chicago." *Chicago Times* 5 November 1989. http://articles.chicagotribune.com/keyword/lynda-barry. Accessed January 2008.

Kean, Benjamin Ong Pang. "Celebrating 120 Years of Komiks from the Phillipines: The History of Komiks." *Newsrama.com* 19 October 2006. http://forum.newsarama.com/showthread.php?t=882322. Accessed 4 January 2008.

Keough, William. "The Violence of American Humor." *What's So Funny: Humor in American Culture.* Ed. Nancy Walker. Wilmington: Scholarly Resources Inc., 1998. 133–43.

Kino, Carol. "How to Think Like a Surreal Cartoonist." *New York Times* 11 May 2008. http://www.nytimes.com/2008/5/11/arts/design/11kino.html. Accessed May 2008.

Kominsky-Crumb, Aline. "Interview." *Guardian* 25 March 2005. http://www.guardian.co.uk/books/2005/mar/25/robertcrumb.comics. Accessed 4 January 2008.

————. *Need More Love.* New York: M Q Publications, 2007.

Lasko-Gross, Miss. *Escape from Special.* Seattle: Fantagraphics, 2007.

————. *A Mess of Everything.* Seattle: Fantagraphics, 2009.

Lefèvre, Pascal. "The Construction of Space in Comics." *A Comics Studies Reader.* Ed. Jeet Heer and Kent Worcester. Jackson: Mississippi UP, 2009. 157–62.

Lewis, Alan. "Pook World Question." 6 March 2008. Newsgroup posting. ernie-pookmoderated@yahoogroups.com. Accessed 21 July 2008.

"Lynda Barry." *World Literature Today* 81.2 (March/April 2007): 32–33.

Martusewicz, Rebecca A. "Maybonne and Me." *Seeking Passage: Post-Structuralism, Pedagogy, Ethics.* New York: Teachers College Press, 2001. 72–100.

Marumaya, Magoroh. "Peripheral Vision: Polyocular Vision or Subunderstanding." *Organization Studies* 25.3 (2004): 467–80.

Matheson, Whitney. "In a Word, Barry's Work Is 'Autobifictionalography." *USA Today* 15 October 2002: Life 7d.

McCloud, Scott. *Reinventing Comics: How Imagination and Technology Are Revolutionizing an Art Form*. New York: Perennial, 2000.

———. *Understanding Comics*. New York: Kitchen Sink P, 1994.

McKeown, Daniel. "Marlysmagazine.com." http://marlysmagazine.com/. Accessed 3 January 2011.

Miller, Ann. *Reading Bande Desineé: Approaches to French-Language Comic Strip*. Chicago: U of Chicago P, 2007.

Miller, Brian. "This Girl's Life: Lynda Barry's Bizarre Brand of Bleakness." 6 October 1999. http://www.seattleweekly.com/1999-10-06/food/thisgirl-s-life.php. Accessed 2 February 2008.

Mitchell, W.J.T. "Beyond Comparison." *A Comics Studies Reader*. Ed. Jeet Heer and Kent Worcester. Jackson: UP of Mississippi, 2009. 116–23.

———. *Iconology: Image, Text, Ideology*. Chicago: U of Chicago P, 1986.

Morgan, Harry. "Graphic Shorthand: From Caricature to Narratology in Twentieth-Century *Bandee desinée* and Comics." *European Comic Art* 2.1 (June 2009): 21–39.

Muscio, Inga. "Lethal Weapons." *Lambda Book Report* July 1999: 20–21.

Naghibi, Nimi, and Andrew O'Malley. "Estranging the Familiar: 'East' and 'West' in Satrapi's *Persepolis*." *SC: English Studies in Canada* 31.2–3 (June/September 2005): 223–47

Nash, Ilana. *American Sweethearts: Teenage Girls in Twentieth-Century Popular Culture*. Bloomington: Indiana UP, 2006.

Øyen, Else. "The Polyscopic Landscape of Poverty Research." Report prepared for the Research Council of Norway. CROP paper. April 2005. www.crop.org. Accessed 3 January 2011.

Parent, Georges-A. "Focalization: A Narratological Approach to Mexican Illustrated Stories." *Studies in Latin American Popular Culture* 1 (1982): 201–15.

Pipher, Mary. *Reviving Ophelia: Saving the Selves of Adolescent Girls*. New York: Ballantine, 1995.

Plimpton, George. "Interview with Mary McCarthy." *Women Writers at Work: The Paris Reviews Interviews*. New York: Modern Library, 1998.

Pope, Alexander. *The Works of Alexander Pope, Esq*. London: Google Books, 1778.

Redi, Francesco. *Bacchus in Tuscany: A Dithyrambic Poem*. Trans. Leigh Hunt. London: J. L. Hunt, 1825.

Robbins, Trina. *A Century of Women Cartoonists*. San Francisco: Chronicle Books, 1993.

———. *From Girls to Grrlz: A History of Women's Comics from Teens to Zines*. San Francisco: Chronicle Books, 1999.

———. *The Great Women Cartoonists*. New York: Watson-Guptill, 2001.

———. *The Great Women Superheroes*. Northampton: Kitchen Sink Press, 1997.

———. *Nell Brinkley and the New Woman in the Early 20th Century*. New York: McFarland, 2001.

Rodi, Rob. "Repeat until Spanked." *Comics Journal* 114 (February 1987): 57–61.

Roth, Robert. Phone interview with author. 19 July 2007.

Round, Julia. "Visual Perspective and Narrative Voice in Comics: Redefining Literary Terminology." *International Journal of Comic Art* 9.2 (2007): 316–29.

Rudd, Gillian. *Managing Language in "Piers Plowman."* Cambridge: Brewer, 1994

Sabin, Roger. *Comics, Comix, & Graphic Novels: A History of Comic Art.* London: Phaidon Press, 1996.

Samanci, Ozge. "Lynda Barry's Humor: At the Juncture of Private and Public, Invitation and Dissemination, Childish and Professional." *IJOCA* 8.2 (Fall 2006): 181–99.

Satrapi, Marjane. *Chicken with Plums.* New York: Pantheon, 2006.

———. *Embroideries.* New York: Pantheon, 2005.

———. *Persepolis.* New York: Pantheon, 2003.

———. *Persepolis 2.* New York: Pantheon, 2004.

Saxton, Ruth O., ed. *The Girl: Constructions of the Girl in Contemporary Fiction by Women.* New York: St. Martin's Press, 1998.

Schrag, Ariel. *Awkward and Definition: The High School Comic Chronicles of Ariel Schrag.* New York: Touchstone, 2008.

———. *Likewise.* New York: Touchstone, 2008.

———. *Potential.* New York: Touchstone, 2008.

Schrag, Ariel, ed. *Stuck in the Middle: 17 Comics from an Unpleasant Age.* New York: Viking, 2007.

Shamoon, Deborah. "Focalization and Narrative Voice in the Novels and Comics of Uchida Shungiku." *International Journal of Comic Art* 5.1 (2003): 147–60.

Shelton, Gilbert, and Paul Mavrides, eds. *The Best Comics of the Decade.* Seattle: Fantagraphics, 1990.

Shifrin, Susan, ed. *Re-Framing Representations of Women.* Burlington: Ashgate, 2008.

Singer, Marc. "Black Skins and White Masks: Comic Books and the Secret of Race." *African American Review* 36.1 (Spring 2002): 107.

Soper, Kerry D. *Garry Trudeau: Doonesbury and the Aesthetics of Satire.* Jackson: UP of Mississippi, 2007.

Stendhal. *The Red and the Black.* Trans. Horace Samuel. New York: E. P. Dutton, 1916.

Stoneley, Peter. *Consumerism and American Girls Literature, 1860–1940.* New York: Cambridge UP, 2003

Tarbox, Gwen Athene. *The Clubwomen's Daughters: Collectivist Impulses in Progressive-Era Girl's Fiction, 1890–1940.* New York: Garland Publishing, 2000.

Tate, Claudia. "Toni Morrison: Interview." *Conversations with Toni Morrison.* Ed. Danille K. Taylor-Guthrie. Jackson: UP of Mississippi, 1994. 156–70.

Tensuan, Theresa. "Comic Visions and Revisions in the Work of Lynda Barry and Marjane Satrapi." *Modern Fiction Studies* 52.4 (Winter 2006): 948–64.

Tinker, Emma. "Selfhood and Trauma in Lynda Barry's Autobifictionalography." *Identity and Form in Alternative Comics, 1967–2007.* Unpublished thesis, 2008. http://emmatinker.oxalto.co.uk/. Accessed 28 November 2010.

Tompkins, Jane. *Sensational Designs: The Cultural Work of American Fiction, 1790–1860*. New York: Oxford UP, 1985.

Tucker, Susan, Katherine Ott, and Patricia P. Buckler, eds. *The Scrapbook in American Life*. Philadelphia: Temple UP, 2006.

Varnum, Robin, and Christina T. Gibbons. "Introduction." *The Language of Comics: Word and Image*. Ed. Robin Varnum and Christina T. Gibbons. Jackson: UP of Mississippi:, 2001. ix–xix.

Walker, Nancy, and Zita Dresner. "Women's Humor in America." *What's So Funny: Humor in American Culture*. Ed. Nancy Walker. Wilmington: Scholarly Resources Inc., 1998. 171–83.

Watson, Nicholas. "The Politics of Middle English Writing." *The Idea of the Vernacular: An Anthology of Middle English Literary Theory, 1280–1520*. Ed. Jocelyn Wogan-Browne et al. University Park: Pennsylvania State UP, 1999. 331–52.

Weissman, Benjamin. "Graphic Stories." *LA Weekly* 17 December 1999: 55.

White, Charlotte. *Growing Up Female: Adolescent Girlhood in American Fiction*. Westport: Greenwood Press, 1989.

Witek, Joseph. *Comic Books as History: The Narrative Art of Jack Jackson, Art Spiegelman, and Harvey Pekar*. Studies in Popular Culture. Jackson: UP of Mississippi, 1989.

Interviews and Profiles

Barry, Lynda. E-mail communication. 9 July 2007.

———. Personal interview with author. Rhinebeck, NY. 19 July 2006.

Borrelli, Christopher. "Being Lynda Barry." *Chicago Tribune* 8 March 2009. http://www.chicagotribune.com/entertainment/chi- mxa0308magazinebarrypg 1322mar08,0,5941014.story?page=1. Accessed May 2009.

Chute, Hillary. "Interview with Lynda Barry." *The Believer* 6.9 (November/December 2006): 47–58.

Coburn, Marcia Froelke. "Her So-Called Life." *Chicago Magazine* March 1997. http://www.marlysmagazine.com. Accessed January 2008.

Cruz, Araceli. "Peek-a-Pook: Lynda Barry Emerges for a Round of Applause." *Village Voice* 27 May 2008. http://www.villagevoice.com/2008-05-27/voice-choices/peek-a-pook/. Accessed 15 June 2008.

Dean, Michael. "Interview." 2 March 2009. *Comics Journal* 296. http://tcj.com/index.php?option=com_content&task=view&id=999&Itemid=48. Accessed January 2008.

Friedman, David. "Leaping off the Page." *LA Times* 19 April 1998. http://articles.latimes.com/1991-04-28/entertainment/ca-1166_1_lynda-barry. Accessed January 2008.

Garden, Joe. "Interview." 8 December 1999. http://www.avclub.com/content/node/24257. Accessed March 2008.

Graham, Rosemary. "Dividing Them from Us within Ourselves: A Conversation with Lynda Barry." *Iris: A Journal About Women* 20 (Fall/Winter 1988): 34–39.

Grossman, Pamela. "Barefoot on the Shag." *Salon.com* 18 May 1999. http://www
.salon.com/books/int/1999/05/18/barry/index.html. Accessed March 2008.

Hambly, Mary. "An Interview with Lynda Barry." *Backbone 4: Humor by Northwest
Women.* Ed. Barbara Wilson and Rachel DaSilva. Emeryville: Seal Press, 1982.

Hempel, Amy. "Laugh Lines." *New York Times Book Review* 27 November 1988.
http://www.nytimes.com/books/97/07/27/reviews/hempel-chast.html.
Accessed March 2008.

Hubbard, Kim. "In Lynda Barry's World, Poodles Are Tough and the Weasels Drink
Daquiris." *People Weekly* 30 March 1987: 109–10.

Independent Publisher Online. "Lynda Barry Faces Her Demons." 2003.
http://www.independentpublisher.com/index.lasso?-database=18news.
fp3&layout=iparticle&-response=art.lasso&-recordID=38795&-search. Accessed
January 2008.

"Interview." *StudioNotes: The Journal for Working Artists* November 1999–January
2000. http://www.marlysmagazine.com/load.html?content=http%3A//www
.marlysmagazine.com/interviews/barry.htm. Accessed January 2008.

La Grone, Paige. "Interview." *Mean Magazine* 6 (1999). www.marlysmagazine.com/
interviews/mean.htm. Accessed January 2008.

Montagne, Renee. "Interview with Renee Montagne." *Listening to America: Twenty-
Five Years in the Life of a Nation, as Heard on National Public Radio.* Ed. Linda
Wertheimer. Boston: Houghton Mifflin, 1995. 292–94.

Neary, Lynn. "Interview with Lynda Barry." *Talk of the Nation* 1 October 2002.

Olson, Tod. "Weird, Cool." *Literary Cavalcade* 52.5 (February 2000): 5–6.

Powers, Thom. "Lynda Barry." *Comics Journal* 132 (1989): 60–75.

Rochlin, Margy. "Lynda J. Barry." *Interview Magazine* November 1985: 119–20.

Rothman, Julia. "*What It Is.*" *Book by Its Cover* 12 May 2008. http://www.book-by-
its-cover.com/comics/what-it-is. Accessed 15 June 2008.

Schappell, Elissa. "A Conversation with Lynda Barry. *Tin House* 29 (Fall 2006): 50–57.

Sebold, Alice. "Writing Outside." *LA Weekly* 30 May 2003: 26.

Shaboy, Benny. "Interview with Lynda Barry." *Studio Notes #27: The Journal for
Working Artists* (November 1999 to January 2000). http://www.marlysmagazine
.com/interviews/barry.htm. Accessed 15 June 2008.

Reviews

Appelo, Tim. "'Good Times' are Getting Better for Lynda Barry." *Seattle Times* 25
April 1991: E1.

Benson, Heidi. "Comic Artist Wrestles with 'Demons' in New Book." *San Francisco
Chronicle* 31 October 2002: D1.

Berson, Misha. "'Good Times' isn't Just Fun and Games, it's Provocative." *Seattle
Times* 23 April 1992: E1.

Brenner, Wayne Alan. "Your Library Wants These Bad: Four Graphic Volumes For
Your Entertainment and Edification." *Austin Chronicle* 1 May 2008.

Chapman, Geoff. "Few Theatrical Good Times in Pubescent Teen Angst Tale." *The Toronto Star* 14 April 1993: B1.

Collins, Glenn. "'Good Times is Hollywood Bound.'" *New York Times* 26 July 1991: C2.

Cooper, Jeanne. "Her Imperfect Life; Cartoonist-Playwright Lynda Barry Turns Adolescent Angst Into Art." *Washington Post* 7 February 1993: G1.

DeFore, John. "Serious Playtime: Lynda Barry's *What It Is*." *San Antonio Current* 28 May 2008. http://www.sacurrent.com/arts/story.asp?id=68777. Accessed 15 June 2008.

Erstein, Hap. "Play's Bittersweet Humor Vividly Depicts Childhood." *Washington Times* 10 February 1993: E1.

Fanger, Iris. "Excellent Cast Makes 'Good Times' Roll." *Boston Herald* 14 May 1993: S20.

Friedlander, Mira. "'Good Times' Teens Can Relate to Lynda Barry's Message." *The Toronto Star* 8 April 1993: WO13.

Gates, David, and Abigail Kuflik. "Edna and Bonna and Lynda." *Newsweek* 19 August 1991: 54.

Goddard, Peter. "Lynda Barry's Rhythm 'n' Rhyme Seeds that Grew into The Good Times are Killing Me Were Planted by Girl Groups of the '60s." *Toronto Star* 10 April 1993: H3.

Hornby, Nick. "Draw What You Know." *New York Times* 22 December 2002: F10.

Hulbert, Dan. "Cartoonists 'Good Times' Evokes Boomers' Nostalgia for '60s Songs." *Atlanta Journal and Constitution* 12 May 1993: B11.

———. "Young Drama Enthusiast Identifies with Play's Theme of Friendship." *Atlanta Journal and Constitution* 2 June 1993: B11.

Jog the Blog. "Come On Come On! Remember to Forget to Forget to Remember!" *Jog the Blog* 25 May 2008. http://joglikescomics.blogspot.com/2008/05/come-on-come-on-remember-to-forget-to.html. Accessed May 2008.

Kennedy, Louise. "At Trinity: Lynda Barry, Queen of Universe; Stage Review The Good Times are Killing Me." *Boston Globe* 3 June 1993: Arts & Film 52.

Kuchwara, Michael. "'The Good Times Are Killing Me' Opens Off-Broadway." *Associated Press* 9 August 1991. Lexis-Nexis. Accessed 14 June 2007.

MCH. "Lynda Barry Off-Broadway." *Comics Journal* 142 (June 1991): 19.

Meek, Heather. "The Comics of Lynda Barry: Novelist, Artist and Autobifictionalographer." 20 July 2007. http://graphicnovelscomics.suite101.com/article.cfm/the_comics_of_lynda_barry. Accessed January 2008.

Morris, Terry. "Sharp Script Makes 'Times' Provocative." *Dayton Daily News* 9 September 1994: Entertainment 2C.

Pasch, Ina. "Playwright's Appearance is a Delight." *Wisconsin State Journal* 28 February 1993: 6G.

"Review of *Cruddy*." *Entertainment Weekly* 10 September 1999. http://marlysmagazine.com. Accessed 23 May 2006.

Rich, Frank. "A Child's Innocence Fights Bias." *New York Times* 19 April 1991: C3.

Rickey, Carrie. "What Is It?" *Philadelphia Inquirer* 4 June 2008. http://www.philly
.com/inquirer/columnists/carrie_rickey/20080604_What_is_it.html. Accessed
June 2008.

Rodi, Rob. "Suburban but Sublime." *Comics Journal* 127 (February 1989): 50–54.

Rogers, Sean. "A Conversation with Lynda Barry." *Walrus Magazine* 17 November
2008. http://www.walrusmagazine.com/blogs/2008/11/17/a-conversation-with-
lynda-barry/. Accessed November 2008.

Rothstein, Mervyn. "From Cartoons to a Play about Racism in the 60's." *New York
Times* 14 August 1991: C11.

Rose, Lloyd, and Pamela Sommers. "The Good Times are Killing Me." *Washington
Post* 12 February 1993: N43.

Sandstorm, Karen. "Vibrant Picture Books Entertain the Adult Child." *Cleveland
Plain Dealer* 11 May 2008. http://www.drawnandquarterly.com/newsList
.php?st=art&art=a45a8141b837f5. Accessed 15 June 2008.

Santos-Taylor, Marcelline. "Demonyos and Duwendes." *Filipino Express* 19.6 (7
February 2005). http://www.filipinoexpress.com/19/06_op-ed.html. Accessed
May 2008.

Schrag, Ariel. "What It Is." *Time Out New York* 29 May 2008. http://newyork.time
out.com/articles/books/29800/what-it-is. Accessed May 2008.

Stead, Deborah. "Small Presses in Short." *New York Times* 20 November 1988:
Section 7, 53.

Stearns, David Patrick. "Playful, Poignant 'Good Times.'" *USA Today* 8 May 1991:
Life 7D.

Sullivan, Darcy. "Kids at the Abyss: Lynda Barry's *Come Over, Come Over*." *Comics
Journal* 140 (February 1991): 43–45.

Tucker, Ken. "*What It Is* Review." 20 May 2008. http://www.drawnandquarterly
.com/newsList.php?item=a4840384f9336d. Accessed May 2008.

Valeo, Tom. "'Good Times Are Killing Me' Slaying Them at Larger Theater." *Crain's
Chicago Business* 25 September 1989: Options 49.

Vance, James. "A 'Good Times' Was Had By All." *Tulsa World* 14 March 1997:
Entertainment 2.

Washington Post. "New in Paperback." *Washington Post Book World* 20 December
1987: X12.

———. "New in Paperback." *Washington Post Book World* 30 October 1988: X16.

Waters, Juliet. "Lynda Barry Explores Creativity and Risk in *What It Is: The Formless
Thing Which Gives Things Form*." *Montreal Mirror* 29 May 2008. http://www
.drawnandquarterly.com/newsList.php?st=art&art=a45a8141b837f5 Accessed 15
June 2008.

West, Phil. "'Good Times' in Tacoma: Barry's Feel-Good Tragedy." *Seattle Times* 18
March 1994: D19.

Winn, Steven. "Recalling 'Good Times' In Concord." *San Francisco Chronicle* 29
August 1995: E1.

Witchel, Alex. "2 Young Actresses And Their 'Good Times.'" *New York Times* 22 May
1991: C11.

INDEX

Page numbers in **bold** indicate an illustration.